FOOD&**WINE**

Wine
Guide
2013

D0006442

by the Editors of Food & Wine and Mary G. Burnham

WINE GUIDE 2013

editor in chief **DANA COWIN**
executive wine editor **RAY ISLE**
deputy editor **CHRISTINE QUINLAN**
art director **COURTNEY WADDELL ECKERSLEY**
designer **MICHELLE LEONG**
volume editor **KRISTEN WOLFE BIELER**
copy editor **ELZY KOLB**
research chief **JANICE HUANG**
researchers **TOM HOLTON, ELLEN MCCURTIN, PAOLA SINGER**
producer relations coordinator **AMY CLEARY**
tastings coordination interns **KAY ISABEL, TIFFANY TERRY**
wine storage **SAN FRANCISCO WINE CENTER**
digital coordinator **JOHN KERN**

design concept **PLEASURE / KEVIN BRAINARD & RAUL AGUILA**

cover photography **CHRISTINA HOLMES**

produced for FOOD & WINE magazine by
gonzalez defino, ny / gonzalezdefino.com
principals **JOSEPH GONZALEZ, PERRI DEFINO**

AMERICAN EXPRESS PUBLISHING CORPORATION

president/ceo **ED KELLY**
chief marketing officer & president, digital media **MARK V. STANICH**
senior vice president/chief financial officer **PAUL B. FRANCIS**
vice presidents/general managers **FRANK BLAND, KEITH STROHMEIER**

vice president, books & products/publisher **MARSHALL COREY**
director, book programs **BRUCE SPANIER**
senior marketing manager, branded books **ERIC LUCIE**
assistant marketing manager **STACY MALLIS**
director of fulfillment & premium value **PHIL BLACK**
manager of customer experience & product development **ELISABETH WILSON**
director of finance **THOMAS NOONAN**
associate business manager **UMA MAHABIR**
operations director (prepress) **ROSALIE ABATEMARCO SAMAT**
operations director (manufacturing) **ANTHONY WHITE**

ISSN 1522-001X
Manufactured in the United States of America.

FOOD&WINE
BOOKS
American Express Publishing Corporation, New York

FOOD&WINE

Wine
Guide

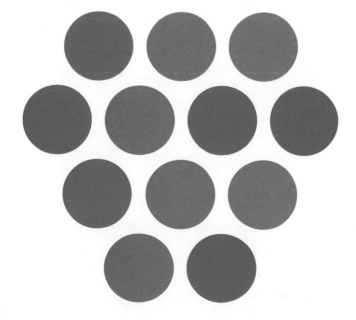

Contents / Wine Guide

OLD WORLD

2013

Foreword

Our 15th annual edition of the FOOD & WINE *Wine Guide* is unlike any other pocket-size book of its kind. Rather than rate or review thousands of individual bottles, we've taken a simpler, smarter approach. The magazine's editors, together with San Francisco–based wine writer Mary G. Burnham, have identified 500 of the world's top wineries, from every significant region. These are producers you can rely on in every vintage, from their most affordable choices to their top bottles. Descriptions of over 1,000 benchmark wines define the wineries' style and approach and provide a better sense of the breadth of their quality. To round out the book, we've added sections on rare and collectible wines from some of the world's premier wine regions, the absolute pinnacles of wine quality, as well as an entirely revised and completely essential primer on pairing wine and food. We feel certain that our 2013 edition is the clearest, most user-friendly wine guide available, and hope that you will, too.

Dana Cowin

Dana Cowin
Editor in Chief
FOOD & WINE

Ray Isle

Ray Isle
Executive Wine Editor
FOOD & WINE

KEY TO SYMBOLS

TYPE OF WINE
- ● RED
- ● ROSÉ
- ○ WHITE

PRICE
- $$$$ OVER $60
- $$$ $30+ TO $60
- $$ $15+ TO $30
- $ $15 AND UNDER

FOR MORE EXPERT WINE-BUYING ADVICE

Join the F&W community at *foodandwine.com*

 Follow us *@fandw*

Become a fan at *facebook.com/foodandwine*

Wine Terms

You won't find much fussy wine jargon in this guide, but some of the terms commonly used to describe the taste of wine might be unfamiliar or used in an unfamiliar way. References in tasting notes to flavors and textures other than "grape" are meant to serve as analogies: All the wines in this guide are made from grapes, but grapes have the ability to suggest the flavors of other fruits, herbs or minerals. Here's a mini glossary to help you become comfortable with the language of wine.

ACIDITY The tart, tangy or zesty sensations in wine. Ideally, acidity brightens a wine's flavors as a squeeze of lemon brightens fish. Wines lacking acidity taste "flabby."

APPELLATION An officially designated winegrowing region. The term is used mostly in France and the U.S. In Europe, a wine's appellation usually reflects not only where it's from but also aspects of how it's made, such as vineyard yields and aging.

BALANCE The harmony between acidity, tannin, alcohol and sweetness in a wine.

BIODYNAMICS An organic, sustainable approach to farming that takes into account a farm's total environment, including surrounding ecosystems and astronomical considerations, such as the phases of the moon.

BODY How heavy or thick a wine feels in the mouth. Full-bodied or heavy wines are often described as "big."

CORKED Wines that taste like wet cork or newspaper are said to be corked. The cause is trichloroanisole (TCA), a contaminant sometimes transmitted by cork.

CRISP A term used to describe wines that are high in acidity.

CRU In France, a grade of vineyard (such as *grand cru* or *premier cru*), winery (such as Bordeaux's *cru bourgeois*) or village (in Beaujolais). Also used unofficially in Italy's Piedmont region to refer to top Barolo vineyards.

CUVÉE A batch of wine. A cuvée can be from a single barrel or tank (*cuve* in French), or a blend of different lots of wine. A Champagne house's top bottling is called a *tête de cuvée*.

DRY A wine without perceptible sweetness. A dry wine, however, can have powerful fruit flavors. *Off-dry* describes a wine that has a touch of sweetness.

EARTHY An earthy wine evokes flavors such as mushrooms, leather, damp straw or even manure.

FILTER/FINE Processes used to remove sediment or particulates from a wine to enhance its clarity.

FINISH The length of time a wine's flavors linger on the palate. A long finish is the hallmark of a more complex wine.

FRUITY A wine with an abundance of fruit flavors is described as fruity. Such wines may give the impression of sweetness, even though they're not actually sweet.

HERBACEOUS Calling a wine herbaceous or herbal can be positive or negative. Wines that evoke herb flavors can be delicious. Wines with green pepper flavors are less than ideal, and are also referred to as vegetal.

LEES The sediment (including dead yeast cells) left over after a wine's fermentation. Aging a wine on its lees (*sur lie* in French) gives wine nutty flavors and a creamy texture.

MINERAL Flavors that (theoretically) reflect the minerals found in the soil in which the grapes were grown. The terms *steely, flinty* and *chalky* are also used to describe these flavors.

NÉGOCIANT In wine terms, a *négociant* (French for "merchant") is someone who buys grapes, grape juice or finished wines in order to blend, bottle and sell wine under his or her own label.

NOSE How a wine smells; its bouquet or aroma.

OAKY Wines that transmit the flavors of the oak barrels in which they were aged. Some oak can impart toast flavors.

OXIDIZED Wines that have a tarnished quality due to exposure to air are said to be oxidized. When intended, as in the case of sherry (see p. 297), oxidation can add fascinating dimensions to a wine. Otherwise, it can make a wine taste unappealing.

PALATE The flavors, textures and other sensations a wine gives in the mouth. The term *mid-palate* refers to the way these characteristics evolve with time in the mouth.

POWERFUL Wine that is full of flavor, tannin and/or alcohol.

RUSTIC Wine that is a bit rough, though often charming.

TANNIN A component of grape skins, seeds and stems, tannin is most commonly found in red wines. It imparts a puckery sensation similar to oversteeped tea. Tannin also gives a wine its structure and enables some wines to age well.

TERROIR A French term that refers to the particular attributes a wine acquires from the specific environment of a vineyard—i.e., the climate, soil type, elevation and aspect.

Wine
Buying Guide

Knowing where and how to shop for wine makes discovering great wines easy and even fun, no matter where you live or what your budget. Take advantage of these tips to shop smarter.

IN SHOPS

SCOPE OUT THE SHOPS Visit local wine shops and determine which ones have the most helpful salespeople, the best selection and the lowest prices. Ask about case discounts, and whether mixing and matching a case is allowed. Expect at least a 10 percent discount; some stores will offer more. These days, many retailers are increasing their discounts and offering one-liter bottles and three-liter wine boxes that deliver more wine for the money. Finally, pay attention to store temperature: The warmer the store, the more likely the wines are to have problems.

ASK QUESTIONS Most wine-savvy salespeople are eager to share their knowledge and recommend some of their favorite wines. Let them know your likes, your budget and anything else that might help them select a wine you'll love.

BECOME A REGULAR The better the store's salespeople know you, the better they can suggest wines that will please you. Take the time to report back on wines they've suggested—it will pay off in future recommendations.

GET ON THE LIST Top wine shops often alert interested customers to special sales, hard-to-find wines or great deals in advance. Ask to get on their e-mail lists.

ONLINE

KNOW YOUR OPTIONS Take advantage of the Internet to easily find the wine you want and get the best price on it. The two most common ways to buy wine online are via online retailers or directly from wineries. Retailers may offer bulk discounts if you buy a case and shipping discounts if you spend a certain amount. Wineries don't often discount, but their wines can be impossible to find elsewhere. A great advantage of online shopping is price comparison: Websites like Wine-Searcher.com allow you to compare prices at retailers around the world.

BE WILLING TO ACT FAST Some of the steepest discounts on prestigious or hard-to-find wines are offered via so-called "flash sales" at sites such as WineAccess.com, WinesTilSoldOut.com and Lot18.com. Announced by e-mail, sales typically last just a day or two, and the best deals might sell out in under an hour.

KNOW THE RULES The difference between browsing for wine online and actually purchasing it has everything to do with where you live and how "liberal" your state is about interstate wine shipments. The laws governing direct-to-consumer inter-state shipments differ from state to state. If you're considering buying wine from an out-of-state vendor, find out first whether it can ship to your state.

KNOW THE WEATHER If you're ordering wine online when it's hot outside, it's worth paying for express delivery: A week spent roasting in the back of a delivery truck risks turning your prized case of Pinot into plonk. Some retailers and wineries offer free storage during the summer months; they'll hold purchased wine until the weather cools and you give the OK to ship.

IN RESTAURANTS

CHECK OUT THE LIST Many restaurants post their wine list online or are happy to e-mail it upon request. Scoping out the wine menu in advance dramatically increases your odds of pick-ing the right wine for your meal. For starters, if the selection looks poor, you can ask about the restaurant's corkage policy and perhaps bring your own bottle instead. A mediocre list might be limited in selection, have a disproportionate number of wines from one producer, fail to specify vintages or carry old vintages of wines meant to be drunk young and fresh. When faced with a bad wine list, order the least expensive bottle that you recognize as being reasonably good.

On the other hand, if the list is comprehensive, you can spend all the time you like perusing it in advance, rather than boring your dining companions while you pore over it at the table. You'll have plenty of time to spot bargains (or overpriced bottles) and to set an ordering strategy based on the list's strengths and your own preferences.

ASK QUESTIONS Treat the wine list as you would a food menu. You should ask how the Bordeaux tastes in comparison to the California Cabernet as readily as you'd ask about the difference between two fish dishes. Ask to speak to the wine director, if there is one. Then, tell that person the type of wine you're look-ing for—the price range, the flavor profile—as well as the dishes you will be having. If you want to indicate a price range without announcing the amount to the table, point to a bottle on the list that costs about what you want to spend and explain that you are considering something like it. And if you're unsure how to describe the flavors you're looking for, name a favorite producer who makes wine in a style you like. With this information, the wine director should be able to recommend several options.

TASTE THE WINE When the bottle arrives, make sure it's exactly what you ordered—check the vintage, the producer and the blend or variety. If it's not, speak up. You may be presented with the cork. Ignore it. Instead, sniff the wine in your glass. If it smells like sulfur, cabbage or skunk, tell your server that you think the wine might be flawed and request a second opinion from the wine director or the manager. If there's something truly wrong, they should offer you a new bottle or a new choice.

OLD WOR

France/
Italy/
Spain/
Portugal/
Germany/
Austria/
Greece

68
ITALY

138
GERMANY

LD

16 FRANCE

108 SPAIN

130 PORTUGAL

148 AUSTRIA

158 GREECE

France

Wine Region

France produces more great wine than any other country. But beyond its benchmark bottlings—the great first-growths of Bordeaux, the *grands crus* of Burgundy, the Cristals and Dom Pérignons of Champagne—France offers a vast number of wines, many of them at surprisingly affordable prices, from thousands of vineyards and producers.

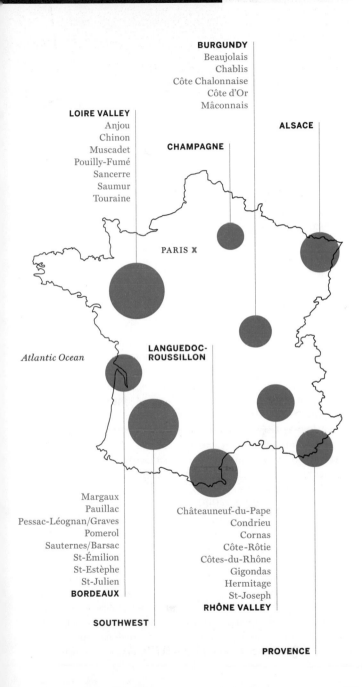

BURGUNDY
Beaujolais
Chablis
Côte Chalonnaise
Côte d'Or
Mâconnais

LOIRE VALLEY
Anjou
Chinon
Muscadet
Pouilly-Fumé
Sancerre
Saumur
Touraine

ALSACE

CHAMPAGNE

PARIS **X**

Atlantic Ocean

LANGUEDOC-ROUSSILLON

Margaux
Pauillac
Pessac-Léognan/Graves
Pomerol
Sauternes/Barsac
St-Émilion
St-Estèphe
St-Julien
BORDEAUX

Châteauneuf-du-Pape
Condrieu
Cornas
Côte-Rôtie
Côtes-du-Rhône
Gigondas
Hermitage
St-Joseph
RHÔNE VALLEY

SOUTHWEST

PROVENCE

France

FRENCH WINE PRODUCTION is huge—more than 1.2 billion gallons a year—and tremendously diverse. France's geography encompasses zones as different as the Atlantic-cooled vineyards of Bordeaux, the limestone-rich soils of Burgundy, the sunny Rhône River regions and the Mediterranean coast.

Many of the world's best grape varieties are French, including Chardonnay, Cabernet Sauvignon, Merlot, Pinot Noir and Sauvignon Blanc. But while the French care about grapes, what really matters to them is *terroir*. The idea of *terroir,* a term that refers to all of the distinguishing elements of a place, such as climate, sun exposure, soil and surrounding flora, is basic to French winemaking. It is the belief that nature makes the wine, not man. In fact, there is no French word for winemaker; someone who makes wine is called a *vigneron,* literally, a "vine grower."

French wine sales have been declining for several years as a result of competition from the New World. In response, French winemakers now travel abroad to learn from others; regulation changes have given vintners more flexibility; and the government has invested in modernizing vineyards and cellars. As a result, established zones such as Bordeaux are turning out more quality wine than ever, and formerly off-the-radar regions, especially in southern France, are making a remarkable number of fine wines.

WINE TERMINOLOGY

Most French wine labels list appellation (i.e., region or subregion) but not the grape used to make the wine. (Alsace labels are an important exception; see p. 20.) A wine bearing its appellation name must meet regulations designed to guarantee authenticity and quality. The hierarchy is:

VIN DE TABLE *Vins de table* labels are not permitted to mention vintages or grapes, or give a place of origin more specific than France. Most are dull, but certain iconoclasts have chosen to ignore some AOC demands (see below) and are making great wines labeled as *vins de table*. The category as a whole is being phased out and incorporated into the *vin de France* category.

VIN DE FRANCE Meant to attract drinkers more interested in grape variety and brand name than origin, this new category allows vintners to blend wines from different regions and still list vintage and variety information on the labels if they choose.

VIN DE PAYS/INDICATION GÉOGRAPHIQUE PROTÉGÉE (IGP) The *vin de pays*/IGP category includes wines from six broadly designated regions (Vins de Pays du Val de la Loire, for example). These wines are subject to lower standards than AOC wines but are allowed to list grape varieties. Most *vins de pays* ("country wines") are forgettable, but as with *vin de table*, some innovative winemakers who wish to work beyond the constraints of AOC rules are producing exemplary wines with this designation.

APPELLATION D'ORIGINE CONTRÔLÉE (AOC/AOP) The AOC ("controlled region of origin") category encompasses most French wines exported to the U.S., and ensures that the wines meet regional requirements. Standards vary by region and typically spell out permitted grapes, winemaking practices, minimum alcohol levels and harvest size (overly large harvests tend to yield dilute wines). There are AOC regions within larger AOC regions as well; generally, the more specific the subregion, the higher the standards (and, often, the price). A new, optional designation for AOC wine is AOP (Appellation d'Origine Protégée), which EU regulators hope all member countries will soon be using; it maintains basically the same requirements as AOC and could provide consistency from country to country.

ALSACE

CLAIM TO FAME

Alsace produces some of the world's finest Rieslings and Gewurztraminers, two Germanic grapes that reflect the bicultural heritage of this eastern border region. Blocked from cool, wet Atlantic weather by the Vosges Mountains, the sunny Alsace climate creates wines that are lusher and more powerful than the German versions. Their combination of zippy acidity, minerality and, often, a hint of sweetness makes them incredibly food-friendly, while their reasonable prices offer terrific value. Alsace wines are also refreshingly easy to identify and understand: Bottled in skinny, tapered green glass, they carry the name of the grape variety (or type of blend) on the label.

KEY GRAPES: WHITE

GEWURZTRAMINER Often made in an off-dry (that is, slightly sweet) style, spicy Alsace Gewurztraminers display flamboyant lychee and floral aromas.

MUSCAT These aromatic wines are actually made from three different, related Muscat varieties; all yield delicate, fruity and usually dry whites.

PINOT BLANC Alsace wines labeled Pinot Blanc often contain a second, similar variety called Auxerrois; winemakers are also allowed to add Pinot Gris and/or Pinot Noir that has been vinified as white wine. Regardless, Pinot Blanc–labeled wines tend to be broad and full-bodied, with musky apple and floral tones, and sometimes have a touch of sweetness.

PINOT GRIS Pinot Gris is the same grape as Italy's Pinot Grigio, yet the wines are very different: Alsace Pinot Gris tends to be creamier and richer than its light, crisp Italian counterparts.

RIESLING The region's most widely planted grape is also arguably its greatest, yielding crisp, medium-bodied wines whose stony flavors reflect the mineral soils. Styles range from bone-dry to sweet, though most Alsace Rieslings are dry. There's no uniform labeling requirement to indicate sugar levels.

SYLVANER, AUXERROIS & CHASSELAS These unexceptional varieties don't generally make great wines on their own and are nearly always blended with more powerful, distinctive types such as Riesling, Gewurztraminer, Muscat and Pinot Gris.

 KEY GRAPES: RED

PINOT NOIR The region's only red grape makes light red and rosé wines defined by their crisp berry character, as well as the rare sparkling Blanc de Noirs of Crémant d'Alsace.

WINE TERMINOLOGY

ALSACE The basic Alsace designation includes nearly all of the region's still wines. Quality standards that these wines must meet include a limit on vineyard yields (lower yields generally mean higher quality) and minimum ripeness levels for grapes.

CRÉMANT D'ALSACE These sparkling wines are usually based chiefly on the Pinot Blanc grape and feature perky acidity and fresh, fruity flavors. (See Other Sparkling Wines, p. 288.)

EDELZWICKER A catchall category for white blends, these are typically simple, zesty white wines that taste best when consumed within a year or so of release.

GENTIL Generally of a higher quality than *edelzwicker* blends (above), *gentil* wines are multivariety blends made to AOC standards, at least 50 percent of which must be some combination of Riesling, Gewurztraminer and Muscat.

GRAND CRU Wines from 51 vineyards may use this relatively recent designation, which comes with limits on vineyard yields. Most of the vineyards are recognized as outstanding, but some producers have protested the inclusion of a handful of controversial sites, and don't use the term *grand cru* on their wines.

RÉSERVE Producers use this term to indicate a higher-quality wine, though its exact meaning is not regulated.

VENDANGES TARDIVES/SÉLECTION DE GRAINS NOBLES These sweet whites are made from very ripe, late-harvested grapes. (See Dessert Wines, p. 304.)

Producers/ Alsace

DOMAINE MARCEL DEISS

Once dismissed by some as eccentric, owner-winemaker Jean-Michel Deiss is now acknowledged by many as a visionary for his progressive, often unorthodox philosophies on vineyard management. A longtime advocate of biodynamic farming, Deiss makes unusual field blends of different grapes harvested and vinified together. His wines are multilayered and intense.

○ **Domaine Marcel Deiss / 2010 / $$**
Thirteen varieties go into this crisp, apple-citrusy blend.

○ **Mambourg Grand Cru / 2008 / $$$$**
Exotically spicy and wildly complex, this luscious white is the pinnacle of Deiss's achievements.

DOMAINE PAUL BLANCK

The Blanck family has been harvesting Riesling in Alsace since Hans Blanck bought his first vines back in 1610. Today brothers Frédéric and Philippe make a broad range of wines, from high-end *grands crus* (which they age in bottle for years beyond the norm) down to everyday wines that deliver terrific value.

○ **Blanck Gewurztraminer / 2010 / $$**
A restrained Gewurztraminer with quince and floral notes.

○ **Blanck Pinot Gris / 2010 / $$**
Like all Blanck wines, this juicy, minerally white comes from vines farmed without chemicals.

○ **Blanck Riesling / 2010 / $$**
Frédéric Blanck crafts Rieslings in a medium-dry, elegant style, exemplified in this apple-driven, entry-level bottling.

DOMAINE SCHOFFIT

In the late 1980s Bernard Schoffit made a name for himself by rehabilitating some abandoned Riesling vines in the *grand cru* of Rangen. The tenacious second-generation vintner (his father founded Domaine Schoffit) soon began making powerful, viscous Rieslings in a sweeter style. Today Schoffit's wines take a more varied approach, with drier, fresher whites joining the lineup.

○ **Schoffit Chasselas Vieilles Vignes / 2010 / $$**
The humble Chasselas grape rarely yields wines as complex as this ripe, satiny version.

○ **Domaine Schoffit Grand Cru Sommerberg Riesling / 2010 / $$$** This suave and seductive Riesling showcases elegant flower, mineral and apricot flavors.

○ **Domaine Schoffit Grand Cru Rangen Clos Saint-Théobald Schistes Riesling / 2010 / $$$$** Schoffit makes several Rieslings from Rangen; Schistes is his driest, offering stony, complex pear and floral tones.

DOMAINE WEINBACH

Colette Faller runs this top estate with daughters Catherine and Laurence. Together they produce some of Alsace's finest wines, including those from the famous Schlossberg, Furstentum and Altenbourg sites. Laurence heads up winemaking, turning out as many as 20 to 25 different lush, voluptuous wines each year. As of 2010 all grapes are sourced from biodynamic vineyards.

○ **Domaine Weinbach Gewurztraminer Réserve Personnelle / 2010 / $$$** Of Weinbach's four Gewurztraminers, this lightly spicy, quince-inflected bottling is the driest.

○ **Domaine Weinbach Cuvée Ste. Catherine Riesling / 2009 / $$$$** Especially ripe grapes go into this slightly sweet Riesling, which is dense but not heavy, with honey-tinged apricot and pear notes.

DOMAINE ZIND-HUMBRECHT

In a region where most wineries count their history in centuries, not decades, Zind-Humbrecht is an upstart. Founded in 1959, this biodynamic producer has quickly become one of Alsace's greatest estates. Some of the world's most sumptuous whites are made here, crafted by Olivier Humbrecht, a Master of Wine.

○ **Domaine Zind-Humbrecht Pinot Blanc / 2010 / $$**
Broad peach and lemon flavors and a zesty, long finish define this blend of Auxerrois and Pinot Blanc.

○ **Domaine Zind-Humbrecht Pinot Gris / 2011 / $$**
Humbrecht's entry-level Pinot Gris is as good as many producer's top bottlings.

○ **Domaine Zind-Humbrecht Turckheim Riesling / 2010 / $$$**
Turckheim's dry, sunny climate explains the ripeness in this succulent Riesling.

HUGEL ET FILS

Among the best-known vintners in Alsace, the Hugel family has
been making wine in the village of Riquewihr since 1639. Their
entry-level Classic wines are dry and food-friendly; the Tradition bottlings are made from estate-grown and purchased fruit.
The finest cuvées, the Jubilee wines, come from the family's 62
vineyard acres, many of which are *grand cru* sites.

○ **Hugel Gentil / 2010 / $**
Gentil blends are all about freshness; this is a floral mix of
Riesling, Gewurztraminer, Pinot Gris, Sylvaner and Muscat.

○ **Hugel Riesling / 2010 / $$**
A graceful, affordable classic, with lemon and apricot notes.

LUCIEN ALBRECHT

Despite this estate's ancient history (the Albrechts were making
wine before Columbus sailed), it offers a modern-style mix of
juicy, affordable wines (the Réserve tier) plus world-class cuvées
from top, estate-owned *grands crus*. Patriarch Jean Albrecht
also creates a line of terrific *crémant* sparkling wines, making
this domaine one of Alsace's most formidable producers.

○ **Lucien Albrecht Cuvée Marie Gewurztraminer / 2009 / $$**
Named for one of Jean Albrecht's daughters, this rose-scented
white has the sweetness and density to stand up to spicy fare.

○ **Lucien Albrecht Réserve Riesling / 2010 / $$**
Crisp and minerally, with pear tones and a hint of sweetness.

MARC TEMPÉ

Marc Tempé is the kind of idiosyncratic, boutique vintner
beloved by hipster sommeliers: Tempé farms his vineyards bio-
dynamically, refuses to add anything to his wines except small
amounts of sulfur (no yeast, no sugar, no acid) and ages them
on their lees for at least two years—an extraordinarily long time.
The result is deeply layered wines of purity and precision.

○ **Marc Tempé Zellenberg Pinot Blanc / 2008 / $$**
Old vines, oak aging and a great vintage create a remarkably
complex and barely sweet Pinot Blanc.

○ **Marc Tempé Zellenberg Gewurztraminer / 2008 / $$$**
Orange and honey notes define this impressively lush white.

○ **Marc Tempé Zellenberg Riesling / 2008 / $$$**
Aging in old, neutral oak gives this satiny Riesling its
unusually broad, expressive dried-pear and mineral tones.

TRIMBACH

Although many Alsace producers have now switched over to
making sweeter wines, Trimbach is a proud holdout, remaining
true to the region's crisply dry, mineral-rich, traditional profile.
Twelfth-generation winemaker Pierre Trimbach crafts pure,
bracingly dry white wines. His most renowned bottling is the
Clos Ste. Hune Riesling; cuvées such as the Frédéric Emile
Riesling deliver nearly as much complexity and pleasure at
more-approachable prices.

O **Trimbach Riesling / 2009 / $$**
Even in a warm vintage like 2009, Trimbach's citrusy,
entry-level Riesling is bright and refreshing.

O **Trimbach Cuvée Frédéric Emile Riesling / 2005 / $$$$**
A mineral-rich, cellar-worthy Riesling sourced from top
vineyards, including *grand cru* sites.

BORDEAUX

CLAIM TO FAME
Bordeaux's stratospherically priced premier red wines—with
names like Lafite, Latour and Pétrus—set the standard by which
other Cabernet Sauvignon- and Merlot-based bottlings pro-
duced around the world are judged. Unfortunately, the Bor-
deaux stars also overshadow the millions of bottles of affordable
and frequently delicious wines that this vast Atlantic region
produces. Its perfect combination of maritime climate (warm
days, cool nights) and wine-friendly soils (gravel and clay) are
suited to dry and sweet whites, too, though reds make up about
90 percent of Bordeaux's output today.

REGIONS TO KNOW
LEFT BANK The gravelly soils deposited on the Garonne River's
western (left) bank are ideal for growing Cabernet Sauvignon,
especially in the Médoc plain, which fans north and seaward
from the city of Bordeaux. Its most famous subregions—Margaux,
Pauillac, St-Julien and St-Estèphe—produce firmly tannic,
cassis- and cedar-inflected reds of impressive structure and
longevity. Less-famous left bank appellations such as Haut-
Médoc, Moulis and Listrac are also worth paying attention to,
as they can produce terrific values.

GRAVES South and inland of Bordeaux proper, the Graves sub-zone is known for three things: tart dry whites based on Sémillon and Sauvignon Blanc; relatively light good-value reds from Merlot, Cabernet Sauvignon and Cabernet Franc; and, most famously, the prestigious subappellation of Pessac-Léognan, home to exalted châteaus such as Haut-Brion.

RIGHT BANK Clay soil mixes with gravel on the Garonne's right (eastern) bank, making this Merlot territory, and making wines from this zone plusher and less tannic than those from the left bank. The Pomerol and St-Émilion subdistricts are the right bank's most prestigious, while regions such as Fronsac, Lussac-St-Émilion, Lalande-de-Pomerol and Côtes de Blaye offer similarly styled wines at much gentler prices.

ENTRE-DEUX-MERS Literally, "between two seas," this sprawling territory between the Gironde and Dordogne rivers produces the bulk of Bordeaux's white wine. Most are crisp, affordable bottlings with straightforward citrus and herb flavors.

CÔTES DE BORDEAUX This new umbrella appellation groups four low-profile subregions occupying hilly slopes (*côtes*) above the Garonne River's tributaries, where a growing number of producers are offering high-quality, value-priced wines.

KEY GRAPES: WHITE
SAUVIGNON BLANC This grape is responsible for the hallmark citrus- and herb-driven aromas and zippy acidity in Bordeaux whites. It is usually blended with Sémillon.

SÉMILLON Rounder than Sauvignon Blanc, Sémillon is marked by minerally fruit and gives Bordeaux's best dry whites their ability to age. Vintners blend it with Sauvignon Blanc to yield medium-bodied, citrusy wines. Sémillon is also the primary grape used to make the sweet wines of Sauternes (see p. 304).

KEY GRAPES: RED
CABERNET FRANC With a handful of mostly famous exceptions (such as the wines of Château Cheval Blanc and Château Ausone), this grape plays a supporting role in Bordeaux's reds, to which it lends its signature sweet tobacco and herb aromas.

CABERNET SAUVIGNON Grown throughout the world, the Cabernet Sauvignon grape comes into its own in Bordeaux—specifically, on the left (western) bank of the Gironde River, where the Médoc subzone turns out wines of peerless finesse and power. In contrast to the vast majority of California Cabernets, Bordeaux examples display more austere, less fruity flavors, with herb-inflected cassis notes and sharper acidity. Nearly all Bordeaux Cabernet gets blended with Merlot to soften its firm tannins and add fruitiness.

MERLOT The most widely planted grape in Bordeaux, Merlot is at its best on the right (eastern) bank of the Gironde River. Less sweetly ripe than Merlot bottlings from the world's warmer regions, Bordeaux versions showcase the grape's characteristically supple tannins and rich plum and black cherry flavors, along with herb and spice notes.

PETIT VERDOT & MALBEC Used by some winemakers in blends, these red varieties are small players in Bordeaux wines today, even though both grapes are native to the region.

WINE TERMINOLOGY
Bordeaux wines are labeled by region; generally, the more specific the regional designation, the better the wine. Wines from Bordeaux's districts—such as Médoc, Graves and St-Émilion—are required to meet higher standards than those labeled Bordeaux or Bordeaux *Supérieur*. Within the districts are communes—Pauillac and Margaux in Médoc, for example—which must meet still more stringent requirements.

BORDEAUX This entry-level category can include wines made anywhere in Bordeaux. Most wines in this category are simple; many are whites from Entre-Deux-Mers.

BORDEAUX SUPÉRIEUR A step up from the basic Bordeaux category, these wines are required to be higher in alcohol, which implies that they were made from riper grapes—historically a measure of higher quality.

CLARET Not legally defined, this is a primarily British term for red Bordeaux wines.

CRU BOURGEOIS This category includes Médoc châteaus that didn't make the cut for *cru classé* (see below) but are still considered good. For various bureaucratic reasons, it is viewed as a stamp of approval rather than a true classification.

CRU CLASSÉ Bordeaux's system for ranking wines, established in 1855, created a hierarchy of wineries (or châteaus) considered superior based on the prices their wines commanded. It applies only to châteaus in Médoc and Sauternes and a single château in Graves. The ranking grouped 61 superior wineries by *cru* (growth), from first (*premier cru*) to fifth. In 1955 a similar system was set up for the St-Émilion district, using just three rankings: *grand cru, grand cru classé* and, at the top, *premier grand cru classé*. It is subject to revision (and inevitable appeal) every 10 years or so. Pay attention to the *classé* on the end—plain old *grand cru* applies to most estate-bottled St-Émilion wine. The famed red wines of Pomerol are not ranked.

MIS EN BOUTEILLE AU CHÂTEAU Only estate-bottled wines made from estate-grown grapes can use this term, meaning "bottled at the winery." Theoretically, these wines are better because of the greater control the producer has over fruit and wine.

Producers/ Bordeaux

CHÂTEAU CANON

St-Émilion's Canon has seen its ups and downs, but is now performing superbly under the ownership of the Chanel fashion house. Managing director John Kolasa has built the château's flagship Merlot–Cabernet Franc blend into one of St-Émilion's finest, and it's priced accordingly.

- Clos Canon / 2009 / Saint-Emilion Grand Cru / $$$
  Canon's second wine is a livelier, juicier rendition of the house style, with ripe, spicy blackberry and cedar notes.
- Château Canon, 1er Grand Cru Classé / 2009 / Saint-Emilion Grand Cru / $$$$ This offers the luscious plum flavors typical of St-Émilion, along with graceful, mineral-edged complexity.

CHÂTEAU CANTEMERLE

With cases of wines from Bordeaux's most prestigious châteaus costing as much as a new car, it's a relief to rely on stalwarts like Château Cantemerle, an Haut-Médoc fifth-growth estate that's a go-to source of reasonably priced, well-made reds. Completely revamped and replanted in the 1980s, Cantemerle has come into its own in the past decade as its vineyards matured. Both the *grand vin* and the second wine, Les Allées de Cantemerle, make smart buys.

● **Château Cantemerle / 2008 / Haut-Médoc / $$$**
In line with Cantemerle's restrained, savory style, this medium-bodied red offers an elegant mix of smoky graphite, herbs and anise-laced black fruit.

CHÂTEAU D'AIGUILHE

This ancient estate is located in the Côtes de Castillon, a low-profile region not far from St-Émilion that's become a source of some of Bordeaux's best value reds. Well-known producer Stephan von Neipperg acquired Château d'Aiguilhe in 1998 and promptly turned it into one of the district's stars, with a signature blend of Merlot and Cabernet Franc that is among the most terrific wines in the region (and a great value, too).

WINE INTEL
Stéphane Derenoncourt, d'Aiguilhe's superstar consultant, masterminds wines for clients in 10 countries but chose Napa Valley for his culty namesake label: Derenoncourt California.

● **Château d'Aiguilhe / 2008 / Côtes de Castillon / $$** The brilliant Stéphane Derenoncourt helps craft this red, a ripe, black cherry–driven, suavely styled wine.

CHÂTEAU DE FIEUZAL

This historic Pessac-Léognan estate produces more red wine than white, but lately Fieuzal's beautifully crafted white—a flavorful blend of Sauvignon Blanc and Sémillon—has generated more excitement. Irish banker Lochlan Quinn purchased the estate more than a decade ago and immediately improved it; one of his wisest moves was hiring talented winemaker Stephen Carrier in 2007.

○ **Château de Fieuzal / 2009 / Pessac-Léognan / $$$**
Aging in new French oak barrels gives this vibrant, citrus- and melon-inflected white a lovely creamy texture and a faint hint of smoke.

CHÂTEAU GLORIA

Although its vineyards consist partly of land that once belonged to famous classified growths, this St-Julien estate was not included in Bordeaux's 1855 classification—because it didn't exist. It wasn't until 1939 that founder Henri Martin began assembling the more than 100 acres that make up Château Gloria, now run by his son-in-law. The estate's combination of top vineyards and no classification means that its wines are often savvy buys.

● **Château Gloria / 2009 / St-Julien / \$\$\$\$**
In a great vintage like 2009, this is an even better value than usual, with bold layers of plush blackberry and spice.

CHÂTEAU GREYSAC

Château Greysac is a standard-bearer for well-made and accessibly priced Bordeaux. The estate, which offers two reds each year (the second is called Château de By), is located north of St-Estèphe in the town of Bégadan. The top wine gets its supple tannins from a higher-than-normal percentage of Merlot in the blend—a full 58 percent in the 2009 vintage, for example.

● **Château Greysac / 2009 / Médoc / \$\$**
The winery bottles only about 70 percent of its production under the Greysac label (and less in off vintages)—which means that only the highest-quality juice is used.

CHÂTEAU LA CONSEILLANTE

The Nicolas family has owned Pomerol's La Conseillante since 1871, which explains the large "N" at the center of the label. The stunning flagship red is a blend of 80 percent Merlot and 20 percent Cabernet Franc. Exceptionally elegant and refined, this first-rate Pomerol comes at a correspondingly hefty price.

● **Château La Conseillante / 2009 / Pomérol / \$\$\$\$**
Stash this bottle away for a toddler's 21st birthday: dense, luscious and plum-driven, this wine will improve for decades.

CHÂTEAU LA CROIX DE GAY

This smallish Pomerol estate turns out a plush, complex red that sells for a fraction of the expected price. Dr. Alain Raynaud (consultant to Napa's Colgin label), whose family rejuvenated the property, ran Croix de Gay for years with his sister, Chantal Lebreton. Raynaud recently sold his share, but Lebreton continues in charge here, producing one stellar vintage after another.

● **Château La Croix de Gay** / 2008 / Pomérol / $$$
Croix de Gay's '08 offers Pomerol's signature plush, dark, spicy fruit character at a very fair price for the region.

CHÂTEAU LAGRANGE

From the Middle Ages to the present, this St-Julien property has seen a succession of owners. Today it is one of the prestigious estates owned or, as in the case of Château Beychevelle, co-owned by Suntory, the Japanese wine and spirits group. Since acquiring Lagrange in 1983, Suntory has spent millions to refurbish it, resulting in wines of intensity and finesse.

● **Château Lagrange** / 2009 / St-Julien / $$$$
Even though there's proportionately more Cabernet than usual in this year's blend, it's still graceful, with lush, mid-weight red currant and mineral flavors.

CHÂTEAU LES ORMES DE PEZ

Beyond the famous names of Bordeaux's classified estates there are terrific under-the-radar châteaus like this St-Estèphe *cru bourgeois*. Owned since 1930 by the Cazes family, Les Ormes de Pez is run today by the dynamic, 39-year-old Jean-Charles Cazes. He manages to keep quality high while also overseeing the family's famous Pauillac *grand cru*, Château Lynch-Bages.

● **Château Les Ormes de Pez** / 2009 / St-Estèphe / $$$
While many Bordeaux reds taste best decades after release, this plump, darkly fruity Cabernet blend is delicious now.

CHÂTEAU MALARTIC-LAGRAVIÈRE

Even in Graves, where both red and white grapes thrive, only a handful of *grand cru* producers, including Malartic-Lagravière, can claim classified wines of both types. This Pessac-Léognan estate came to prominence only recently, after the Belgian Bonnie family bought it in 1996. They've invested in the estate, even bringing in famed enologist Michel Rolland as a consultant. The Bonnies have turned this into a Bordeaux house to watch.

○ **Château Malartic Lagravière Grand Cru Classé de Graves** / 2010 / Pessac-Léognan / $$$ Sauvignon Blanc gives this creamy white its melon-citrusy flavors; Sémillon gives it weight.

● **Château Malartic Lagravière Grand Cru Classé de Graves** / 2009 / Pessac-Léognan / $$$$ Sustainably farmed grapes yield this intense, minerally red, redolent of black currants.

CHÂTEAU PALMER

Named for a British major general who acquired the estate in 1814, spent a fortune and ran it into the ground, Château Palmer is today among the stars of Margaux. It's now owned by the Sichel and Mähler-Besse families, who have kept the long-lived *grand vin* on a steady course while introducing a second wine, Alter Ego, which delivers plenty of class at a more modest price.

● **Alter Ego / 2009 / Margaux / $$$$**
For about one-fifth the price of Château Palmer, you can buy this richly textured, aromatic and seriously structured red.

● **Château Palmer / 2009 / Margaux / $$$$**
Low yields, minerally soils and a warm vintage show in this tightly coiled, firmly built blend. Give it time, or a steak.

CHÂTEAU PHÉLAN SÉGUR

Businessman and investor Xavier Gardinier sold two Champagne houses (Pommery and Lanson) in order to acquire this St-Estèphe estate in 1985. Though it's not a classified growth, Phélan Ségur is now performing like one, thanks at first to Gardinier's management, and now to that of his sons. Consultant Michel Rolland helps craft the wines—hence their rich, powerful fruit character.

● **Château Phélan Ségur / 2006 / St-Estèphe / $$$**
Made with just a bit more Cabernet than Merlot, this is classic St-Estèphe with a slightly modern edge; loads of black fruit and tobacco are woven with olive tapenade and licorice notes.

CHÂTEAU PICHON LONGUEVILLE COMTESSE DE LALANDE

Better known by its shorter nickname, Pichon-Lalande, this benchmark Pauillac producer owes its modern prominence to May-Éliane de Lencquesaing, who brought it to the forefront of Pauillac's great estates before selling it to Champagne Louis Roederer in 2007. Since then, Roederer has tweaked a few things—letting Cabernet play an increasing role in the elegantly styled blend, for example—and naming Philippe Moreau the new winemaker in 2011.

● **Château Pichon Longueville Comtesse de Lalande / 2009 / Pauillac / $$$$** This layered red—powerful yet immensely graceful—makes a compelling argument that now is the time to splurge on Bordeaux, and this is a bottle on which to do so.

CHÂTEAU RAUZAN-SÉGLA

The Wertheimer brothers (owners of the fashion house Chanel) bought this 350-year-old Margaux estate (plus Château Canon, p. 28) in the mid-'90s and tapped former Latour director John Kolasa to manage both properties. Made with moderate amounts of new oak, the Cabernet-driven blend exhibits classic Margaux grace and is a credit to Kolasa's keen sense of restraint.

● **Château Rauzan-Ségla, Grand Cru Classé / 2009 / Margaux / $$$$** There's a liqueur-like richness (but no heaviness) to this seductive red, which gets its soft, velvety tannins from a generous portion of Merlot.

BURGUNDY

CLAIM TO FAME

Burgundy's inconsistent weather means that vintages can vary wildly in quality from one year to the next, and its patchwork of regions (and subregions, and sub-sub-subregions) takes devoted effort to grasp. Why bother? Because no place on Earth can match Burgundy for the alluring grace of its best wines. In great vintages its ethereal, smoky reds and majestic whites offer both polish and power.

REGIONS TO KNOW

CHABLIS This cool northern subregion is geologically more similar to Champagne than it is to the rest of Burgundy, giving its wines—all made with Chardonnay—a stony austerity. Unlike other white Burgundies, the majority of Chablis wines are unoaked, resulting in fresh, pure whites with steely crispness. The region's best bottles are labeled with their *grand* or *premier cru* vineyard names, followed by the Chablis appellation; lesser wines are labeled simply Chablis. Petit Chablis wines are from less prestigious subregions.

CÔTE CHALONNAISE Though much red is made here, affordable Chardonnay has long been the hallmark of this region located on the Côte d'Or's southern border. While values can still be had, prices have crept up, and wines from its four top villages— Givry, Mercurey, Montagny and Rully—are the most expensive. Mercurey and Givry also make worthwhile reds.

CÔTE D'OR This high-rent region is split in two: northern Côte de Nuits and southern Côte de Beaune. The Côte de Nuits specializes in Pinot Noir and contains most of Burgundy's red *grands crus,* including those in legendary villages like Chambolle-Musigny, Gevrey-Chambertin and Nuits-St-Georges. The Côte de Beaune produces some of the planet's most compelling Chardonnays, from villages such as Puligny-Montrachet and Meursault, and a single *grand cru* red, Corton.

MÂCONNAIS At Burgundy's southern extreme, the Mâconnais is a go-to source of affordable, largely reliable whites. Though much basic entry-level wine gets made here, a growing number of ambitious, small-scale producers are pushing quality to new levels. Its most acclaimed offerings come from Pouilly-Fuissé.

❧ KEY GRAPES: WHITE
CHARDONNAY Most Burgundy whites are made from Chardonnay, though styles differ greatly among subregions. They range from the flinty, high-acid whites of Chablis in the north to the rich oak-aged offerings of the Cote d'Or, and reflect varying climates and soils as much as different winemaking traditions.

SAUVIGNON BLANC & ALIGOTÉ Small amounts of these grapes grow in a few spots around Burgundy: Sauvignon in the northern village of St-Bris, and Aligoté in the Côte Chalonnaise.

❧ KEY GRAPES: RED
PINOT NOIR With its silky texture, effortless depth and aromas of violets, cherries and earth, good red Burgundy is the ultimate in Pinot Noir. Unfortunately, bad red Burgundy can be just as expensive as the good, so choosing bottles wisely is key. Pinot Noir vines planted in well-drained limestone soils on sunny slopes tend to produce the most powerful, long-lived wines.

WINE TERMINOLOGY
Burgundy ranks wines by the vineyards from which they originate, not by the producer who made them (as in Bordeaux). Burgundy labels list the region; some also list the subregion, and the most prestigious include a vineyard name. Generally, the more specific the locality on a label, the finer the wine, but vintage is also very important when assessing quality.

BOURGOGNE Burgundy's most basic wines are labeled with just the name of the region, Bourgogne, and occasionally with the grape. Quality ranges from so-so to solid.

DISTRICT A district appellation (such as Chablis or Mâconnais) is the next step up in quality after AOC Bourgogne. The grapes must be grown exclusively in the named district.

VILLAGE A wine may take the name of a specific village if all of its grapes have been grown within that village's boundaries; for instance, Meursault or Nuits-St-Georges. These are more prestigious than district-wide appellations, but not necessarily better. Those from multiple villages within a larger region can append "Villages" to that region, as in Côte de Nuits–Villages (used for reds and a bit of white) and Côte de Beaune–Villages (always red). Côte de Nuits–Villages are terrific introductory wines and offer the best values in this pricey slice of Burgundy.

PREMIER CRU The second-highest distinction, *premier cru* vineyards have a lengthy history of producing superior wines. These wines must be made only with grapes grown in the designated vineyards, whose names are typically noted right after the village name (e.g., Meursault *Premier Cru* Genevrières).

GRAND CRU The highest classification in Burgundy, *grand cru* vineyards are so elite that some, like Montrachet, don't even include the *grand cru* title on their wine labels—their fame is presumed. To capitalize on their prestige, some villages added the name of the local *grand cru* vineyard to their own names. (For example, the wines from the town of Chassagne became Chassagne-Montrachet. While many are indeed superb, they're not true Montrachet.)

MONOPOLE A vineyard belonging to a single owner. In Burgundy, *monopoles* are rare. One of the most famous is La Tâche, a *grand cru* site in the Côte de Nuits belonging to Domaine de La Romanée Conti.

NÉGOCIANTS Merchants who buy wine, grapes or must (freshly pressed juice) from small growers and/or producers and create wines under their own names.

Producers/
Burgundy

BOUCHARD PÈRE & FILS

Bouchard has been on a roll lately. A relatively new winery (courtesy of the Henriot family, which bought Bouchard in 1995) contains all of the high-tech tools that winemakers covet, while land purchases have made the firm the largest vineyard owner in the Côte d'Or. Bouchard pays for purchased grapes based on ripeness, not weight, which helps keep quality high.

○ **Bouchard Père & Fils Pouilly-Fuissé / 2010 / Pouilly-Fuissé / $$** This lightly nutty white comes from Pouilly-Fuissé, the top subzone of the Mâconnais region.

○ **Bouchard Père & Fils Réserve Chardonnay / 2010 / Burgundy / $$** With its fresh, appley flavors, this Chardonnay is an affordable introduction to Burgundy's whites.

CHANSON PÈRE & FILS

Although its estate, which dates back to 1750, includes prime Côte de Beaune vineyards, Chanson's modern reputation sagged until the Bollinger Champagne group acquired it from the Chanson family in 1999. By rejecting purchased grapes of lower quality and fine-tuning farming and winemaking, Bollinger has transformed Chanson's lineup from ho-hum to first rate.

● **Domaine Chanson Clos des Mouches / 2009 / Beaune Premier Cru / $$$$** Textbook Burgundy, with intense yet graceful red berry flavors and a seductive texture.

DOMAINE BONNEAU DU MARTRAY

Charlemagne reportedly owned the parcel of the fabled Corton hill that's now in possession of the Bonneau du Martray family. As befits the former property of a king, it's one of the largest and best sites on Corton, which explains why Bonneau du Martray's Corton-Charlemagne is one of Burgundy's longest-lived and most storied *grands cru* whites.

○ **Domaine Bonneau du Martray / 2009 / Corton-Charlemagne Grand Cru / $$$$** The initial satiny texture is deceiving—with its dense flavor and vibrant acidity, this wine will age for years.

DOMAINE CHARLES AUDOIN

Savvy Burgundy buyers look to subzones such as Marsannay, in the Côte de Nuits, for great value. A case in point: the wines of the Audoin family. Charles and Marie-Françoise Audoin and their son Cyril create a number of single-vineyard wines as well as regional blends that compete with bottlings from more prestigious appellations, but at more accessible prices.

● **Domaine Charles Audoin Cuvée Marie Ragonneau / 2009 / Marsannay / $$$** This rich, velvety, spicy wine is packed with fruit and offers a depth rare for Marsannay reds.

DOMAINE CHRISTIAN MOREAU PÈRE & FILS

This is a newish domaine from an old Chablis family: The Moreaus sold their J. Moreau et Fils wine-merchant business in 1985, but held on to a few top vineyards. Today Christian Moreau, along with his son Fabien (whose experience includes a winemaking stint in New Zealand) and Christian's Canadian wife, Christine, turns out fine offerings from these prime sites.

○ **Domaine Christian Moreau Père & Fils / 2010 / Chablis / $$** This entry-level white exemplifies Moreau's flinty, racy style.

○ **Domaine Christian Moreau Père & Fils Vaillon / 2010 / Chablis Premier Cru / $$$** Amazingly fresh and bright, with stony mineral, lemon and saline notes.

○ **Domaine Christian Moreau Père & Fils Les Clos / 2010 / Chablis Grand Cru / $$$$** A thrillingly intense, firm and chalky white from the most prestigious *grand cru* in Chablis.

DOMAINE DE LA ROMANÉE-CONTI

Known by wine geeks everywhere simply as DRC, this estate exhausts superlatives: Its wines rank among the most expensive, coveted and collectible on the planet. Managed by the dapper, scholarly Aubert de Villaine and owned jointly by the de Villaine and Roch, Leroy and Bize families, the estate's jewel-like collection of organically farmed vineyards encompass legendary sites like La Tâche and the original Romanée-Conti plot.

● **Domaine de la Romanée-Conti Corton Prince Florent de Mérode / 2009 / Corton / $$$$** The first Corton made by DRC, this is darkly luscious and flamboyant.

● **Domaine de la Romanée-Conti Richebourg / 2009 / Richebourg / $$$$** This profound Burgundy is incredibly intense, but it's a baby. Cellar it for a decade, at least.

DOMAINE DE LA VOUGERAIE

The prominent Boisset family began buying pieces of some of Burgundy's most coveted vineyards years ago, including prized *grands crus* like Clos du Roi. They collected these crown jewels into one estate and baptized it Domaine de la Vougeraie, producing the first wines under this young label in 1999. Offerings include an impressive cross section of cuvées from the Côte d'Or, all biodynamically farmed.

○ **Le Clos Blanc de Vougeot Monopole / 2009 / Vougeot Premier Cru / $$$$** This dense, beautifully crafted white comes from a rare plot of Chardonnay on the famous Clos du Vougeot hill.

● **Les Marconnets / 2009 / Savigny-lès-Beaune Premier Cru / $$$** Marked by elegant floral and spice notes, this velvety red delivers a lot of refinement for the price.

DOMAINE GEORGES ROUMIER

The Roumier name is synonymous with superlative wines from Chambolle-Musigny, a part of the Côte de Nuits that, thanks to limestone-rich soils, yields some of Burgundy's most profound and delicate wines. Christophe Roumier's revered reds (and one white) come from small parcels of vines in famous appellations like Morey-Saint-Denis and Bonnes Mares, as well as the flagship *premiers crus* of Chambolle-Musigny.

● **Domaine G. Roumier / 2009 / Chambolle-Musigny Premier Cru / $$$$** Sourced from several vineyard sites around the village of Chambolle, this is easier to find than Roumier's single-vineyard cuvées.

● **Domaine G. Roumier Amoureuses / 2009 / Chambolle-Musigny Premier Cru / $$$$** Roumier's Amoureuses bottling is legendary for its elegant perfume and silky finesse; a single case costs a small fortune.

DOMAINE JEAN-MARC BOILLOT

With assorted cousins and siblings making wine up and down Burgundy's storied slopes, the Boillots can be hard to keep straight. Jean-Marc Boillot is a family star: After leaving his father's estate in 1984 and working for famed Burgundy vintner Olivier Leflaive for a time, he parlayed vineyards inherited from his grandparents into a larger, much-admired domaine of his own. Signature bottlings include lavish whites from Puligny-Montrachet and full-flavored reds from Pommard.

RARITIES & COLLECTIBLES

DOMAINE COCHE-DURY Rare and ravishing, Coche-Dury's *grand cru* Corton-Charlemagne is one of Burgundy's most coveted whites—recent vintages sell for upwards of $1,700 a bottle. Its fame (and that of Coche-Dury's whites overall) sometimes makes people overlook how good the domaine's reds are, too.

DOMAINE COMTE GEORGES DE VOGÜÉ This iconic Chambolle-Musigny property has been run by the same family for more than half a millennium, and has been making wines from Chambolle for the same length of time. It owns almost 18 acres in the famed *grand cru* of Musigny—nearly 80 percent of the site.

DOMAINE FRANÇOIS RAVENEAU Chablis at its peak, Raveneau's Les Clos is the top wine from the region's most renowned producer. Even its *premiers crus* have the ability to age gracefully for years.

○ **J.M. Boillot** / 2010 / **Montagny Premier Cru** / **$$**
Montagny is a subzone of the Côte Chalonnaise, a source of good values—like this juicy, green apple–driven bottling.

○ **Domaine J.M. Boillot Champ-Canet** / 2010 / **Puligny-Montrachet Premier Cru** / **$$$$** Puligny-Montrachet whites offer a rare combination of structure, density and raciness, evident in this muscular *premier cru*.

DOMAINE MATROT

Though this Meursault-based domaine produces wines spanning a range of prices and vineyards—from humble to haute—it's the entry-level bottlings that often stand out. For legal reasons, there are technically two domaines here, though everything is made by Thierry Matrot, whose style is pure and vibrant, thanks to a restrained use of oak barrels. His approach works especially well with basic offerings like his generic white Burgundy, which is usually a terrific value. That said, pricier village-level and *premier cru* wines are typically top-notch, too.

○ **Thierry et Pascale Matrot Chardonnay** / 2010 / **Bourgogne** / **$$** There's far more finesse to this vibrant, pear-inflected white than its humble regional label suggests.

○ **Thierry et Pascale Matrot Les Chalumeaux** / 2010 / **Puligny-Montrachet Premier Cru** / **$$$$** A tour de force of silky power and steely acidity, this extraordinary white exhibits a captivating mix of fruit, flowers and mineral notes.

DOMAINE RIJCKAERT

Belgian Chardonnay specialist Jean Rijckaert helped make boutique *négociant* Maison Verget famous, then left in the late 1990s to start this small estate in southern Burgundy. While his home address is best known for expertly crafted, affordable whites from estate vineyards in Burgundy's Mâconnais and in the Jura (plus an elegant bed-and-breakfast), Rijckaert also buys grapes from prestigious *crus* to create a few sumptuous cuvées.

○ **Rijckaert L'Épinet / 2009 / Viré-Clessé / $$**
The newish Mâconnais zone of Viré-Clessé yields zesty, flinty whites; Rijckaert's '09 adds succulent pear fruit to the mix.

○ **Rijckaert Les Croux Vieilles Vignes / 2009 / Pouilly-Fuissé / $$$** Old vines and a warmer vintage created this unusually round, fleshy Mâcon white.

DOMAINE SERVIN

François Servin could have kept making the same respectable wines his family's Chablis estate was known for, but instead he took a risk. His modifications—like pouring money into a high-tech winery and densely replanting vines—have made Domaine Servin a candidate for Chablis's "most improved" award, with a crop of top-flight bottlings that compete with the region's best.

○ **Domaine Servin Les Pargues / 2010 / Chablis / $$**
This single-vineyard white invites contemplation, with stony, savory lemon and mineral flavors that unfold in the glass.

○ **Domaine Servin Les Clos / 2010 / Chablis Grand Cru / $$$$**
Aging in oak has helped soften this broad, rich white, which comes from Chablis's greatest *cru*.

DOMAINE TAUPENOT-MERME

With 30 vineyard acres spread over 19 appellations, Taupenot-Merme is relatively large by Burgundy standards. Since taking over the family domaine in 1998, siblings and seventh-generation vintners Romain and Virginie Taupenot have brought finesse to the varied portfolio, which includes a stellar selection of top *crus*.

● **Domaine Taupenot-Merme / 2008 / Mazoyères-Chambertin Grand Cru / $$$$** Even in average vintages, the Taupenots turn out stunning wines, like this firm, meaty *grand cru*.

● **Domaine Taupenot-Merme La Riotte / 2009 / Morey-Saint-Denis Premier Cru / $$$$** Old vines in the tiny La Riotte vineyard yielded about 11 barrels of this gorgeous red.

JEAN-MARC BROCARD

The affable Jean-Marc Brocard started this label with a few acres of vines in the 1970s. Today he makes a range of terrific, unoaked wines from nearly 450 acres of vineyards spread throughout Chablis and beyond. His son Julien is converting the estate to biodynamic farming; look for ladybugs or moons on the labels of wines from environmentally green sites.

○ **Jean-Marc Brocard Domaine Sainte Claire / 2010 / Chablis / $$** A fresh, chalky white from the heart of Brocard's estate, near the village of Préhy.

○ **Jean-Marc Brocard Montée de Tonnerre / 2009 / Chablis Premier Cru / $$$** Of Chablis's 17 *premiers crus,* Montée de Tonnerre is one of the best, as this pure, stony bottling attests.

LES HÉRITIERS DU COMTE LAFON

With Dominique Lafon as managing director, this historic estate now manages all of its own vineyards, extracting top-tier wines from prized Côte de Beaune *crus* including Meursault and Montrachet. While these whites are the stars, Lafon also applies his viticultural skill (and biodynamic farming) to his other Mâconnais vineyards with great results—and better prices.

○ **Les Héritiers du Comte Lafon Mâcon-Villages / 2010 / Mâcon-Villages / $$** Very low yields in 2010 translated to extra concentration in this plump, zesty white.

○ **Les Héritiers du Comte Lafon Viré-Clessé / 2010 / Viré-Clessé / $$$** Few Mâcon wines are as voluptuous as this silky, old-vine Chardonnay.

LOUIS MICHEL & FILS

Chablis vintner Louis Michel gave up using barrels to age his wines four decades ago, preferring the freshness and mineral drive of whites fermented and matured entirely in stainless steel. With incredible vineyard holdings that span humble Petit Chablis to three prestigious *grands crus,* his portfolio offers exciting options for any Chablis fan, regardless of budget.

○ **Louis Michel & Fils / 2010 / Chablis / $$**
This white possesses the characteristically mineral, saline edge that makes Chablis the ideal wine for seafood.

○ **Louis Michel & Fils Vaudésir / 2009 / Chablis Grand Cru / $$$$** The warmth of the '09 vintage shows in the broad, lush stone-fruit flavors that define this *grand cru.*

MAISON JOSEPH DROUHIN

Since 1880, the Drouhin family has steadily added to its collection of Côte d'Or vineyards, which include parts of such legendary plots as Musigny and Vosne-Romanée. Today more than half of Drouhin's Burgundy offerings are made with estate grapes, all organically farmed. That control, plus the family's focus on quality, keeps Drouhin among Burgundy's finest producers.

○ **Joseph Drouhin Morgeot Marquis de Laguiche / 2010 / Chassagne-Montrachet Premier Cru / $$$$** The village of Chassagne produces superlative whites, like this satiny, peach-laden example.

● **Joseph Drouhin / 2010 / Côte de Beaune / $$$**
Adding fruit from *premier cru* vines gives this gently spicy red more depth than its Côte de Beaune label suggests.

● **Joseph Drouhin / 2010 / Vosne-Romanée / $$$$**
This muscular, violet-scented red comes from Vosne-Romanée, one of the world's greatest spots for Pinot Noir.

MAISON LOUIS JADOT

Few producers anywhere match this *négociant's* ability to turn out both reliably tasty, value-packed everyday wines and world-class cuvées. This is due partly to the skill of Jacques Lardière, Louis Jadot's recently departed technical director of 30-plus years, and to the inarguable quality of the company's fruit, which it sources from every major zone in Burgundy, including Beaujolais and Chablis.

○ **Louis Jadot / 2009 / Meursault / $$$**
This rich, toasty Chardonnay is a solid example of the famously elegant white wines of Meursault.

● **Château des Jacques / 2010 / Moulin-à-Vent / $$**
Jadot bought this estate in 1996 and imparts these Beaujolais reds with noticeable Burgundian power and ageability.

SIMONNET-FEBVRE

This ancient Chablis producer is a great source not just of minerally, Chardonnay-based wines, but also of sparkling *crémants* (see p. 290) and, more unusually, Sauvignon-led whites from the Yonne district. Beaune-based Louis Latour acquired the estate from the Simonnet family in 2003, providing an influx of cash and expertise that has unlocked the potential of the winery's formidable vineyard sources.

○ **Simonnet-Febvre Sauvignon / 2010 / Saint-Bris / $**
A juicy, melon-inflected white from the only zone in Burgundy that allows Sauvignon Blanc.

○ **Simonnet-Febvre / 2010 / Chablis / $$**
Like all of the winery's offerings, this intro-level Chablis is made without oak, keeping its fruity flavors clean and pure.

○ **Simonnet-Febvre Vaillons / 2010 / Chablis Premier Cru / $$**
A top *premier cru* from a winning vintage, this powerful, vibrant and minerally white represents an incredible value.

TRÉNEL FILS

This up-and-coming Mâcon-based *négociant* has been reborn under the direction of Gilles Meimoun, who came on board in 2006 and now heads it up. Under Meimoun's enthusiastic direction, Trénel's Mâcon and Beaujolais wines have become dependable classics, owing to major changes in everything from farming (with an emphasis on organics) to vinification.

○ **Trénel / 2010 / Mâcon-Villages / $**
A straightforward, appealing Mâcon at a good price, with brisk, bright apple and citrus notes.

○ **Trénel Hommage à André Trénel / 2010 / Saint-Véran / $$**
Aging half of this organically grown Chardonnay in barrels gives it a polished texture and a hint of creaminess.

VINCENT GIRARDIN

His wines may seem traditional, but Vincent Girardin is a thoroughly modern winemaker. Made in a state-of-the-art facility in Meursault, Girardin's seductive, fruit-driven Côte d'Or reds and whites—mostly *grands* and *premiers crus*—have made his reputation, while his entry-level Mâconnais whites offer great value.

○ **Vincent Girardin Cuvée Saint-Vincent Chardonnay / 2010 / Burgundy / $$** Girardin's basic white is made with grapes from the pricey Chassagne-Montrachet and Meursault districts, which explains its silky finesse.

○ **Vincent Girardin Vieilles Vignes / 2010 / Rully / $$**
Crisp apple, floral and mineral tones are the signature of Rully's whites; old vines give this example an added density.

● **Domaine Vincent Girardin Santenay Les Gravières / 2009 / Santenay Premier Cru / $$$** A plush, structured red that shows how top *crus* in less prestigious regions—like Santenay's Les Gravières—can deliver bang for the buck.

WILLIAM FÈVRE

Sometimes selling out to a larger company improves a winery. That's exactly what happened at this already-terrific Chablis estate after William Fèvre sold it in 1998 to the Henriot Champagne company. Henriot sent in winemaker Didier Séguier, who increased grape quality by reducing vineyard yields and decreased the amount of new oak used for aging. The result has been more complex wines with purer, fresher flavors.

○ **Domaine William Fèvre / 2010 / Chablis / $$**
Made from estate-owned grapes, this zesty, lemon-edged bottling offers impressive focus for not a lot of money.

○ **William Fèvre Champs Royaux / 2010 / Chablis / $$**
Exactly what basic Chablis should be: refreshing, minerally and highly delicious.

BURGUNDY

BEAUJOLAIS

CLAIM TO FAME
Though considered part of Burgundy, Beaujolais has a different climate (warmer) and a different soil (granite, schist and sandstone) from the rest of the region. It also features a different signature grape: Gamay. Responsible for tanker-loads of the grapey, simple red called Beaujolais Nouveau, Gamay also yields the deeply lush, floral-edged reds of Beaujolais's 10 *crus*, which are some of the most underrated wines on the planet.

KEY GRAPES: RED
GAMAY Supple tannins and juicy, exuberant fruit define this easy-to-love variety. Lighter wines from cooler vintages showcase tangy cranberry and strawberry tones; riper, more concentrated grapes yield medium-bodied, graceful red wines loaded with mouth-filling raspberry and cherry flavors.

WINE TERMINOLOGY
BEAUJOLAIS NOUVEAU Designed to be consumed within weeks of harvest, Beaujolais Nouveau is as light-bodied and simple as red wine gets. By French law, it is released the third Thursday of every November, conveniently coinciding with the start of the U.S. holiday season.

BEAUJOLAIS Wines labeled Beaujolais offer slightly more substance than Beaujolais Nouveau, with fruity berry flavors and succulent acidity.

BEAUJOLAIS-VILLAGES Only wines made with grapes sourced from 38 villages occupying gentle hills at the center of the region can be designated Beaujolais-Villages. Typically produced with more care and precision than basic Beaujolais, these wines exhibit bright, red berry flavors as well as an added depth of mineral and spice.

CRU BEAUJOLAIS The region's finest wines come from 10 hillside villages in the northern part of Beaujolais, where granite and schist soils and sunny slopes yield riper, more concentrated wines. Deep flavors and ample tannins give the best bottles the ability to age, unlike other Beaujolais. *Cru Beaujolais* labels often list only the village name: Brouilly, Chénas, Chiroubles, Côte de Brouilly, Fleurie, Juliénas, Morgon, Moulin-à-Vent, Régnié or St-Amour.

Producers/ Beaujolais

CHÂTEAU THIVIN

The oldest estate on Mont Brouilly—an extinct volcano whose southern slopes yield some of Beaujolais's best wines—Château Thivin dates its origins to the 15th century. The Geoffray family purchased it in 1877 and, over generations, helped turn the Côte de Brouilly into a much-respected appellation and Château Thivin into its star. Claude Geoffray and son Claude-Edouard continue the legacy today.

● **Château Thivin / 2010 / Brouilly / $$**
Harvested from vines grown in pink, granite-rich sand, Thivin's Brouilly inflects Gamay's exuberant fruitiness with spicy white pepper notes.

● **Château Thivin / 2010 / Côte de Brouilly / $$**
A distinctive mineral edge underscores this red's classically buoyant, graceful berry and floral notes.

DOMAINE DU VISSOUX

Pierre-Marie Chermette is one of Beaujolais's best-known "naturalist" winemakers, eschewing common techniques such as adding yeast or sulfites to his wines. Thanks to super-low yields, prime vineyards and labor-intensive farming, Chermette's grapes get so ripe that, unlike most of his neighbors, he adds little or no sugar. The resulting wines display a profound sense of place.

● **Domaine du Vissoux Cuvée Traditionnelle Vieilles Vignes / 2010 / Beaujolais / $$** Loaded with deep red berry flavors— the result of very old vines—this is pure pleasure.

● **Vissoux Les Trois Roches / 2010 / Moulin-à-Vent / $$** This bottling showcases Beaujolais's ability to age, with broad black cherry and mineral tones that only improve with time.

GEORGES DUBOEUF

Even more remarkable than this *négociant*'s huge output (some 2.5 million cases of Beaujolais wine yearly) is that so much of it is so delicious. Duboeuf helped to create the Beaujolais Nouveau craze in the 1970s; today its lineup also includes many Beaujolais-Villages bottlings (with the well-known "Flower Label"), plus *cru* wines offering more-serious drinking pleasure.

● **Georges Duboeuf "Flower Label" / 2010 / Beaujolais-Villages / $** Straightforward and affordable, this is overflowing with fresh red and black berry flavors.

● **Georges Duboeuf "Flower Label" / 2010 / Fleurie / $** Thanks to its juicy, focused plum and spice tones, the Fleurie "Flower Label" pairs well with many different foods.

LOIRE VALLEY

CLAIM TO FAME

White wines star in this meandering river valley, the longest (and probably most château-dotted) in France. In fact, the Loire Valley produces more whites than any other French region. They range from the flinty, citrusy Sauvignon Blancs of Sancerre and Pouilly-Fumé to complex Chenin Blancs in Vouvray to brisk, oyster-friendly bottlings at the coast, where the Loire River meets the cold Atlantic just past Muscadet. But don't overlook Loire red wines: Thanks to the valley's cooler climate, reds here are refreshingly crisp and food-friendly.

REGIONS TO KNOW

ANJOU & SAUMUR For quality wine production, Chenin Blanc is the most important grape in these central Loire regions. In Anjou it often gets made into well-respected sweet wines. Savennières, a small Anjou subzone, uses Chenin Blanc to create incredibly concentrated dry (as well as sweet) whites that are among the greatest examples of the grape. Red and rosé wines from Anjou and Saumur highlight the fresh side of Loire Cabernet Franc, with bright acidity and green herb notes. Saumur-Champigny is exclusively a red wine region.

MUSCADET The largest white wine appellation in France, Muscadet relies entirely on the Melon de Bourgogne grape variety, which thrives in the region's relatively cool, coastal climate and sandy soil that would prove disastrous for most grapes. However, the best Muscadet bottlings come from grapes grown on rocky soil, not sand, and in 2011, three new designations based on soil types, called *crus communaux*, were created. (See Wine Terminology, p. 48.)

SANCERRE & POUILLY-FUMÉ Benchmark whites made from Sauvignon Blanc are the calling card of these sister appellations in the upper Loire. Sancerres tend to be lighter and more perfumed, while Pouilly-Fumés are often fuller-bodied, with smoky mineral, herb and citrus tones. For Sauvignon Blanc made in a similar style at a more affordable price, look to the satellite regions of Menetou-Salon, Quincy and Reuilly. Though famous for white wines, Sancerre produces small amounts of rosé and red wine from Pinot Noir.

TOURAINE This large region centered around the midvalley town of Tours grows a dizzying array of red and white grapes, including Sauvignon Blanc, Gamay, Pinot Noir, Cabernet Sauvignon, Malbec (known locally as Côt) and a local specialty, Pineau d'Aunis. But none of the wines made from them compare to the legendary Chenin Blanc–based white wines of the premier subregion, Vouvray. Whether bone-dry or sweet, sparkling or still, they're among the world's most enthralling (and long-lived) whites. Touraine is also responsible for the Loire Valley's best red wines (in the subregions of Chinon and Bourgeuil), smoky renditions of Cabernet Franc.

❦ KEY GRAPES: WHITE

CHENIN BLANC Is there a grape more versatile than Chenin Blanc? Its wines veer from light and mouth-puckeringly tart to sweet, full and rich, and come in sparkling, still and dessert bottlings. Their common thread: bright acidity, which gives the best Chenin Blancs amazing longevity.

MELON DE BOURGOGNE Coastal Muscadet's signature grape yields light-bodied, fairly neutral and refreshing whites with light citrus flavors and a hint of salty sea spray. Top bottles from a few select producers buck the norm, making small-lot cuvées from old vines that offer intense, chalky minerality and richer fruit.

SAUVIGNON BLANC In contrast to more exuberantly tropical and herbaceous Sauvignon Blancs from elsewhere in the world, Loire examples combine the grape's refreshing acidity and trademark citrus tones with smoky mineral and chalk aromas.

❦ KEY GRAPES: RED

CABERNET FRANC The Loire's most distinctive red variety turns out wines with red-fruit, herb and pepper notes typical of cool-climate reds, and often, a smoky tobacco edge. Their high acidity and sometimes astringent tannins mean they're built for food.

WINE TERMINOLOGY

CRUS COMMUNAUX Located within Muscadet's largest and best-known subregion, Sèvre et Maine, this new designation identifies that region's top *terroirs* and enforces strict quality controls on wines labeled with it. Three *crus communaux*—Clisson, Gorges and Le Pallet—were approved in 2011; more are expected.

SEC Meaning "dry," this is a key term to look for when shopping for Vouvray, Savennières or other Chenin Blanc–based whites.

DEMI-SEC Though the term translates as "half-dry," demi-sec wines actually taste sweet (but are not dessert wines).

SUR LIE Appearing on Muscadet's better bottles, this term indicates that a wine has been aged on its lees, which are sediments left over after a wine's fermentation. The dead yeasts give a wine a creamier texture and a light, nutty edge.

VIN DE PAYS DU VAL DE LOIRE Much of the Loire's inexpensive, everyday wine gets pumped out under this massive, region-wide designation, which is also an umbrella region for many smaller *vin de pays* designations within it. These wines list a grape variety as well as a vintage.

Producers/ Loire Valley

CHÂTEAU DE LA RAGOTIÈRE

The three Couillaud brothers purchased this sprawling, ancient Muscadet estate 30-odd years ago and have spent the decades since transforming it into an impressive quality leader. Their innovative Chardonnays have shown that grape's surprising affinity for the region's soil, but it's their classic, zesty Muscadets that are most worth a hunt.

○ **Château de la Ragotière Muscadet / 2010 / Muscadet-Sèvre et Maine / $$** Old vines in the best subregion yield an unusually intense white, redolent of stony minerals, citrus and peach.

DOMAINE DE LADOUCETTE

Based in a turreted château in Pouilly-Fumé that could serve as an inspiration for a Disney castle, this family-owned winery is one of the Loire's largest, offering terrific wines under a handful of labels from across the valley's appellations, including De Ladoucette (Pouilly-Fumé), Comte LaFond (Sancerre), Les Deux Tours (Touraine), Marc Brédif (Vouvray) and La Poussie (a single stellar Sancerre site), plus another cuvée from the home estate in Pouilly-Fumé, Baron de L.

○ **Marc Brédif / 2010 / Vouvray / $$**
It's a mystery why Chenin Blanc isn't more popular, especially with juicy, affordably wonderful examples like this around.

○ **Comte LaFond / 2010 / Sancerre / $$$**
This offers all the zesty, herb- and lime-tinged notes you expect from Sauvignon, plus a mouth-filling lushness.

○ **de Ladoucette / 2009 / Pouilly-Fumé / $$$**
The warmer '09 vintage added richness to this elegant, intense Sauvignon's crisp citrus and melon flavors.

DOMAINE DES AUBUISIÈRES

Since inheriting this estate from his father in 1982, Bernard Fouquet has elevated Aubuisières to one of Vouvray's best. His dry, off-dry and sparkling wines are all made from Chenin Blanc but come from two types of soil, each yielding fruit with distinctive flavors. With some wines aged in steel and others in oak, Fouquet's range showcases the chameleon character of Chenin Blanc—at great value.

○ **Domaine des Aubuisières Cuvée de Silex / 2010 / Vouvray / $$** There's a delicate, lightly floral edge to this precise, very pure and fresh white.

○ **Domaine des Aubuisières Les Girardières / 2010 / Vouvray / $$** This single-vineyard Chenin Blanc offers a quintessential Vouvray mix of penetrating minerality and a hint of sweetness, plus juicy pear notes.

DOMAINE DES CORBILLIÈRES

Domaine des Corbillières produces some of the greatest values coming out of the Touraine region today. The estate's ridiculously affordable and delicious wines obtain their rare intensity from old vines and their finesse from skilled proprietors Dominique and Véronique Barbou.

● **Domaine des Corbillières Rosé / 2011 / Touraine / $** Aromatic, strawberry-inflected flavors and a great price make this a fine candidate for a house rosé.

● **Domaine des Corbillières Cuvée Demoiselles / 2009 / Touraine / $** This juicy, dense blend of three red varieties offers proof that the best Touraine reds are underestimated and underpriced.

DOMAINE DIDIER DAGUENEAU

Didier Dagueneau, the prodigiously bearded wild man of the Loire, made some of the best Pouilly-Fumés and Sancerres ever. He died when his ultralight plane crashed in 2008, but his son, Benjamin, has kept the wines at the same level. Extremely low vineyard yields and, most unusual, aging in oak barrels result in some of world's greatest Sauvignons.

○ **Silex par Louis-Benjamin Dagueneau / 2009 / Blanc Fumé de Pouilly / $$$$** Flint-rich soils (silex) give this distinctive white its pronounced stone flavors; its silken texture comes from being fermented and aged in oak.

DOMAINE DU CLOSEL/CHÂTEAU DES VAULTS

This benchmark Savennières estate has been known as Château des Vaults for more than 500 years and in more recent decades has gone by both names. Owned today by Evelyne de Jessey, it boasts organically cultivated vineyards that include a substantial portion of the exalted Clos du Papillon site. The winery's classic Savennières bottlings rank among the world's finest examples of Chenin Blanc.

○ **Domaine du Closel La Jalousie** / 2010 / Savennières / $$
Made from the estate's youngest vines (which are still 20-plus years old), this shows honeyed apple notes and bright acidity.

○ **Domaine du Closel Les Caillardières** / 2009 / Savennières / $$ Typically, this wine has a touch of sweetness, but in '09 its pear-liqueur flavors are completely dry.

DOMAINE FRANÇOIS CHIDAINE

The Chidaine family comes from Montlouis, regarded in Vouvray as the wrong side of the Loire River. Yet François Chidaine makes some of the region's freshest, most compelling whites, both from family vineyards and more recently acquired sites in a handful of the Loire's top subzones. Biodynamic farming and a light hand in the cellar give Chidaine's wines a freshness and minerality evident even in his basic Touraine bottlings.

Francois Chidaine Rosé / 2011 / Touraine / $
Chidaine boosts the flavor of this dry, brisk rosé by blending Grolleau, a local grape, with Pinot Noir for more depth.

DOMAINE PASCAL JOLIVET

Pascal Jolivet comes from a winemaking family, but he started his own wine business from scratch in the 1980s, buying grapes from all over Sancerre and Pouilly-Fumé. These regions are still his portfolio's focus, but now Jolivet also owns substantial vineyard acreage, allowing him to fine-tune the farming of his grapes.

○ **Pascal Jolivet** / 2010 / Sancerre / $$
Redolent of melon and citrus, this fruity, focused white drinks well on its own or with a wide array of foods.

○ **Pascal Jolivet Terres Blanches** / 2010 / Pouilly-Fumé / $$$
A single-vineyard Sauvignon, sleekly styled and mineral-laden.

○ **Pascal Jolivet Exception Blanc** / 2010 / Sancerre / $$$$
The firm acidity and tightly wound flavors of Jolivet's top cuvée make it one of Sancerre's most ageworthy whites.

DOMAINE VACHERON

Since taking over this respected Sancerre estate from their fathers, Vacheron cousins Jean-Laurent and Jean-Dominique have made it one to watch. Low yields, biodynamic farming, and handpicked fruit are among the factors that keep upping quality. Vacheron sources grapes from 100 acres of prime vineyards—mainly old vines and mostly located on flint-rich rock.

○ **Domaine Vacheron Blanc / 2011 / Sancerre / $$$**
Tangy acidity and a grapefruit-peel scent define Vacheron's entry-level Sancerre.

○ **Domaine Vacheron Les Romains / 2010 / Sancerre / $$$$**
One of Vacheron's most admired wines, this minerally single-vineyard Sauvignon has been made since 1997.

● **Domaine Vacheron Rosé / 2011 / Sancerre / $$**
A silky bottling made from Pinot Noir, like all Sancerre rosés.

HENRI BOURGEOIS

This 10th-generation *négociant* defies stereotypes: Despite its considerable size, it makes high-quality wines across a range of prices; despite its age, it's one of the region's most progressive estates. Owner Jean-Marie Bourgeois led the company's foray into screw-caps, and even founded a winery in New Zealand.

○ **Henri Bourgeois / 2011 / Pouilly-Fumé / $$**
Aging this fragrant Sauvignon entirely in tanks (not barrels) highlights its refreshing citrus notes.

○ **Henri Bourgeois La Côte des Monts Damnés / 2010 / Sancerre / $$** This powerful white comes from a Chavignol vineyard that has yielded remarkable Sauvignon for centuries.

YANNICK AMIRAULT

Making stellar Cabernet Franc in the Loire every year is incredibly hard. Yet Yannick Amirault's wines are good no matter what the vintage. Since taking over his family estate at 22, the prodigiously talented Amirault has improved existing vineyards and added new ones, sourcing grapes from both of the top Cabernet Franc zones: St-Nicolas-de-Bourgueil and Bourgueil.

● **Yannick Amirault La Mine / 2009 / St-Nicolas-de-Bourgueil / $$** A serious, food-friendly red with polished, spicy plum tones.

● **Yannick Amirault La Petite Cave / 2009 / Bourgueil / $$$**
The perfect wine to convince someone how good Loire reds can be, with generous boysenberry notes and a firm structure.

RHÔNE VALLEY

CLAIM TO FAME

From the exalted, powerful reds of the tiny Hermitage appellation in the north to the southern Rhône's suppler, berry-rich red blends, the Rhône offers some of the best quality for price in all of France. Northern Rhône reds get their spice and brooding dark-fruit flavors from the dominant Syrah grape; in contrast, the reds of the warmer, far larger southern Rhône are multivariety blends based chiefly on Grenache. White wines often get overshadowed by both region's reds, but can be terrific values.

REGIONS TO KNOW

NORTHERN RHÔNE A narrow, 50-or-so-mile stretch of steep and often terraced hills, the northern Rhône occupies a transitional zone between cooler-climate Burgundy to the north and the sunnier Mediterranean climes to the south—a position that's reflected in its wines' alluring mix of finesse and robust flavor. Though responsible for less than 5 percent of the Rhône's total production, the northern Rhône is the source of many of its most celebrated wines. Its top subregions for reds include Côte-Rôtie ("roasted slope," for its sunny exposure), Cornas, and the legendary Hermitage hill, whose wines were a favorite of Louis XIII. For whites, the tiny Condrieu appellation produces coveted, voluptuous wines from Viognier. The northern Rhône's largest subzone, Crozes-Hermitage, is responsible for about half of the region's wine. Much of it is ordinary, but values abound.

SOUTHERN RHÔNE Some 30 miles south of the northern Rhône, the sunnier southern Rhône begins. Many grapes are permitted in various subregions across the southern Rhône, most selected for their ability to withstand the hotter Mediterranean climate—in Châteauneuf-du-Pape, the most prestigious district, 13 varieties are allowed. The Gigondas and Vacqueyras appellations produce mostly red wines similar to (but less profound and expensive than) those of Châteauneuf-du-Pape. Across the river, the Lirac and Tavel districts are best known for outstanding rosés and increasingly some reds. And farther afield the satellite regions of Ventoux, Luberon and Costières de Nîmes make wines similar to basic Côtes-du-Rhône (see p. 54).

❦ KEY GRAPES: WHITE

GRENACHE BLANC, CLAIRETTE & BOURBOULENC Used only in the southern part of the Rhône Valley, these plump grape varieties typically get blended with Marsanne, Roussanne and Viognier to create the region's medium-bodied, white peach– and citrus-inflected wines.

MARSANNE & ROUSSANNE These fragrant varieties are usually blended together to make the full-bodied, nutty, pear-scented white wines of the northern Rhône Valley's Hermitage, Crozes-Hermitage and St-Joseph appellations. In the southern Rhône, they are often used to complement Viognier. Though they're not high in acidity, the resulting wines often have the ability to age for a decade or more.

VIOGNIER Lush and fragrant, the honeysuckle-scented Viognier is responsible for celebrated whites of the northern Rhône's Condrieu appellation.

❦ KEY GRAPES: RED

GRENACHE The southern Rhône's darkly fruity, full-bodied red wines are made primarily with Grenache, which gets bolstered with a combination of Cinsaut, Syrah, Mourvèdre and/or Carignane in a typical blend.

SYRAH The only red grape variety permitted in the production of northern Rhône reds, Syrah can achieve fabulous power and complexity, expressing a captivating mix of dark fruit accented by black pepper and meat flavors. Most northern Rhône red wines are allowed to include regional white grapes, except in Cornas, where Syrah must stand alone.

WINE TERMINOLOGY

CÔTES-DU-RHÔNE Côtes-du-Rhône is the southern Rhône's most basic category, and represents the vast majority of wines produced here. Most Côtes-du-Rhône wines come from the south, although the entire Rhône Valley is permitted to use the designation. Very little basic Côtes-du-Rhône wine comes from the northern Rhône; most northern Rhône bottlings meet higher standards and are entitled to label their wines with one of the region's eight *crus*.

CÔTES-DU-RHÔNE VILLAGES This designation identifies wines made from grapes grown in the dozens of southern Rhône villages that satisfy stricter quality requirements than those for the basic Côtes-du-Rhône designation. Eighteen high-quality villages have earned the right to append their name to the wine label, for example Côtes-du-Rhône Villages Cairanne.

Producers/ Rhône Valley

ALBERT BELLE

Albert Belle's family used to grow grapes for the local co-op; today this northern Rhône vintner's reds are among the best in the large Crozes-Hermitage appellation (the estate extends into Hermitage as well). Along with son Philippe, Belle produces traditionally crafted Syrahs that display a rare mix of concentration and finesse; his rich yet balanced whites are a blend of Roussane and Marsanne grapes.

- **Domaine Belle Cuvée Louis Belle** / 2009 / Crozes-Hermitage / $$ Belle's top-tier cuvée offers a deep, mineral-inflected richness that evokes wines from the more prestigious Hermitage appellation.
- **Domaine Belle Les Pierelles** / 2009 / Crozes-Hermitage / $$ Smoky and spicy, Belle's Les Pierelles delivers the flair and complexity of a much pricier wine.

CHÂTEAU D'AQUÉRIA

Château d'Aquéria is the leading estate in Tavel, a tiny subregion that produces some of the world's greatest rosés. Rich with history, d'Aquéria takes its name from one Count Louis Joseph d'Aquéria, who reportedly planted the estate's first grapes in 1595; its neoclassical château dates to the 18th century. The current owners, the de Bez family, focus most of their production on a single, reliably elegant rosé.

- **Château d'Aquéria** / 2011 / Tavel / $$ D'Aquéria's juicy, coral-colored dry rosé is substantial enough to stand in for red wine at the dinner table—and it is fabulously food-friendly, too.

CHÂTEAU DE BEAUCASTEL/PERRIN & FILS

One of most revered names in Châteauneuf-du-Pape, Château de Beaucastel is the southern Rhône's flagship producer. The Perrin family owns more than a thousand acres and produces a huge variety of wine, ranging from the value Vieille Ferme label to such cult classics as the Mourvèdre-based Hommage à Jacques Perrin—a wine as legendary for its price as for its power.

- La Vieille Ferme / 2010 / Ventoux / $
  Plum and spice define this easy-drinking four-variety blend.
- Famille Perrin Les Cornuds / 2009 / Vinsobres / $$
  This Syrah-Grenache blend comes from Vinsobres, recently promoted from a basic village rank to its own *cru*.
- Château de Beaucastel / 2008 / Châteauneuf-du-Pape / $$$$
  Great producers make superb wine even in tough years. This complex, violet-scented red is a perfect example.

CHÂTEAU DE SAINT COSME

Winemaker Louis Barruol's family acquired this legendary Gigondas estate in 1490—but the property dates to Roman times (a tasting-room wall was built in the second century). The Barruols offer a supremely well-crafted lineup. Château de Saint Cosme wines come from its organic estate; Saint Cosme and Little James' Basket Press bottlings are made from purchased grapes.

- ○ Saint Cosme / 2011 / Côtes-du-Rhône / $$
  Louis Barruol says that the obscure Picpoul grape saved this four-variety blend, lending it freshness in a warm vintage.
- Saint Cosme / 2011 / Côtes-du-Rhône / $$
  Using only Syrah for this wine means that it's spicier and more structured than most Côtes-du-Rhônes.
- Château de Saint Cosme / 2010 / Gigondas / $$$
  This profound Gigondas shows tremendous sophistication and has the firmness to age effortlessly for many years.

CHÂTEAU GUIOT

Château Guiot helped put the Costières de Nîmes region on the world's fine-wine radar. This slice of Provence used to be considered part of the Languedoc but was elevated in 2004 to the more esteemed Rhône appellation. Sylvia Cornut makes the wines, while husband François tends their 200-plus vineyard acres. Top red cuvées are dense blends; the two Vins de Pays du Gard bottlings (under the Mas de Guiot label) are great values.

RARITIES & COLLECTIBLES

CHÂTEAU RAYAS This estate's two Châteauneuf-du-Pape reds, a namesake flagship and Pignan, command cultlike devotion. For a more affordable introduction to vigneron Emmanuel Reynaud's style and sensibility, look for the family's Château des Tours Vacqueyras.

DOMAINE HENRI BONNEAU Tradition-minded Bonneau still ages his legendary Châteauneuf cuvées—among them the profound, and dauntingly priced, Réserve des Célestins—for up to 10 years in an ancient underground cellar behind his house.

J.L. CHAVE Hermitage reaches its apogee in the top-tier reds and whites of this acclaimed estate, now run by Jean Louis Chave (whose family established it in 1481). Chave's most sought-after wine, the ultra-rare Cuvée Cathelin, is made only in the best years.

- **Château Guiot / 2011 / Costières de Nîmes / $**
Refreshing watermelon flavors make this estate-grown rosé a great summer wine staple.
- **Mas de Guiot Cabernet-Syrah / 2009 / Vin de Pays du Gard / $$** A blend of two bold red grape varieties, this exuberant bottling shows the warmth of southern France in its rich plum and berry flavors.

CHÂTEAU MONT-RÉDON

The largest single-estate vineyard of Châteauneuf-du-Pape, Mont-Rédon commands more than 200 acres of vineyards, with vines that average 45 years of age and include all of the 13 grape varieties approved in the region, a rare occurrence today. Mont-Rédon manages its historic vineyards with modern, quality-improving technology, like grape-sorting that's assisted by computer imaging of the berries.

- **Château Mont-Rédon / 2010 / Châteauneuf-du-Pape / $$$**
This graceful, lavender-edged blend is an outstanding example of a Châteauneuf white.
- **Château Mont-Rédon / 2010 / Côtes-du-Rhône / $$**
The brilliant 2010 vintage shows in this polished red, which is elegant beyond its price.
- **Château Mont-Rédon / 2007 / Châteauneuf-du-Pape / $$$**
Mont-Rédon's premier bottling has layers of spice and supple plum and berry flavors.

CLOS DES PAPES

Vintner Paul-Vincent Avril inherited both this ancient and well-regarded Châteauneuf-du-Pape estate and a knack for excelling with red and white wines. These factors mean that obtaining a taste of any of his acclaimed cuvées—especially the rare whites—can be tough. But wines from Clos des Papes are worth the splurge: Under Avril, recent offerings are world-class.

○ **Clos des Papes / 2010 / Châteauneuf-du-Pape / $$$$**
A flamboyant, full-bodied white with lingering honeysuckle, citrus and beeswax notes.

● **Le Petit Vin d'Avril / NV / Vin de Table / $$**
An insider's stealth choice, this compulsively drinkable red is disguised behind a humble, nonvintage label.

● **Clos des Papes / 2009 / Châteauneuf-du-Pape / $$$$**
Captivating aromas of incense and dried violets are just the introduction to this definitive Châteauneuf.

DELAS FRÈRES

The all-star team at this well-known *négociant*—including enologist Jacques Grange and winemaker Jean-François Farinet—has transformed a once-lackluster portfolio into a treasure trove of memorable wines. Their talent, plus an infusion of cash from corporate parent Louis Roederer, means that this *négociant* is at last living up to the potential of its vineyards. With a home base close to St-Joseph, it offers great wines from both northern and southern Rhône regions.

● **Delas Frères / 2010 / Ventoux / $**
The Rhône's less prestigious Ventoux zone is a great source of value-driven reds, as this soft, plummy bottling demonstrates.

● **Delas Frères Haute Pierre / 2009 / Châteauneuf-du-Pape / $$$** Unlike most Châteauneuf-du-Papes, the Haute Pierre is made almost entirely with Grenache, making it especially plush and generous.

DOMAINE DU PÉGAU

Domaine du Pégau crafts its wonderfully voluptuous, modern-style Châteauneuf-du-Pape wines the old-fashioned way: Winemaker Laurence Féraud does little more than bring in grapes, crush them and let them ferment. She attributes the fabulous concentration of Pégau's much-coveted, top-tier wines to extremely low yields and old vines.

- **Domaine du Pégau Cuvée da Capo** / 2010 / **Châteauneuf-du-Pape** / **$$$$** Cuvée da Capo was the first modern prestige cuvée in Châteauneuf-du-Pape; the clove-scented 2010 lives up to its exalted reputation.
- **Domaine du Pégau Cuvée Reservée** / 2010 / **Châteauneuf-du-Pape** / **$$$$** The opulent Cuvée Reservée is built to last, with deep red fruit and tannins that need time to soften.

DOMAINE GRAND VENEUR

Like many Rhône winegrowing dynasties, Alain Jaume's family first planted grapes in Châteauneuf in the early 1800s. The estate stands out, however, for its ability to produce such consistently terrific wines year after year. Jaume and his sons—Christophe and Sébastien—are meticulous winemakers with access to excellent vineyards, which they farm organically.

- ○ **Domaine Grand Veneur La Fontaine** / 2010 / **Châteauneuf-du-Pape** / **$$$** This minerally white blend is ravishing, marked by silky quince and lemon curd notes.
- **Domaine Grand Veneur Clos de Sixte** / 2010 / **Lirac** / **$$** A highlight of the portfolio, this affordable Lirac has rich blackberry flavors and stony minerals.
- **Domaine Grand Veneur Vieilles Vignes** / 2010 / **Châteauneuf-du-Pape** / **$$$$** A superb Châteauneuf with layered tones of red and black fruit, spice and fruitcake.

DOMAINE LES APHILLANTHES

Before 1999 Daniel Boulle sold all of his fruit to the local cooperative, but he now crafts his impeccable Grenache, Syrah and Mourvèdre into a series of distinctive Côtes-du-Rhône cuvées. Boulle's dark, rich and structured reds offer phenomenal satisfaction for the price—even rivaling wines from some of the region's more lofty real estate.

- **Domaine Les Aphillanthes Cuvée 3 Cépages** / 2010 / **Côtes-du-Rhône Villages** / **$$** Equal parts Grenache, Mourvèdre and Syrah, this balanced red is exuberantly fruity.
- **Domaine Les Aphillanthes Le Cros** / 2010 / **Côtes-du-Rhône** / **$$** This offers a big step up in structure and intensity from Boulle's entry-level reds, for just a few more dollars.
- **Domaine Les Aphillanthes Vieilles Vignes** / 2010 / **Côtes-du-Rhône Villages** / **$$** Old vines give this muscular bottling extra-concentrated blackberry notes.

DOMAINE PAUL AUTARD

It's no accident that Paul Autard is an insider favorite among sommeliers: He crafts his wines in a classically balanced style (read: not superripe or super-oaky), which renders them ideal partners for food. Instead of sheer power and concentration, Autard's four rich estate-grown wines (three Châteauneufs and a Côtes-du-Rhône) hinge on balance and finesse.

● **Domaine Paul Autard Cuvée La Côte Ronde / 2010 / Châteauneuf-du-Pape / $$$$** This fragrant, dark blend of Grenache and Syrah is unusually rich (like many 2010 Rhônes).

DOMAINE RASPAIL-AY

The small scale of this Gigondas estate—8,000 cases a year— means that Dominique Ay can focus intensely on his two wines. He also experiments: Ay ages his Grenache-based red in large, old oak tanks (instead of in conventional barrels), and he makes his rosé by tinting white wine with a dash of red (rather than fermenting red grapes with minimal skin contact).

● **Domaine Raspail-Ay / 2009 / Gigondas / $$$** More delicate and vivid than most Gigondas reds, with refined red fruit and juicy acidity.

DOMAINE ROGER SABON

Even by French standards the Sabon winemaking family ranks as ancient—its first recorded vineyard in Châteauneuf-du-Pape dates to 1540. Grenache is at the heart of the reds, including the famous Le Secret des Sabon bottling. Produced from centenarian vines, it's among the region's benchmark wines but tough to find in the U.S. Instead, look for the terrific Châteauneuf-du-Pape, Côtes-du-Rhône and Lirac bottlings.

● **Domaine Roger Sabon Prestige / 2008 / Châteauneuf-du-Pape / $$$$** Eight different grape varieties give complexity to this rich, savory, berry-filled Châteauneuf.

E. GUIGAL

A Côte-Rôtie specialist, Guigal makes more northern Rhône wine than any other producer—including some of the region's definitive wines. Crowned by three pricey Côte-Rôtie bottlings from the La Turque, La Mouline and La Landonne vineyards (famously nicknamed "the LaLas"), Guigal's portfolio offers a tableside tour of every key Rhône appellation.

○ **E. Guigal / 2009 / Côtes-du-Rhône / $$**
Widely available, very affordable and flat-out delicious.

○ **E. Guigal / 2010 / Condrieu / $$$**
Condrieu is the source of the world's greatest Viogniers, and Guigal's—like this silky, minerally example—are classics.

JEAN-LUC COLOMBO

Jean-Luc Colombo owns a 49-acre estate in Cornas and a thriving *négociant* business. But his real influence is as a consultant, passing on his secrets for making the kind of flashy, concentrated wines he's known for. Colombo's famous Cornas bottlings include a handful of intense, brooding estate cuvées; his great array of *négociant* wines deliver value.

● **Colombo Cape Bleue / 2011 / Vin de Pays de la Méditerranée / $** Floral and a little spicy, this delicious rosé comes from coastal hills near Marseille.

● **Colombo Les Abeilles / 2010 / Côtes-du-Rhône / $**
Mature Grenache, Syrah and Mourvèdre vines contribute equally to this sturdy red with deep plum and stone flavors.

● **Colombo Terres Brûlées / 2009 / Cornas / $$$**
The local term *terres brûlées*—"burnt lands"—refers to the fierce sunshine in Cornas, the source of this powerful Syrah.

M. CHAPOUTIER

Michel Chapoutier's spectacular estate wines from Hermitage and Châteauneuf-du-Pape are so celebrated that they divert attention from this superstar's great lineup of affordable reds and whites. These reasonably priced wines come from vineyards elsewhere in the Rhône Valley and southern France. An ardent proponent of biodynamic farming, the prolific Chapoutier also makes wine in Portugal and Australia.

○ **La Ciboise / 2010 / Luberon / $**
This unpretentious, melony white blend pairs especially well with seafood dishes.

● **La Ciboise / 2009 / Luberon / $$**
A straightforward blend of Grenache and Syrah with blackberry and red cherry flavors and firm tannins.

● **M. Chapoutier Monier de la Sizeranne / 2007 / Hermitage / $$$$** A benchmark bottling from a master winemaker, La Sizeranne delivers the power, richness and spicy complexity typical of great Hermitage.

PAUL JABOULET AÎNÉ

Jaboulet is arguably the most important Rhône wine house of the past century. Its Hermitage La Chapelle set a world-class standard, and basic cuvées such as Parallèle 45 are seemingly ubiquitous. From a Tavel rosé to a definitive Châteauneuf, Jaboulet wines represent every major subzone. After an unstable period in the early 2000s, Jaboulet has rebounded under Denis Dubourdieu's direction and the ownership of the Frey family, which bought the winery in 2006.

- ● **Paul Jaboulet Aîné Domaine de Terre Ferme / 2009 / Châteauneuf-du-Pape / $$$$** First planted by Romans, the incredibly steep Terre Ferme yields a single, powerhouse red.
- ● **Paul Jaboulet Aîné Domaine de Thalabert / 2009 / Crozes-Hermitage / $$$$** This deliciously smoky Syrah comes from a site that Jaboulet has been farming since 1834.

VIDAL-FLEURY

The oldest producer in the Rhône has grown steadily over centuries into a formidable *négociant,* offering wines that span the region. A value-priced Côtes-du-Rhône red is a favorite of big-box retailers, but Vidal-Fleury also offers many more serious wines, including a Côte-Rôtie from its original vineyards, where Thomas Jefferson first encountered the wines.

- ○ **Vidal-Fleury / 2010 / Côtes-du-Rhône / $**
  Winemaker Guy Sarton du Jonchay created a vibrant, melon-inflected white that's absurdly good for the price.
- ● **Vidal-Fleury / 2009 / St-Joseph / $$**
  One of St-Joseph's most reliable reds, with remarkably seductive layers of spicy, lightly gamey black fruit.

SOUTHERN FRANCE

CLAIM TO FAME

France's Mediterranean coast and southwest regions were long known for the quantity, not the quality, of their wines. But global demand for affordable wines spurred a dramatic change. While southern France still churns out uninteresting bulk wine, it's also a source of exciting cuvées made from ancient, rediscovered vineyards and ambitious new ones. Its vast reach and varied geography means that nearly any grape can thrive here.

REGIONS TO KNOW

LANGUEDOC-ROUSSILLON France's Mediterranean coast produces vast amounts of mostly red wine, including many terrific values. Both the Roussillon (which lies closer to Spain) and the Languedoc (at the center of the coastal arc) are turning out increasingly complex wines at prices that don't carry the prestige tax of its northern neighbors. Unlike most parts of France, the Languedoc grows a range of grapes—some native to the region, others from different French regions. Look to subregions like Corbières, Côtes du Roussillon, Faugères and Fitou for great red blends, often based on old-vine Carignane and Grenache.

PROVENCE Known for its herb-edged dry rosés, especially those from the Bandol appellation (rosés from Côtes de Provence and Coteaux d'Aix-en-Provence can also be excellent), Provence is also an overlooked source of bold reds. Go-to regions include Bandol, Les Baux de Provence and Coteaux d'Aix-en-Provence. Whites are citrusy and soft; the best come from Cassis.

THE SOUTHWEST Outshone by those of neighboring Bordeaux, the wines of France's southwest are little known in the U.S., but that is changing. Bergerac reds are made with the same grapes as Bordeaux—Cabernet, Merlot, Malbec and Cabernet Franc—and can exhibit a similar finesse. Vintners in Cahors craft reds of massive power from the Malbec grape. In Madiran, winemakers produce dark, full-bodied and tannic wines. The Basque Country's hearty wines are made from a blend of local grapes; Jurançon, for example, is a full-bodied white wine produced from Petit and Gros Manseng grapes in dry and sweet styles.

KEY GRAPES: WHITE

CHARDONNAY Much of southern France is too warm for fine Chardonnay, though straightforward value versions abound.

GRENACHE BLANC One of the Languedoc's most widely planted white grapes, this fairly neutral variety is usually bottled as part of a blend, contributing softness and mouth-filling body.

MACCABÉO This medium-bodied, floral-edged grape is known as Viura in Spain's Rioja, where it stars, but it's also common in Roussillon and the Languedoc.

MARSANNE, ROUSSANNE & VIOGNIER Best known as Rhône varieties, these grapes do well in the warm regions farther south, producing round, lush and sometimes spicy whites.

PICPOUL BLANC Meaning "lip-stinger," this minerally grape is behind some of the Languedoc's incredibly refreshing, zesty whites, especially those grown near the town of Pinet.

ROLLE, BOURBOULENC, CLAIRETTE, SÉMILLON & UGNI BLANC Along with Grenache Blanc and Marsanne and a few others, these local grapes create Provence's white blends, with different zones specializing in different grape combinations. Rolle is also common in the Roussillon, where it yields zesty whites similar to Italy's Vermentino (they are thought to be the same grape).

🍇 KEY GRAPES: RED

AUXERROIS Known elsewhere as Malbec or Côt, this smoky red (not to be confused with a white variety of the same name) stars in the southwest's Cahors region. Unlike the fruity, supple Malbecs of Argentina, Cahors reds are spicy, earthy and tannic.

CABERNET SAUVIGNON & MERLOT This duo is mostly used for inexpensive wines destined for export. While a few regions (such as parts of Provence) and a few top producers succeed with more ambitious versions, most of these wines are fruity and simple.

CARIGNANE This widely planted red dominates France's southernmost territory, especially the Roussillon. While much Carignane wine is simple and rustic, it can make great fruity, spicy reds. The best come from old vines in Languedoc's Corbières.

CINSAUT Native to Provence (and eaten locally as a table grape), Cinsaut is the signature variety of the region's fresh, fruity rosés. In the Languedoc it's often blended with Carignane to add perfume to the reds of Minervois, Corbières and Fitou.

GRENACHE & SYRAH Fruity Grenache and firm, tannic Syrah are blended throughout the south. In both the Languedoc and the Roussillon they are combined with Mourvèdre to create hearty, fruity reds, such as the blends of Minervois and Fitou. In Provence they're responsible for noted rosé and red wines.

MOURVÈDRE The calling card grape of Provence's prestigious Bandol region (and the same as Spain's Monastrell), Mourvèdre yields spicy, rich reds and robust rosés on its own. Elsewhere it's often blended with Grenache and Syrah.

TANNAT Widely planted in the southwest, this tough, tannic grape does best in the Madiran subregion.

Producers/ Southern France

CAZES

The fact that this Roussillon estate manages about 500 acres of vines (biodynamically, no less) only makes it more impressive that Cazes is able to offer such quality. Famous for a sweet, fortified wine called Muscat de Rivesaltes, Cazes is a sometimes-overlooked source of stellar dry wines, too.

○ **Domaine Cazes Le Canon du Maréchal Muscat-Viognier / 2010 / Vin de Pays des Côtes Catalanes / $** Two floral grapes yield one very floral blend, uplifted with refreshing acidity.

● **Domaine Cazes Le Canon du Maréchal Syrah-Merlot / 2010 / Vin de Pays des Côtes Catalanes / $** Syrah gives this supple, plum-driven red its peppery edge.

CHÂTEAU DE LANCYRE

When the Durand and Valentin families purchased this Languedoc estate in 1970, they inherited a winemaking history dating to the 1550s—the winery still has some medieval-era stone fermentation vats. The families transformed the dilapidated property into one of the leading names in up-and-coming Pic-St-Loup by offering outstanding Syrahs and a range of modern, well-priced bottlings.

● **Château de Lancyre / 2011 / Pic-St-Loup / $$** Warm days and cool nights in Pic-St-Loup created a mouth-filling, exceedingly food-friendly rosé.

● **Château de Lancyre Vieilles Vignes / 2009 / Pic-St-Loup / $$** Lancyre's ripe, herb-edged flagship blend combines the fruity exuberance of Grenache with Syrah's firm tannins.

DOMAINE D'AUPILHAC

Sylvain Fadat grew melons, asparagus and peaches on his family's farm northwest of Montpellier before taking a chance on wine grapes in 1989. Planted in soils rich in prehistoric oyster fossils (ideal for wine grapes), Fadat's initial vintages proved so successful that three years later he abandoned all other crops in favor of vines. Today his hand-picked, organically grown grapes make some of the Languedoc's best wines.

● **Domaine d'Aupilhac Lou Maset** / 2010 / **Coteaux du Languedoc** / $$ Fadat's wines offer value up and down the price scale, and this blend of Rhône varieties is no exception.

DOMAINE GAUBY

This winery in southwest Roussillon—not far from the Spanish border—helped prove that this overlooked region could produce refined dry reds and whites in addition to the sweet wines and rustic, high-alcohol bottlings that were its signature. Since releasing its first experimental estate wines in the late 1980s, Gauby has migrated to an increasingly elegant, less rustic style—one that makes it a benchmark for the region.

○ **Domaine Gauby Les Calcinaires** / 2010 / **Vin de Pays des Côtes Catalanes** / $$ An odd blend of five varieties (Muscat, Chardonnay, Maccabéo, Grenache Gris and Vermentino) creates a lush, vibrant white redolent of melon and citrus.

● **Domaine Gauby La Muntada** / 2009 / **Côtes du Roussillon Villages** / $$$$ One of the Roussillon's priciest reds, this delivers enough smoky black fruit and firm tannins to age well for many years.

DOMAINE LÉON BARRAL

Didier Barral, the owner of this Faugères-district estate, gets assistance in his vineyards from a team of weed-munching horses and cows. They graze on cover crops planted between rows of vines, all of which are pruned into traditional, back-breaking bush shapes. Old vines, wild yeasts and minimal winemaking intervention add up to robust, deeply flavored reds (plus one rare white) with a captivating sense of place.

● **Domaine Léon Barral Valinière** / 2009 / **Faugères** / $$$$ This brooding, intense red is one of the great examples of Mourvèdre outside of Bandol. The addition of 20 percent Syrah contributes a nice spicy character.

DOMAINES OTT

Long a source of some of Provence's most ambitious and pricey rosés, in recent years Domaines Ott has introduced more accessibly priced wines under its Les Domaniers label. Premier cuvées come from three distinct estates, each the source of a noted rosé: Château de Selle, Château Romassan and Clos Mireille. Ott's three red wines and two whites prove this quality-focused estate has an adept hand with colors beyond pink.

Ott Sélection Les Domaniers / 2011 / Côtes de Provence / $$
This elegant, strawberry-inflected rosé is wonderfully food-friendly, but delicious sipped on its own, too.

Domaines Ott Château de Selle / 2011 / Côtes de Provence / $$$ Any rosé priced north of $40 should deliver complexity plus refreshing charm—and this lovely example does the job.

Domaines Ott Château Romassan / 2011 / Bandol / $$$
Bandol's rosés tend to be bolder than those of the Côtes de Provence, as this savory and lightly spicy bottling shows.

DOMAINE TEMPIER

The leading estate in the Bandol region, Domaine Tempier makes some of the world's finest Mourvèdre-based reds. But its best-known bottling is its dry rosé—a multifaceted, flat-out delicious wine that proves rosé can be complex. Owned for generations by the Péyraud family, the estate has gained momentum in recent years under winemaker Daniel Ravier, who has improved the single-vineyard cuvées.

Domaine Tempier / 2011 / Bandol / $$$
Reliably muscular (yet silky smooth), this is a definitive Bandol rosé, with bright fruit and great acidity.

Domaine Tempier Cabassaou / 2008 / Bandol / $$$$
Pure old-vine Mourvèdre forms the heart of this densely styled, ageworthy red, which comes from vines more than a half-century old.

Italy
Wine Region

The variety offered by Italian wine
is so extensive that even experts
have trouble keeping track of how
many official wine regions exist
in the country. From the foothills
of the Alps in the north to the
island of Sicily in the south, Italy's
wealth of great reds and whites
seems to increase each year,
especially as top winemakers
experiment more and more with
the country's vast number of
indigenous grape varieties.

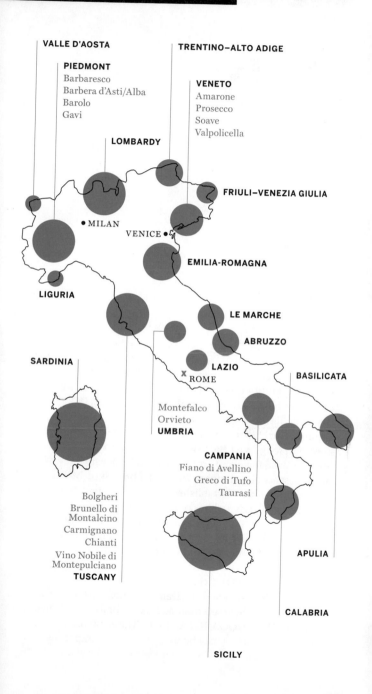

VALLE D'AOSTA

TRENTINO—ALTO ADIGE

PIEDMONT
Barbaresco
Barbera d'Asti/Alba
Barolo
Gavi

VENETO
Amarone
Prosecco
Soave
Valpolicella

LOMBARDY

FRIULI—VENEZIA GIULIA

• MILAN

VENICE •

EMILIA-ROMAGNA

LIGURIA

LE MARCHE

ABRUZZO

SARDINIA

LAZIO

✗ ROME

BASILICATA

Montefalco
Orvieto
UMBRIA

CAMPANIA
Fiano di Avellino
Greco di Tufo
Taurasi

Bolgheri
Brunello di
Montalcino
Carmignano
Chianti
Vino Nobile di
Montepulciano
TUSCANY

APULIA

CALABRIA

SICILY

69

Italy

AN ANNUAL DUEL between Italy and France determines the year's top exporter of wine to the U.S. In 2010, it was Italy; in 2011, France won. What this year will bring is unclear, but it's certain that the quality of Italian wine is at an all-time high. Italy has more than 300 DOC and DOCG zones (see Wine Terminology, below), but two regions are preeminent: Piedmont, in the northwest, where the Nebbiolo grape yields powerful, long-lived Barolos and Barbarescos; and Tuscany, home of the Sangiovese grape, which is responsible for two of Italy's most acclaimed wines, Chianti and Brunello di Montalcino. Southern Italy has reestablished its fine-wine tradition, while in the north the crisp whites of Friuli and Trentino–Alto Adige have become go-to wines for many sommeliers. Central Italy beyond Tuscany also has a lot to offer, including Umbria's dark Sagrantino di Montefalco and Lazio's lighter wines.

WINE TERMINOLOGY

Italy's regulatory system is the Denominazione di Origine Controllata (DOC), which sets basic standards for four main quality categories: DOC, DOCG, IGT and VdT. These standards include which grape varieties may be used, where the grapes must be grown, how much a vineyard can grow (lower yields create more-concentrated, higher-quality wines), as well as a finished wine's alcohol content. Most Italian wines are labeled by region; some list the grape if it defines a region, such as Montepulciano d'Abruzzo, made from the Montepulciano grape in Abruzzo.

VINO DA TAVOLA (VDT) Translating literally as "table wine," this category is for everyday wines that don't adhere to DOC or DOCG standards. It is also used by some vintners who buck traditional DOC/G rules to make ambitious, experimental bottlings.

DENOMINAZIONE DI ORIGINE CONTROLLATA (DOC) This more regulated category includes the majority of Italy's quality wine.

DENOMINAZIONE DI ORIGINE CONTROLLATA E GARANTITA (DOCG) This, the strictest classification, includes Italy's most prestigious wines. DOCG wines must pass a blind taste test by a panel of experts appointed by Italy's Ministry of Agriculture.

INDICAZIONE GEOGRAFICA TIPICA (IGT) Although used for many regional table wines, the IGT classification also includes better wines that don't qualify for higher designations because of the use of unorthodox grape varieties or production methods.

CLASSICO A prestigious subregion, often the original and oldest part of a region whose boundaries were later enlarged.

RISERVA This term indicates a wine that has been aged for a longer period than basic wines of the same designation. Exact requirements differ by region.

SUPERIORE Denotes a wine with a higher alcohol content and more concentration, made from grapes grown in a top subzone.

PIEDMONT

CLAIM TO FAME
Piedmont's most sought-after reds, Barolo and Barbaresco, are revered for their ageworthy structure and complex aromatics. But don't overlook Barbera and Dolcetto, the food-friendly, supple red wines that the Piemontesi drink every day.

REGIONS TO KNOW

BAROLO & BARBARESCO Sourced from a small number of vineyards in the hills around the town of Alba, Nebbiolo-based reds from these two zones have steep price tags reflecting their scarcity. Barolos must be aged three years, two in barrel, before release; Barbarescos must be aged two years, one in barrel. Many don't reach their prime until after a decade or more of age.

DOGLIANI & ALBA Both sources of top Dolcettos; Alba is also known for good values in Nebbiolo.

GAVI Gavi's melony whites are lively enough to serve as an aperitif and substantial enough to accompany a wide range of foods.

LANGHE, GATTINARA & GHEMME Go-to zones for Nebbiolo-based reds that offer a taste of this compelling grape at a lower price than Barolo and Barbaresco.

ROERO This subregion's zesty, minerally, Arneis-based whites are becoming easier to find in the U.S.

🍇 KEY GRAPES: WHITE

ARNEIS The almond-flavored Arneis grape has come back from near extinction; its best wines are from the Roero subregion.

CHARDONNAY Many prominent Piedmont vintners produce worthwhile Chardonnays; they tend to be rich, fruity and fresh.

CORTESE A specialty of southeast Piedmont, Cortese yields tart, citrusy and mostly inexpensive whites. The best come from hillside vines in Gavi, where riper grapes yield fruitier wines.

🍇 KEY GRAPES: RED

BARBERA & DOLCETTO Two of Piedmont's most popular wines, these reds offer soft tannins, berry flavors and juicy acidity.

NEBBIOLO The grape behind the majestic wines of Barolo and Barbaresco, Nebbiolo has high tannins and acidity, which makes it hard to drink when young. With savory, floral aromatics (think tar and roses), it's crafted in a range of styles, from traditional (firm, austere and earthy) to modern (smoother and fruitier).

Producers/ Piedmont

BRAIDA

In 1982, Braida's Giacomo Bologna set a new benchmark for Barbera d'Asti when he created Bricco dell'Uccellone, a pioneering and instantly sought-after French oak–aged wine made from a single spectacular vineyard. Though site-specific, barrel-aged Barberas are common today, Bricco dell'Uccellone remains one of the best. Bologna's children, Raffaella and Giuseppe, apply the same standards to a wide-ranging portfolio that includes both native and foreign grapes.

● **Braida Montebruna / 2010 / Barbera d'Asti / $$$**
This polished Barbera comes from a site near the renowned Uccellone vineyard and features similarly lush flavors, but at less than half the price.

● **Braida Bricco dell'Uccellone / 2009 / Barbera d'Asti / $$$$**
It's easy to see why this wine revolutionized the reputation of the Barbera grape: Rich, complex and velvety, it's the antithesis of the thin, acidic Barberas of decades past.

BROGLIA

In a perfect world, more Gavi producers would make wines like those from the Broglia family, which show just how delicious Piedmont's Cortese grape can be. Broglia specializes in the production of Gavi, while many Piedmont vintners treat it as an afterthought. Crop yields are kept very low, which means all of Broglia's succulent wines possess concentration and depth.

○ **Broglia Il Doge / 2010 / Gavi / $$**
Made from the estate's youngest Cortese vines, this minerally, entry-level white is more delicate than the La Meirana bottling.

○ **Broglia La Meirana / 2011 / Gavi / $$**
Broglia's premier Meirana vineyard is the source of its compulsively drinkable flagship wine. It offers all the refreshing qualities you want in a Gavi, plus loads of juicy fruit flavors.

○ **Broglia Bruno / 2010 / Gavi / $$$**
Most Gavi wines are light and delicate, but this crisp, lemon- and peach-inflected cuvée has a pleasing intensity.

CASCINA BONGIOVANNI

With a tiny production from 15 acres of family vineyards, Cascina Bongiovanni is among the smallest of Piedmont's top producers. Davide Mozzone, whose grandfather planted the estate's original Nebbiolo vineyard in 1950, released Cascina Bongiovanni's first estate reds in 1993; plush and aged in French oak, they established the family label firmly in Barolo's modernist camp.

○ **Cascina Bongiovanni / 2011 / Langhe Arneis / $$**
This lively, pear-scented Arneis is a textbook rendition of Piedmont's most appealing white variety.

● **Cascina Bongiovanni / 2008 / Barolo / $$$$**
Exuberant fruit is a hallmark of Bongiovanni's Barolos, and this firm, violet-scented '08 is no exception.

CAVALLOTTO

Although the Cavallotto family produces 11 different wines, its output is small: fewer than 10,000 cases a year. For some reason, this estate remains oddly underappreciated, despite producing superlative wines. The upside? Cavallotto's wines sell for less than those of more renowned estates, but rival them in quality—especially its Barolos from the Bricco Boschis vineyard.

● **Cavallotto Bricco Boschis Vigna del Cuculo / 2008 / Barbera d'Alba / $$$** Bricco Boschis is planted mostly to Nebbiolo, but this velvety red comes from a nearly five-acre plot of Barbera.

● **Cavallotto Bricco Boschis Riserva Vigna San Giuseppe / 2005 / Barolo / $$$$** Made from the best grapes from Bricco Boschis, this masterful *riserva* tastes amazingly youthful.

CA' VIOLA

Beppe Caviola first made a name for himself with his complex wines from the Dolcetto grape—a remarkable feat given that Dolcetto doesn't get the respect that more powerful grapes like Nebbiolo command. Still, Caviola's wines made him famous and he's now an in-demand consultant. At his home base in Dogliani, he produces five reds, with two made from Dolcetto.

● **Ca' Viola Barturot / 2008 / Dolcetto d'Alba / $$**
Beppe Caviola gives Dolcetto's smooth tannins and fresh berry tones a boost of smoky richness in this single-vineyard red.

● **Ca' Viola Brichet / 2009 / Barbera d'Alba / $$$**
The sunny, south-facing slopes of the Brichet vineyard make it one of Alba's top spots, as this dense, satiny Barbera shows.

CERETTO

Compared with most prestigious Piedmont estates, Ceretto is vast, encompassing 300 acres. Its wines are consequently easier to find, though Ceretto's top Barolos like Bricco Rocche are still scarce. Vintner Marcello Ceretto and his brother Bruno helped drive the craze for single-site Nebbiolos in the 1970s; today the next generation crafts wines in the same fruit-focused style.

○ **Ceretto Blangè / 2010 / Langhe Arneis / $$**
Ceretto's crisp, apple- and citrus-scented Arneis is delicious.

● **Ceretto Asij / 2008 / Barbaresco / $$$**
Grapes from Ceretto's famed Asiji vineyard go into this fragrant, medium-bodied Barbaresco.

● **Ceretto Zonchera / 2007 / Barolo / $$$**
Made from a blend of estate Bricco Rocche vines, the dense, flavorful Zonchera is a great value in the portfolio.

CONTERNO FANTINO

Few vintners can claim the instant success of Claudio Conterno and Guido Fantino. The first wine that the childhood friends crushed together—a 1982 Barolo from the Sorì Ginestra vineyard—landed on the cover of a high-profile wine magazine. They're still in the vanguard of Barolo's modern wine style; Guido's son Fabio now helps oversee the stellar lineup.

● **Conterno Fantino Vignota / 2010 / Barbera d'Alba / $$$**
Plush and seductive, with ripe tannins and floral plum notes.

● **Conterno Fantino Sorì Ginestra / 2008 / Barolo / $$$$**
The 2008 Sorì Ginestra lives up to its storied history, with a phenomenal mix of richness, minerality and structure.

COPPO

Coppo is one of the finest wineries in Canelli, the center of sparkling Moscato d'Asti production. While Coppo's Moscato is terrific, the Coppo family focuses its efforts on reds—especially Barbera. Except for the flagship Pomorosso bottling, Coppo's expertly made Barberas are priced for everyday drinking.

● **Coppo L'Avvocata / 2009 / Barbera d'Asti / $**
Coppo's intro-level Barbera is exuberantly fruity, with ripe red berry flavors and easygoing charm.

● **Coppo Camp du Rouss / 2008 / Barbera d'Asti / $$**
Spicy and smooth, this oak-aged red outclasses its price with layers of ripe, smoke-tinged cherry.

FONTANAFREDDA

Fontanafredda has long been known for making lots of good but rarely great wines that cover Piedmont's major bases: Barolos, Barberas, Barbarescos and Dolcettos, plus whites and sparklers. But when ambitious entrepreneur Oscar Farinetti bought the estate with a partner in 2008, quality improvements that had been in progress for some years kicked into high gear. Today this is a winery to watch.

● **Fontanafredda Briccotondo Barbera** / 2010 / Piedmont / $
This berry-flavored, rich Barbera tastes better than ever but sells for around the same price as previous vintages, making it a great bargain.

● **Fontanafredda Serralunga d'Alba** / 2007 / Barolo / $$$
Classic violet, ripe red cherry and spice notes define this introductory Barolo.

GIACOMO CONTERNO

Giacomo Conterno is one of the greatest names not only in Piedmont but in all of Italy. Conterno's famed Barolo wines—topped by the legendary Monfortino bottling—are standard-bearers of the traditionalist school, meaning they're aged in massive old Slavonian oak casks and require many years of aging to soften. Roberto Conterno is in charge of the estate today, employing the same uncompromising standards that made the Conterno label legendary.

● **Conterno Cascina Francia** / 2007 / Barolo / $$$$
A harmonious, almost sweet-seeming Barolo, until the potent Nebbiolo tannins kick in at the end.

● **Conterno Monfortino Riserva** / 2004 / Barolo / $$$$
A truly great Barolo; even its perfumed fragrance—wild strawberries, cherries, menthol, earth—is intoxicating.

LA SPINETTA

The single-vineyard Moscato d'Asti bottlings introduced by La Spinetta in 1978 redefined what the grape variety—and the region—were capable of. Since then, the Rivetti family has turned its attention to Barbera, Barbaresco and finally Barolo in a series of ambitious cuvées. Today the Rivetti brothers are among Piedmont's brightest stars. Low yields, oak aging and a focus on vineyards is the Rivetti formula; showy, fruit-driven wines are the result.

RARITIES & COLLECTIBLES

BRUNO GIACOSA A go-to source for definitive Barbarescos and Barolos from the regions' finest *crus* for half a century. Giacosa bottles his top *cru* wines only in the best vintages, and the cost reflects that; for a more moderately priced introduction to his style, look for his Nebbiolo d'Alba Valmaggiore.

CANTINA MASCARELLO This benchmark producer—now led by winemaking legend Bartolo Mascarello's daughter, Maria Teresa—creates a single, superlative Barolo each year, always in a traditional style.

GAJA Angelo Gaja became famous (or, to traditionalists, notorious) for planting Cabernet in Piedmont. Still, his reputation rests on his profound Barbarescos, along with his single-vineyard Sori Tilden and Sori San Lorenzo wines.

● **La Spinetta Vigneto Gallina Vürsù** / 2008 / Barbaresco / $$$$ One of a trio of pricey Barbarescos, this comes from the prestigious Gallina vineyard in the commune of Neive and was the first Barbaresco that La Spinetta ever made; it features ripe, smoky currant and sweet herb notes.

● **La Spinetta Vigneto Garretti** / 2008 / Barolo / $$$$ The Garretti Barolo comes from earlier-ripening grapevines in the Rivetti's Campe vineyard, hence its impressively elegant, medium-bodied style.

MARCARINI

Marcarini is famous for an exceptional, traditionally made Barolo from the Brunate vineyard, but this smallish La Morra label succeeds with each of Piedmont's greatest grapes, including traditional red varieties plus Arneis and Moscato. Its consistency comes from many years of expertise—fifth-generation winemaker Luisa Marchetti's ancestor founded the estate—and from amazing vineyards on some of the region's best slopes.

● **Marcarini Fontanazza** / 2010 / Dolcetto d'Alba / $$ Marcarini's tasty intro-level Dolcetto is unoaked, which keeps its grape and floral flavors incredibly vivid.

● **Marcarini Brunate** / 2008 / Barolo / $$$ The 1958 Brunate was La Morra's first single-vineyard Barolo to carry the vineyard name on the label. Fifty vintages later, this outstanding red still sets an example.

MARCHESI DI GRÉSY

The noble di Grésy family has grown grapes on its sprawling Martinenga estate for centuries, but it wasn't until 1973, when the current marquis built a winery, that the di Grésys became commercial vintners. The Marquis di Grésy quickly augmented well-situated family vineyards with some of Piedmont's best Barbaresco sites, making that wine the venture's calling card.

● **Marchesi di Grésy / 2009 / Barbera d'Asti / $$**
Oak aging gives this fresh, cherry-driven red a smoky note.

● **Marchesi di Grésy Camp Gros / 2006 / Barbaresco / $$$$**
Made only in the best vintages, this famous Barbaresco comes from a small selection of di Grésy's Martinenga vineyards.

PAITIN DI PASQUERO ELIA

Although this estate is ancient, in the 1990s, Paitin's showy Barbarescos were among the most modern in the region. Two decades later, brothers Giovanni and Silvano Pasquero Elia (descendants of Paitin's 1796 founders) have re-embraced traditional techniques. The result is wines that strike a deft balance between earthy, old-school bottlings and superripe extremes.

● **Paitin Ca Veja / 2009 / Nebbiolo d'Alba / $$**
A ripe, raspberry-tinged red, highly drinkable and well priced.

● **Paitin Sorì Paitin / 2006 / Barbaresco / $$$**
The estate's best-known wine comes from its original vineyard, which yields firm, concentrated Barbarescos.

PIO CESARE

When Giuseppe Boffa took over Pio Cesare from his father-in-law in the 1940s, the winery produced large amounts of wine from purchased grapes. Boffa turned it into a more quality-focused estate responsible for some of Piedmont's most prized Barolos. Boffa's son, Pio, is now the winemaker, and though he's added new cuvées, he has preserved the estate's structured style.

● **Pio Cesare / 2009 / Barbera d'Alba / $$**
This vibrant, silky red shows ripe plum, anise and cedar notes.

● **Pio Cesare Fides / 2009 / Barbera d'Alba / $$$**
Boffa lavishes this dense Barbera with care usually reserved for Nebbiolo, including 20 months of aging in French oak.

● **Pio Cesare / 2007 / Barolo / $$$$**
The 2007 harvest yielded Barolos with ripe tannins and bold fruit, qualities on display in this big, cherry-infused red.

PRODUTTORI DEL BARBARESCO

Cooperative wineries are often known for tanker-loads of plonk, but Produttori del Barbaresco is a splendid exception. This co-op not only makes some of Italy's best Barbarescos but also has helped drive Piedmont's trend toward site-specific winemaking. The winery's single-vineyard cuvées are outstanding, while a multivineyard Barbaresco and a Langhe red offer great value.

● **Produttori del Barbaresco Vigneti in Moccagatta Riserva /
2005 / Barbaresco / $$$$** This masterful '05 Barbaresco is just hitting its stride, with rich cherry and mineral flavors that are seemingly endless.

● **Produttori del Barbaresco Vigneti in Pora Riserva / 2005 /
Barbaresco / $$$$** There's a captivating purity to this refined single-vineyard *riserva,* which comes from a prime site once owned by the winery's founder.

VIETTI

Vietti is famous for its traditionally styled single-vineyard Barolos. Beyond the top-end wines are a compelling array of Piedmont classics, including a bright Arneis, the native white grape that owner Alfredo Currado rescued from near extinction in the 1960s. Son Luca Currado—an alumnus of California's Opus One and Bordeaux's Mouton Rothschild—runs the winery today.

● **Vietti Tre Vigne / 2009 / Barbera d'Asti / $$**
Supple berry tones, sweet spice and food-friendly acidity make this a textbook Barbera.

● **Vietti Castiglione / 2008 / Barolo / $$$**
The Castiglione provides a taste of Vietti's beautifully refined style at a fraction of the price of its single-vineyard Barolos.

OTHER NORTHERN ITALY

REGIONS TO KNOW

FRIULI–VENEZIA GIULIA The hill country of northern Friuli is dominated by small, high-quality wineries that produce vivid, mineral-laden whites—many from obscure native grapes—plus a few reds, including the violet-hued Refosco. Collio and Colli Orientali del Friuli are the premier subregions. The gravelly plains in the warmer southern subregions grow most of Friuli–Venezia Giulia's Merlot and Cabernet Sauvignon.

LOMBARDY Surrounding Milan in north-central Italy, Lombardy derives its reputation for quality wine primarily from the Franciacorta region, which makes superb sparklers (see p. 289). The Oltrepò Pavese region, a longtime bulk district, is also starting to make fine wine, including reds from the spicy Bonarda grape.

TRENTINO–ALTO ADIGE Although the names of these adjacent Alpine provinces are typically hyphenated, they make distinctly different wines. Trentino is known for its fresh, fruity reds made from native grapes, while the mostly German-speaking Alto Adige produces terrific whites, including crisp Gewürztraminers and compelling Pinot Grigios and Pinot Biancos.

VENETO In addition to sparkling Prosecco (see p. 289), the Veneto offers three signature wines: Amarone, Valpolicella and Soave. Made from sweet, partially dried grapes, Amarones are high-alcohol reds with luscious depth and body. Based on the same grapes, Valpolicella is a younger, drier version of Amarone. Top vintners often infuse their Valpolicellas with leftover grapes from making Amarone—a process known as *ripasso*—to create wines that, at their best, are among Italy's great underrated reds. Soave's Garganega-based whites are often bland, yet those made in small amounts from low-yielding, well-situated vineyards (especially in the original *classico* subregion) can be zippy and delicious.

🍇 KEY GRAPES: WHITE

CHARDONNAY Northern Italy's Chardonnays display crisp acidity, thanks to shorter summers and cooler temperatures.

FRIULANO, RIBOLLA GIALLA, MALVASIA ISTRIANA & PICOLIT These aromatic natives are Friuli–Venezia Giulia specialties.

GARGANEGA Veneto's Soave wines get their lemon and almond flavors from this indigenous variety.

GLERA Formerly called Prosecco, this grape is the basis for the sparkling wines of the Prosecco region.

MÜLLER-THURGAU, SYLVANER, RIESLING & GEWÜRZTRAMINER The prevalence of these Germanic varieties in Trentino–Alto Adige reflects the region's proximity to Austria and Switzerland.

PINOT GRIGIO, PINOT BIANCO & SAUVIGNON (BLANC) These international varieties thrive in northern Italy, where they yield whites with intense minerality and a crisp, Alpine freshness.

❦ KEY GRAPES: RED

CORVINA, MOLINARA AND RONDINELLA This trio of indigenous red varieties provides the basis for three very different Veneto wines: bold, complex Amarone; juicy, medium-bodied Valpolicella; and lighter Bardolino. Using partially raisined grapes for fermentation creates Amarone's sweet-tart flavor and full body.

PINOT NERO Northern Italian Pinot Noir (Pinot Nero) is typically racy and light. Top regions for the grape include Lombardy's Oltrepò Pavese and Alto Adige.

REFOSCO Friuli–Venezia Giulia's best-known red grape yields plummy, dry wines that range from medium- to full-bodied.

SCHIAVA, LAGREIN & TEROLDEGO These Alto Adige varieties are well adapted to the region's short summers. Schiavas are often light and simple; Lagrein and Teroldego offer more tannins and body plus crisp acidity.

Producers/ Other Northern Italy

ABBAZIA DI NOVACELLA

Augustinian monks established this monastery and winery in Alto Adige's remote Isarco Valley in 1142, and it's been in operation ever since. Perhaps competitive pricing has helped keep Novacella in business for eight centuries—the wines are terrific bargains. Its pricier Praepositus cuvées can age beautifully.

○ **Abbazia di Novacella Praepositus Kerner** / 2010 / Alto Adige / $$ Novacella excels with the obscure, aromatic Kerner grape; this citrus-laden bottling is no exception.

● **Abbazia di Novacella Kalterersee Schiava** / 2010 / Alto Adige / $ Straightforward red berry flavors, supple tannins and food-friendly acidity make this a versatile red at the table.

ALOIS LAGEDER

Alois Lageder's Alto Adige wines are not only eco-friendly, they're some of Italy's best. Lageder's brother-in-law, Luis von Dellemann, makes the wines in the region's first carbon-neutral winery; the Tenutae Lageder label is crafted from biodynamically farmed estate grapes. Dellemann's minerally whites and refined reds show why Alto Adige is one of the world's great wine regions.

○ **Tenutae Lageder Porer Pinot Grigio / 2010 / Alto Adige / $$**
Drinking beautifully now, this unusually intense, peach-inflected Pinot Grigio can be aged for a few years, too.

● **Alois Lageder Lagrein / 2009 / Alto Adige / $$**
A terrific example of the native Lagrein grape, with zesty plum fruit and supple tannins.

ANSELMI

Roberto Anselmi could stake a claim to the title of Soave's finest producer, except that he dropped the Soave designation from his wines in 2000. Instead, Anselmi uses the humble Veneto IGT classification, mostly as a protest against Soave's lax production standards. Anselmi is a rebel with a cause: His whites, made mostly from low-yielding Garganega vines—many from single vineyards—continue to raise the bar for the region.

○ **Anselmi Capitel Croce / 2009 / Veneto / $$**
Treated like a Burgundy (oak aging, lees stirring), this smooth, fresh and dense white is redolent of spice and almonds.

○ **Anselmi Capitel Foscarino / 2010 / Veneto / $$**
A minerally, apricot-edged white from some of the best vineyards in the Soave Classico zone.

AZIENDA AGRICOLA GINI

The dynamic Gini brothers—Sandro and Claudio—come from an ancient line of Soave vintners. But like some of the region's elite producers, they use modern techniques to make luscious, complex wines. Both of Gini's higher-end Soaves (La Froscà and Contrada Salvarenza) get richness from aging in small barrels.

○ **Gini La Froscà / 2010 / Soave Classico / $$**
The Froscà hillside has been yielding opulent, exceptional wines—like this plump, almond-edged offering—for centuries.

○ **Gini Contrada Salvarenza Vecchie Vigne / 2009 / Soave Classico / $$$** Made from 80-year-old vines, this concentrated Soave is a revelation for anyone used to bulk versions.

BERTANI

Veneto-based Bertani has long been a pioneer: In the 1850s, two Bertani brothers imported cutting-edge Burgundian practices; in 1958 the winery made one of the first commercial Amarones. While Bertani continues to innovate, its oldest wine is still its most famous. In production for some 150 years, Secco-Bertani advanced the *ripasso* technique: refermenting Valpolicella with dried grapes left over from Amarone to impart richness and color.

● **Bertani Secco-Bertani Ripasso / 2009 / Valpolicella Valpantena / $$** This cherry-rich *ripasso* blend is juicy, spicy and supremely food-friendly.

● **Bertani / 2004 / Amarone della Valpolicella Classico / $$$$** Powerful and gorgeously perfumed, this Amarone still tastes youthful, with layers of velvety cherry and spice.

INAMA

Stefano Inama's remarkable Soaves taste nothing like most wines bottled under the same regional name. Inama sources Garganega grapes from only the small, hilly *classico* subzone; he farms his vines for quality, not quantity, and ages some cuvées in French oak. The combination of intensely flavorful fruit and modernist winemaking yields wines of distinctive richness.

○ **Inama Vin Soave / 2011 / Soave Classico / $**
Zesty and silky, this unoaked intro-level bottling is a steal.

○ **Inama Soave Vigneti di Foscarino / 2009 / Soave Classico / $$** Aging this lively single-vineyard wine in barrels gives its apricot and floral flavors a creamy texture.

J. HOFSTÄTTER

One of the largest family wineries in Alto Adige, Hofstätter is the only estate to own property on both sides of the Adige valley. Different growing conditions in its scattered vineyards allow the Foradori family to cultivate an impressive range of grapes. Highlights in the comprehensive lineup include one of Italy's finest Pinot Noirs, the Barthenau Vigna San Urbano.

○ **J. Hofstätter Joseph Pinot Bianco / 2010 / Alto Adige / $$** There's a steely Alpine freshness to this impressive Pinot Bianco's intense apple and herb flavors.

● **J. Hofstätter Barthenau Vigna S. Urbano / 2008 / Alto Adige / $$$$** Plush black cherry and mineral notes define this vibrant, single-vineyard Pinot Noir.

MASI

Masi is one of the most famous names in Amarone. Responsible for 20 percent of the Veneto's Amarone output, this family winery maintains high quality across its wide portfolio, thanks to patriarch Sandro Boscaini's fierce insistence on technical rigor (he even founded a wine research institute). Masi's five velvety, seductively styled bottlings are decidedly modern, emphasizing rich fruit character and intensity.

● **Masi Campofiorin / 2008 / Rosso del Veronese / $$**
Made using the skins of Amarone grapes, this earthy, cherry-rich red is an affordable alternative to its pricey big brother.

● **Serego Alighieri Vaio Armaron / 2005 / Amarone della Valpolicella Classico / $$$$** One of Masi's top Amarones, it carries its power with grace, offering cherry, fig and tea notes.

NINO NEGRI

No one paid the remote Alpine region of Valtellina much mind, wine-wise, until Casimiro Maule started crafting head-turning reds and whites from the century-old Nino Negri estate. Maule's deft touch with Nebbiolo—known locally as Chiavennasca—has made him a star, with the 5 Stelle his most famous creation.

● **Nino Negri Quadrio / 2008 / Valtellina Superiore / $$**
A touch of Merlot fleshes out leaner Chiavennasca in this crisp, cherry-driven blend.

● **Nino Negri 5 Stelle / 2007 / Sfursat di Valtellina / $$$$**
For his five-star (*stelle*) wine, Maule crushes partly raisined grapes, then ferments their juice to create a concentrated, completely dry red redolent of plums, spices and toast.

SAN MICHELE-APPIANO

A model for cooperative winemaking, this century-old Alto Adige producer turns out terrific wines at modest prices. Based near the town of Appiano (Eppan in German), San Michele claims more than 350 members. Featuring every important regional grape, the co-op's portfolio offers a tableside tour of Alto Adige.

○ **St. Michael-Eppan Pinot Bianco / 2010 / Alto Adige / $$**
Alto Adige yields exceptionally fresh, bright Pinot Biancos (a.k.a. Pinot Blancs), as this silky, pear-driven bottling shows.

● **St. Michael-Eppan Lagrein / 2009 / Alto Adige / $$**
The Lagrein grape's firm tannins are svelte and ripe in this vibrant, plummy example.

TIEFENBRUNNER

The Tiefenbrunner estate has been making wine since the 1300s, but it wasn't until 1968 that Hilde and Herbert Tiefenbrunner began to bottle wine commercially. The estate now produces about three-quarters of a million bottles of almost 30 different wines each vintage; bright, lively whites are its specialty.

○ **Tiefenbrunner Pinot Bianco / 2010 / Alto Adige / $**
Tiefenbrunner's entry-level whites are aged in tanks (not oak), which emphasizes this wine's minerally apple and citrus tones.

○ **Tiefenbrunner Kirchleiten Sauvignon / 2010 / Alto Adige / $$**
An amazingly rich and zesty Sauvignon from a stellar vineyard.

TUSCANY

CLAIM TO FAME

Few wine regions have the instant name recognition of Tuscany's Chianti, first legally defined in 1716 (but recognized as a wine region as early as the 13th century). While the boundaries of that original growing region define today's *classico* subzone, the vastly expanded Chianti territory now includes seven more subregions. Some of Chianti's most acclaimed wines, however, don't carry its name. Only reds based on the Sangiovese grape can be called Chianti. Ambitious, rule-breaking Super-Tuscans, most often based on international grapes such as Cabernet, Merlot and Syrah, carry the humbler "IGT Toscana" designation.

REGIONS TO KNOW

CHIANTI There has never been a better time to drink Chianti. Spurred by international competition, its vintners have replanted vineyards and adopted new techniques—like aging wines in small French oak barrels instead of giant old vats. Of Chianti's eight subzones, Chianti Classico is the original and most prestigious. Only Chianti Rufina, located at a higher altitude than most of Tuscany, routinely produces wines to rival Chianti Classico's top bottles. Most wineries use 100 percent Sangiovese, or blend it with Cabernet, Merlot or native grapes such Canaiolo and Colorino. (In Chianti Classico, these grapes can make up no more than 20 percent of the wine.) Generic Chianti, with no subzone, is the simplest. *Riserva* Chiantis require at least two years of aging and are more powerful as a result.

MONTALCINO Vineyards around the town of Montalcino produce Tuscany's greatest wine, Brunello di Montalcino, from a local Sangiovese clone, Brunello. Made from the same grape, Rosso di Montalcino reds are younger, lighter versions of Brunellos.

MONTEPULCIANO Though not far from Montalcino, Montepulciano produces lighter wines that can include small amounts of other grapes along with Sangiovese (known locally as Prugnolo Gentile). Vino Nobile di Montepulciano wines must be aged two years (three for *riservas*). Like Montalcino, Montepulciano releases younger, "baby brother" reds under *rosso* designations.

MAREMMA In the coastal Maremma district, pioneering producers broke with tradition to create the original Super-Tuscan wines in the late 1960s. The Maremma's most famous subregions are Bolgheri and the single-estate Bolgheri Sassicaia DOC.

CORTONA Established in 1999, this DOC in Tuscany's southwestern corner is devoted chiefly to international grapes, and has become a source of exciting Syrahs.

CARMIGNANO Vintners in the town of Carmignano have been boosting their Sangiovese-based wines with Cabernet Sauvignon since the 1700s—long before these blends became known as Super-Tuscans. As a result, their reds typically feature lower acidity and firmer tannins than those of Chianti Classico.

SCANSANO The hilly area around the Maremma village of Scansano makes reds based on Sangiovese, known locally as Morellino. Basic Morellino di Scansano has improved a great deal lately. It's generally aged in tanks, which keeps it vibrant and fresh.

 ## KEY GRAPES: WHITE

TREBBIANO Tuscany's main white grape makes mostly light, unremarkable wines, though quality is improving.

VERMENTINO A white grape full of minerality and zesty lime, Vermentino thrives in milder, coastal subregions like Maremma.

VERNACCIA A specialty of the hilltop town of San Gimignano, this grape yields crisp, full-bodied and nutty whites.

KEY GRAPES: RED

CABERNET, MERLOT AND SYRAH These international varieties are popular blending grapes for native Sangiovese.

CANAIOLO, MAMMOLO AND COLORINO Vintners typically blend these native red varieties with Sangiovese.

SANGIOVESE Sangiovese is king in Tuscany, where it yields high-acid, cherry- and herb-inflected reds in a range of styles. Local synonyms include Brunello, Morellino and Prugnolo Gentile.

Producers/ Tuscany

ANTINORI

Although the Antinori dynasty spans more than 600 years of family winemaking, this iconic label is one of Italy's most dynamic. The very modern portfolio includes Tignanello, which effectively created the Super-Tuscan category. While its empire includes estates in many Italian regions (and partnerships around the globe), Tuscany remains Antinori's center of gravity.

> **WINE INTEL**
> For the first time in its history, Antinori is opening its cellars to the public: A new facility between Florence and Siena, opening in 2013, will enhance production and welcome tourists.

● **Villa Antinori / 2009 / Tuscany / $$**
Cabernet and Merlot give depth to Sangiovese in this red blend, a Tuscan stalwart since 1928.

● **Marchese Antinori Riserva / 2007 / Chianti Classico / $$$**
This features firm, cedar-tinged plum and black cherry flavors.

BADIA A COLTIBUONO

A former monastery, this sprawling Chianti Classico estate is devoted now to the secular pursuit of great wine and food. The Stucchi Prinetti family bought the property in 1846 and, more recently, converted the monastic quarters into a hotel and cooking school. Classic Sangiovese-based reds are the winery's focus.

● **Badia a Coltibuono / 2009 / Chianti Classico / $$**
Made from organically grown grapes, this elegant red features Chianti's hallmark bright cherry and floral tones.

BARONE RICASOLI

The Ricasoli family essentially invented Chianti wine as we know it: A famous ancestor pioneered the formula that became the basis for today's Chianti Classico. Now Ricasoli reds again rank among Chianti's best, thanks to the dynamic 32nd Baron Ricasoli, who bought back the family brand from an international conglomerate in 1993. He slashed production, replanted vineyards and restored greatness to Italy's oldest wine estate (some 900 years and counting).

● **Barone Ricasoli Colledilà / 2008 / Chianti Classico / $$$$**
This vibrant single-vineyard red features herb-edged wild cherry flavors that are remarkably complex.

BORGO SCOPETO

With its own post office and church, plus residences and an inn for tourists, Scopeto deserves the moniker of *borgo* ("hamlet"). Bologna-born businesswoman Elisabetta Gnudi Angelini (who also owns prestigious Montalcino properties Altesino and Caparzo) purchased the hillside estate outside Siena in 1999; she has added a respected *riserva* and a Super-Tuscan to the lineup, while refining its single Chianti Classico.

● **Borgo Scopeto / 2008 / Chianti Classico / $$**
Scopeto's basic *classico* is a polished, anise-perfumed beauty.

BOSCARELLI

When the De Ferrari Corradi family bought this small estate in Montepulciano in 1962, the rustic hill town was known for its *vin santo* dessert wines. It's now famous for stylish, Sangiovese-based reds, due in part to Boscarelli, whose indisputably outstanding wines helped galvanize a generation of vintners and transform Montepulciano into one of Tuscany's elite subzones.

● **Boscarelli de Ferrari / 2009 / Tuscany / $$**
Prugnolo Gentile—a Sangiovese clone native to Montalcino— takes center stage in this fresh, overachieving red.

● **Boscarelli / 2009 / Vino Nobile di Montepulciano / $$$$**
Boscarelli's minerally, zesty Vino Nobile is one of Montepulciano's most famous reds.

● **Boscarelli Nocio dei Boscarelli / 2006 / Vino Nobile di Montepulciano / $$$$** Winemaker Maurizio Castelli produces this single-vineyard Sangiovese only in top vintages; the '06 is marked by fresh violet notes and plush fruit.

CAPARZO

With its breathtaking grounds, Caparzo's cypress-studded, hilltop estate may be most recognizable as the cinematic setting of the 2010 Amanda Seyfried rom-com, *Letters to Juliet*. Equally stunning, however, are Caparzo's well-crafted Brunellos, which are made with grapes from vineyards on all five sides of the famous hill of Montalcino. Caparzo's non-Brunello wines are less well known but equally worthwhile, including some blends of local and French grape varieties.

- **Caparzo / 2009 / Tuscany / $**
  Sangiovese comes together with four other varieties in this lightly oaked, plummy red.
- **Caparzo / 2006 / Brunello di Montalcino / $$$**
  Caparzo's Brunello aims for grace over power, with lots of cherry-driven Sangiovese character.

CASANOVA DI NERI

Like most top Montalcino wineries, Casanova di Neri is young (by Italian standards, at least): Giovanni Neri established his namesake estate in 1971. Neri steadily built its reputation for impeccable wines, but it took his talented son, Giacomo, to lift the estate to international stardom with a series of stellar Brunellos, beginning a decade after he took over the winery in 1991. Made in a flashy, concentrated style, they're among Montalcino's most collectible reds.

- **Casanova di Neri Tenuta Nuova / 2007 / Brunello di Montalcino / $$$$** Very low vineyard yields give this opaque Brunello its formidable concentration.

CASTELLARE DI CASTELLINA

Wildly successful journalist turned media magnate Paolo Panerai has a golden touch: Even his wine hobby turned into a thriving business, with Tuscany's substantial Castellare just one of three notable Panerai estates. One key to the quality of its wines is its prime location, perched in hills outside Siena where nighttime temperatures cool grapes and slow down the ripening process; another factor is winemaker Alessandro Cellai, one of Tuscany's rising stars.

- **Castellare / 2009 / Chianti Classico / $$**
  Vineyards at 1,300 feet and very low yields help explain Castellare's dark intensity.

CASTELL'IN VILLA

Two characteristics distinguish Castell'in Villa's Chiantis: their generally traditional style (meaning vibrant cherry flavors and dusty minerality) and their long aging. Greek-born, Swiss-raised proprietress Princess Coralia Pignatelli della Leonessa prefers the mellower flavors extra aging brings, which is why she often releases wines many years later than is typical.

- **Castell'in Villa Chianti Classico / 2008 / Chianti Classico / $$**
  Sangiovese's bright fruit and acidity shine in this spicy red.
- **Castell'in Villa Poggio delle Rose / 2003 / Tuscany / $$$$**
  A modern-style outlier in a traditional portfolio, this Sangiovese has gained gorgeous aromas with a decade of age.
- **Castell'in Villa Santacroce di Castell'in Villa / 2003 / Tuscany / $$$$** A flagship blend of Cabernet and Sangiovese that's built to last, with firm tannins and deep red fruit.

CASTELLO BANFI

U.S. importers John and Harry Mariani weren't content to just sell Italian wine; they wanted to make it. In 1978 they bought a chunk of Montalcino; today their holdings include an entire hamlet surrounding a medieval fortress they named Castello Banfi. With thousands of acres across Tuscany, Banfi makes a huge amount and range of wines, crowned by pricey Brunellos.

- ○ **Castello Banfi San Angelo Pinot Grigio / 2010 / Tuscany / $$**
  Pinot Grigios this rich and delicious are rare finds in Tuscany.
- **Castello Banfi Poggio alle Mura / 2006 / Brunello di Montalcino / $$$$** Ageworthy and complex, Poggio alle Mura combines spicy black cherry and star anise notes.

CASTELLO DI AMA

Castello di Ama's single-vineyard Chianti Classicos and its voluptuous Merlot-based L'Apparita come from the winery's Gaiole estate, and are as scarce as they are costly. Luckily, vintner Marco Pallanti also makes other wines, including an entry-level Chianti Classico, a white blend and a rosé, all offered at gentler prices.

- **Castello di Ama / 2010 / Tuscany / $$**
  This substantial rosé tastes best when sipped with food, which brings out its fruity side.
- **Castello di Ama / 2007 / Chianti Classico / $$$**
  The high altitude (up to 1,700 feet) and low yields of di Ama's vineyards are two keys to its Chianti's suave, complex flavors.

CASTELLO DI MONSANTO

This estate's groundbreaking top wine, Il Poggio Riserva, was the original single-vineyard Chianti Classico. First made in 1962, it remains one of Tuscany's finest wines. Owner Fabrizio Bianchi and daughter Laura, along with ex-Ornellaia winemaker Andrea Giovannini, also make a high-end Cabernet (called Nemo), a Chardonnay and a range of Sangiovese-based reds.

● **Castello di Monsanto Riserva / 2008 / Chianti Classico / $$**
Exactly what a great Chianti should be: racy, juicy and supremely food-friendly.

CONTI COSTANTI

Tito Costanti was the first to officially bottle and market the distinctive Sangiovese grapes of Montalcino into single-variety, unblended wines. By dubbing the 1865 and 1869 vintages *Brunello* for a wine exhibition in Siena, Costanti essentially invented modern Brunello di Montalcino, Tuscany's most esteemed wine. Andrea Costanti runs the respected winery today, with an assist from well-known consultant Vittorio Fiore.

● **Conti Costanti / 2009 / Rosso di Montalcino / $$$**
There's an intangible handmade quality to this dense, ripe red's earthy strawberry and cherry flavors.

● **Conti Costanti / 2007 / Brunello di Montalcino / $$$$**
An elegant, classically styled Brunello from a glorious vintage.

FATTORIA DEI BARBI

True to its name—*fattoria* means "farm"—this centuries-old Montalcino estate produces specialties like cured meat and pecorino cheese, which pair perfectly with the traditional wines also made here. Long a regional quality leader, Barbi was exporting its wines as far back as 1817. It remains an evangelist for ambitious Brunello, but Barbi's everyday wines are terrific, too.

● **Brusco dei Barbi / 2008 / Tuscany / $$**
This entry-level Sangiovese has the powerful structure of a more expensive wine.

● **Fattoria dei Barbi / 2009 / Rosso di Montalcino / $$**
A baby brother to Barbi's Brunellos, this easy-drinking red shows fresh rose and red cherry flavors.

● **Fattoria dei Barbi Riserva / 2004 / Brunello di Montalcino / $$$$** This powerful, broad-shouldered Brunello is just beginning to soften, and will improve for years to come.

FATTORIA SELVAPIANA

Selvapiana's firm, ageworthy reds are reference points in Chianti Rufina, a small subzone with high-elevation vineyards and cold nights. This microclimate allows proprietor Francesco Giuntini Antinori and his adopted heirs, siblings Federico and Silvia Giuntini Masetti, to create bold, expressive reds. With the help of leading consultant Franco Bernabei, Selvapiana makes two Sangiovese-based wines and two outstanding blends.

● **Fattoria Selvapiana / 2010 / Chianti Rufina / $$**
Selvapiana is one of the Chianti Rufina region's best producers; this expressive, beautifully structured wine shows why.

FATTORIA VITICCIO

Lucio Landini had a successful career as an emigrant engineer for cement factories in Venezuela. But as soon as he could, he returned to Italy with his family and spent his life savings purchasing this Greve estate in the early 1960s. Viticcio found its place among Chianti Classico's leading wineries in the past decade under Alessandro Landini, Lucio's son, whose rigor (low yields, organic farming) and pursuit of quality (e.g., hiring prominent consultant Gabriella Tani) has paid dividends.

● **Viticcio Bere / 2009 / Tuscany / $**
The Landinis blend Cabernet and Merlot from their Bolgheri vineyard with Sangiovese to create this bright, well-priced red.

● **Viticcio / 2008 / Chianti Classico / $$**
Fragrant violet notes introduce this sleek Chianti Classico, which has a touch of Merlot for softness.

LE MACCHIOLE

Unlike many Bolgheri estates, Le Macchiole was founded by a native of the region, Eugenio Campolmi. He brought in consulting winemaker Luca D'Attoma in 1991, and their success with Cabernet Franc, Merlot and Syrah launched Le Macchiole into the ranks of Tuscany's most esteemed modern estates. D'Attoma still helps craft the wines, which include four rich, elegant reds.

○ **Le Macchiole Paleo / 2010 / Tuscany / $$$$**
Lovely lemon and spiced pear notes mark this full-bodied Sauvignon Blanc–Chardonnay blend.

● **Le Macchiole Paleo / 2009 / Tuscany / $$$$**
This is one of the world's great Cabernet Francs, with flavors that recall dark chocolate and cherries.

RARITIES & COLLECTIBLES

BIONDI SANTI This eminent Montalcino producer created the Brunello di Montalcino category in the late 1800s, and its traditionally styled, ageworthy Brunello Riserva is still a benchmark for the region.

SOLDERA Gianfranco Soldera's subtle, layered Brunellos are so sought-after, and produced in such small quantities, that he essentially handpicks his customers (as well as his grapes). But the wines can occasionally be found at top Italian restaurants.

TENUTA SAN GUIDO The Bolgheri estate sold its Cabernet-based Sassicaia only to friends and family for the wine's first 15 vintages. When Tenuta San Guido began releasing Sassicaia to the public in 1968, it instantly became a legend (and more or less created the Super-Tuscan wine category).

LISINI

Sangiovese from rugged old vines is the specialty of this Montalcino producer, one of the region's stalwart names since its emergence in the 1970s. Under matriarch Elina Lisini, and with the aid of prominent consultants such as Giulio Gambelli, Lisini wines have come to epitomize traditional, high-quality Brunello.

- **Lisini / 2009 / Rosso di Montepulciano / $$$**
  A deliciously fresh, raspberry-inflected Sangiovese.
- **Lisini / 2006 / Brunello di Montalcino / $$$$**
  Great balance and a firm structure make this tangy, cherry-driven Sangiovese a great candidate for the cellar.

MARCHESI DE' FRESCOBALDI

With five estates, the Frescobaldi family is Tuscany's largest vineyard owner—and growing. Yet size doesn't detract from their winemaking precision or taste for innovation: Frescobaldi wines, including traditional regional bottlings from Nipozzano, still win acclaim, and the family has pioneered progressive ventures like Luce Estate and the recent launch of Tenuta dell'Ammiraglia.

- **Frescobaldi Rèmole / 2010 / Tuscany / $**
  This blend of Cabernet Sauvignon and Sangiovese is a reliable weekday red with genuine Tuscan character.
- **Tenuta Frescobaldi di Castiglioni / 2009 / Tuscany / $$**
  Though made chiefly from Bordeaux grapes (Cabernet, Merlot, Cabernet Franc), this juicy, dark red tastes distinctly Italian.

POGGIO ANTICO

Paola Gloder Montefiori's Milanese parents were so captivated by the remoteness of this Montalcino estate that they bought it in 1984. Their youngest daughter was enthralled, too: When just in her 20s, she gave up city life to run the winery. With vineyards averaging nearly 1,500 feet in altitude, Poggio Antico occupies prime Sangiovese territory, turning out a trio of exceptionally refined Brunellos, a Rosso and admired Super-Tuscans.

● **Poggio Antico / 2007 / Brunello di Montalcino / $$$$**
A suave, gorgeously polished Brunello defined by floral, smoke and dense red-fruit notes.

● **Poggio Antico Madre / 2009 / Tuscany / $$$$**
First made in 2001, this premier red is a vibrant, smoky blend of equal parts Sangiovese and Cabernet.

RUFFINO

Ruffino is one of the most consistent large Chianti producers, turning out a vast range of wines sourced from across Chianti and beyond, plus estate bottlings from farms in Chianti Classico, Montalcino and Montepulciano. Launched as a *négociant* in 1877, the company was owned for nearly a century by the Folonari family, which turned it into one of Italy's megabrands before selling it to beverage giant Constellation Brands in late 2011.

● **Ruffino Modus / 2008 / Tuscany / $$**
Juicy Sangiovese, firm Cabernet and fruity Merlot create a seamless—and reasonably priced—blend.

TENUTA DELL'ORNELLAIA

Inspired by the success of his uncle, Mario Incisa della Rocchetta, who created the seminal cult wine Sassicaia (first vintage, 1968), Marquis Lodovico Antinori started Ornellaia by planting Bordeaux vines in the same neighborhood, coastal Maremma, near Bolgheri. Ornellaia's current owners, the Frescobaldi family (see p. 93), retain the Antinori vision, with winemaker Axel Heinz crafting profound reds from estate and some purchased grapes.

● **Le Volte / 2009 / Tuscany / $$$**
This velvety, artful combination of Merlot, Cabernet and Sangiovese comes at a very fair price.

● **Le Serre Nuove / 2009 / Bolgheri / $$$$**
Axel Heinz gives a taste of Ornellaia's profound pleasure in the estate's second wine, a complex Bordeaux blend.

TENUTA DI NOZZOLE

The Folonari family (see Ruffino, opposite) acquired this prime Chianti Classico estate in 1971, and with it, 700 years of wine-making history. Deep pockets, great vineyards and ambitious winemaking result in a range of compelling wines including three traditional Sangiovese-based reds plus international blends.

● **Tenuta di Nozzole Riserva / 2008 / Chianti Classico / $$**
This *riserva* seduces with concentrated fruit and savory spice.

● **Tenuta di Nozzole Villa Nozzole / 2009 / Chianti Classico / $$**
Black currant and tobacco notes are the hallmarks of this ultra-ripe, nearly black Sangiovese.

● **Tenuta di Nozzole Il Pareto / 2008 / Tuscany / $$$$**
Nozzole's bold Super-Tuscan Cabernet boasts deep blackberry notes, firm tannins and toasty oak.

TERRABIANCA

Roberto Guldener left his family's Zurich clothing shop in 1988 for life as a winemaker with his wife, Maja, in Chianti Classico. He replanted the Terrabianca vineyards (which feature chalky soils, hence the estate's name, meaning "white earth"), installed a new winery and hired star consultant Vittorio Fiore to help make the impressive wines.

● **Terrabianca Scassino / 2009 / Chianti Classico / $$**
This elegant Chianti has juicy red fruit and fine tannins.

● **Terrabianca Campaccio Riserva / 2006 / Tuscany / $$$$**
The 2006 Campaccio is a blockbuster Sangiovese-Cabernet blend with briary berry fruit and a firm structure.

VILLA CAFAGGIO

This Chianti Classico estate offers some of the best-priced wines coming off the Conca d'Oro, an amphitheater-shaped slope outside Panzano famous for yielding some of Tuscany's finest reds. Paolo Farkas bought and rehabilitated the ancient estate in 1967; his son, Stefano, realized its potential. Key to its success has been the financial backing of *négociant* Casa Girelli, now owned by the Trentino-based Gruppo La-Vis.

● **Villa Cafaggio / 2009 / Chianti Classico / $$**
Winemaker Stefano Chioccioli makes this zesty Chianti in a traditional style, with savory red fruit and notable tannins.

● **Villa Cafaggio Riserva / 2008 / Chianti Classico / $$**
A well-priced *riserva* offering firm tannins and dark, spicy fruit.

OTHER CENTRAL ITALY

REGIONS TO KNOW

ABRUZZO Led by its signature bottling, Montepulciano d'Abruzzo, this mountainous region has become a terrific source of value-priced reds. Often a simple wine with soft, straightforward berry and plum flavors, Montepulciano d'Abruzzo can also be remarkably robust, spicy and tannic. Top vintners are showcasing the grape's polished side at both ends of the style (and price) spectrum. Whites are steadily improving; look for those made from the local Pecorino and Passerina varieties.

EMILIA-ROMAGNA Emilia-Romagna's wines are not as famous as its meats and cheeses (e.g., Prosciutto di Parma and Parmigiano-Reggiano) but are still worth discovering. Its most prominent bottling is Lambrusco, a fizzy, often sweet wine that's usually red but ranges in color from white to deep purple. The best are dry and come from small producers. Quality-focused wineries are also turning out fine offerings made from white grapes like Albana, Chardonnay and Malvasia, and reds based on Sangiovese, Barbera, Cabernet Sauvignon and Pinot Nero (Pinot Noir).

LAZIO Lazio's prolific vineyards on the outskirts of Rome have supplied the city's taverns and trattorias with wine for millennia. The region's defining wine, Frascati, is a ubiquitous, crisp, citrusy white that's often thin and innocuous, but it can deliver complexity when made with care. Authorities approved two new DOCGs, Frascati Superiore and Cannellino Frascati, in 2011, which will, in theory, guarantee higher quality, though it's too early to tell. Reds based on the Cesanese grape have been gaining attention since the Cesanese del Piglio zone was promoted to DOCG status in 2008.

LE MARCHE Le Marche sticks out from Italy's eastern coast like the shapely calf in the peninsula's boot. The region's top reds are made from Sangiovese (Tuscany's signature variety) or Montepulciano, a grape that bursts with soft plum and berry. Blends of the two grapes are the specialty of Rosso Piceno, a DOC near the port city of Ancona; Rosso Conero is a bold, smoky red made chiefly from Montepulciano. Le Marche's top white is the zesty, mouth-filling Verdicchio; the best versions come from the hill-top subzone of Verdicchio dei Castelli di Jesi Classico. Wines made from little-known native white grapes, such as Pecorino and Passerina, are showing up more frequently in the U.S.

UMBRIA The green hills of landlocked Umbria are home to Orvieto, a light-bodied, usually inexpensive white made from a blend of local grapes. Mass-produced bottlings, made chiefly with the Trebbiano grape, are generally forgettable; look instead for versions sourced from old Grechetto vines grown in the soft volcanic rock of Orvieto's *classico* subzone, which can be fantastic. Umbria's best-known reds are forceful, bold examples of the Sagrantino grape.

❧ KEY GRAPES: WHITE

GRECHETTO A white variety presumed to be native to Greece (hence its name), Grechetto is grown chiefly in Umbria and yields refreshing, lime- and peach-flavored bottlings.

PASSERINA & PECORINO Found mainly in Abruzzo and Le Marche, the appley Passerina and mineral-driven Pecorino are increasingly being bottled on their own to make some of central Italy's most appealing whites.

TREBBIANO A handful of quality-driven vintners (mostly in Abruzzo) are proving that the Trebbiano grape, widely used for characterless bulk wines, can indeed yield whites of character.

VERDICCHIO Once bottled chiefly in amphora-shaped bottles, Verdicchio-based wines are typically almond-scented, crisp and citrusy; they're among the world's most seafood-friendly whites.

❧ KEY GRAPES: RED

MONTEPULCIANO Not to be confused with the Tuscan town of the same name, where the wines are made from Sangiovese (see p. 86), the plummy, spicy Montepulciano grape is behind some of central Italy's best reds.

SAGRANTINO A native of Umbria, this grape yields powerful, tannic and long-lived reds. Full of spice, earth and plum notes, Sagrantino thrives around the Umbrian village of Montefalco.

Producers/ Other Central Italy

ANTONELLI SAN MARCO

After years of making bulk wine at their Umbrian estate, the Antonelli family turned to quality production in 1979—about the same time the Sagrantino di Montefalco appellation, where their vineyards are located, was granted DOC status (DOCG came along in 1992). Today this winery is an Umbrian star, thanks to modern winemaking techniques applied to native grapes.

● **Antonelli / 2007 / Sagrantino di Montefalco / $$$** It takes a lot of talent to get the tannic Sagrantino grape to taste as smooth as this rich, seamless red.

ARNALDO CAPRAI

Marco Caprai and his late father, Arnaldo, are famous for reviving Sagrantino, a red grape unique to Umbria. Sagrantino's firm tannins, dusty plum flavors and food-friendly acidity are beautifully showcased in Caprai's top wine, Sagrantino di Montefalco 25 Anni, one of Umbria's most esteemed reds.

○ **Arnaldo Caprai Grecante / 2011 / Grechetto dei Colli Martani / $$** Umbria's most distinctive white grape, Grechetto, yields this lively, peach-inflected bottling.

● **Arnaldo Caprai 25 Anni / 2007 / Sagrantino di Montefalco / $$$$** Impenetrable now, this benchmark Sagrantino needs aging to reveal its full complexity.

CANTINE GIORGIO LUNGAROTTI

Giorgio Lungarotti founded his winery in the early 1960s in Torgiano, Umbria, and his innovative Sangiovese blend, Rubesco Riserva, put the region on the wine world's map. Now led by his daughters, the winery is Umbria's most prolific producer; the San Giorgio and Vigna Monticchio blends are its showcase wines.

○ **Lungarotti Torre di Giano / 2010 / Umbria IGT / $$** A fresh, delicate blend of Trebbiano and Grechetto.

● **Lungarotti San Giorgio / 2004 / Umbria IGT / $$$$** Combining Cabernet with Sangiovese and Canaiolo makes this tannic red the Umbrian equivalent of a Super-Tuscan.

FONTANA CANDIDA

Fontana Candida is both the leading producer of Frascati—the fragrant, soft white from the countryside outside Rome—and its biggest champion. Much Frascati is still characterless, but with winemaker Mauro Merz at the helm, Fontana Candida is restoring the wine's true charm. Merz selects vineyards for the quality, not the quantity, of the grapes they produce, and he ferments them at cool temperatures to protect the fruit's delicate citrus flavors.

○ **Fontana Candida / 2011 / Frascati / $**
Juicy lemon and citrus notes define this zesty, reliable Frascati.

○ **Fontana Candida Terre dei Grifi / 2010 / Frascati Superiore / $**
The Terre dei Grifi boasts fleshier, sweeter fruit than most Frascati, but it's still perfectly refreshing.

LA MONACESCA

La Monacesca's remote location—a high, secluded valley in the Marche region—originally attracted Benedictine monks, who built a monastery and gave rise to the estate's name. Altitude plays a key factor in the quality of its wines: Chilly evening temperatures slow grapes' ripening, while warm days speed it up, an ideal mix of conditions. The Marche's great white grape, Verdicchio, stars in the winery's signature bottling.

○ **La Monacesca / 2010 / Verdicchio di Matelica / $$**
Di Matelica is one of just two official Marche zones for Verdicchio. This steely, lemony rendition is ideal with seafood.

○ **La Monacesca Ecclesia / 2008 / Marche / $$$**
This unoaked, peach-scented Chardonnay gets its flavor complexity from eight different clones of the variety.

LA VALENTINA

Though wine quality has risen all over Abruzzo in recent decades, La Valentina's Sabatino Di Properzio has been consistently ahead of the curve. He's helped show the complex side of what's often a simple regional red—Montepulciano d'Abruzzo—by keeping vineyard yields low and using only estate grapes. The most famous site is a 10-acre vineyard from which Di Properzio produces a definitive Montepulciano called Binomio.

● **La Valentina Spelt / 2007 / Montepulciano d'Abruzzo / $$**
A baby brother to Binomio, this muscular red has intense black fruit, great structure and a wallet-friendly price.

MORODER

Consultant Roberto Cantori lends his polished touch to Moroder's wines, which helps explain both their deliciousness and their renown. Alessandro and Serenella Moroder have converted their cliff-top Marche estate to organic farming, and they continue to focus on Montepulciano, a variety that the Moroder family has specialized in for centuries.

○ **Moroder Elleno / 2011 / Marche Bianco / $$**
Drink this Malvasia as young as possible to make the most of its lightly floral pear flavors.

● **Moroder / 2009 / Rosso Conero / $$**
Made from the plummy Montepulciano grape, this is a spicy, eminently food-friendly red.

● **Moroder Dorico / 2007 / Rosso Conero Riserva / $$$**
With its classic structure and long finish, Moroder's flagship red shows just how great the Montepulciano grape can be.

UMANI RONCHI

For 50 years, the Bianchi-Bernetti family has devoted most of its energy to producing the Marche region's two signature wines: Verdicchio (a zesty white) and Rosso Conero (a Montepulciano-based blend). Michele Bernetti, a member of the most recent generation to head the estate, has fine-tuned the vineyards and the winery, and the wines taste better than ever.

○ **Umani Ronchi Casal di Serra / 2010 / Verdicchio dei Castelli di Jesi Classico Superiore / $$** This generously fruity, crisp Verdicchio comes from Italy's top zone for the grape.

● **Umani Ronchi San Lorenzo / 2009 / Rosso Conero / $$**
This spicy red comes from the San Lorenzo vineyard, where south-facing slopes yield perfectly ripe Montepulciano.

● **Umani Ronchi Cúmaro / 2007 / Rosso Conero Riserva / $$$**
Also from the San Lorenzo vineyard, this intense Montepulciano is made only in exceptional years, from the best barrels.

VILLA BUCCI

No winery has mastered the Verdicchio grape like Villa Bucci. Located in Le Marche's prestigious Castelli di Jesi subregion, where Verdicchio is the chief white grape, Villa Bucci produces two benchmark Verdicchios as well as two Rosso Piceno reds (blends of Montepulciano and Sangiovese), all shaped by the legendary Giorgio Grai, the winery's longtime consultant.

○ **Bucci / 2010 / Verdicchio Classico dei Castelli di Jesi / $$**
This elegant, citrus-driven white gets a lovely, silky texture from a half year of barrel aging.

● **Bucci Pongelli / 2009 / Rosso Piceno / $$**
Fruit-forward Montepulciano softens juicy Sangiovese in this robust (but not overoaked) blend.

SOUTHERN ITALY

CLAIM TO FAME
Once known for its bulk wine, southern Italy is now a source of high-quality bottlings, often made from grapes found nowhere else. There's still disappointing wine here, but the region's best vintners offer compelling wines that frequently deliver great value.

REGIONS TO KNOW
APULIA This is the home of Primitivo, a plush grape that has gained fame as Zinfandel's Italian twin. Less well known are the excellent reds of the Salice Salentino and Copertino subzones, both made primarily from the dark-skinned Negroamaro grape.

BASILICATA The spicy, Aglianico-based reds of Basilicata make this region's best case for greatness, especially those from Aglianico del Vulture, where vineyards planted on the slopes and foothills of the extinct Monte Vulture volcano yield potent wines. Newer DOCs, Terre dell'Alta Val d'Agri and Matera, offer red, white and rosé blends based on grapes other than Aglianico.

CALABRIA Cirò, a delicate, floral-scented red based on the Gaglioppo grape, is Calabria's best wine.

CAMPANIA This region is a leader in southern Italy's native grape revival. Campania's *terroir*-driven wines include powerful Aglianico reds (top, ageworthy examples come from the Taurasi DOCG) and three distinctive whites: the expressive Falanghina; lush, nutty Fiano di Avellino; and floral, zesty Greco di Tufo.

SARDINIA The twin stars of this Mediterranean isle are its fresh Vermentino whites and spicy, supple Cannonau (Grenache) reds, the best of which come from old, low-yielding "bush" vines.

SICILY Though international grapes like Cabernet and Chardonnay have gained a foothold here, Sicily's most interesting wines are made from native varieties. Fruity Nero d'Avola is its signature red grape, and when blended with Frappato is responsible for Cerasuolo di Vittoria, the island's only DOCG wine. From Mount Etna's slopes, reds designated Etna Rosso offer powerful tannins and savory red-fruit flavors. White grapes grown in Etna's black soils, particularly Carricante, can yield fresh, mineral-rich wines. Elsewhere, standouts include citrusy whites made from Catarratto, Grillo and Inzolia, and reds based on Frappato.

❧ KEY GRAPES: WHITE

FALANGHINA, FIANO DI AVELLINO & GRECO DI TUFO Wines made from these varieties share crisp floral and mineral notes and are usually well priced.

VERMENTINO Grown up and down Italy's coasts, Vermentino produces whites whose racy, lime- and herb-scented zesty flavors make them a terrific match for seafood.

❧ KEY GRAPES: RED

AGLIANICO Responsible for the top reds of Basilicata and Campania, this inky, earthy variety possesses high tannins and acidity that give its wines the ability to age.

CANNONAU, CARIGNANO & MONICA Sardinia's Spanish- and French-influenced history shows in its plantings of these foreign red varieties. Cannonau, known elsewhere as Grenache or Garnacha, bursts with supple red-fruit flavors; the island's top Carignano (Carignane) wines stand among the best examples of this often tough and rustic variety. The Monica grape generally makes simple reds.

FRAPPATO Sicily's Frappato yields alluring, light- to medium-bodied reds with fragrant, silky red-fruit tones.

GAGLIOPPO Wines made from this Calabrian grape are perfumy and supple, with sweet red cherry and floral notes.

NEGROAMARO Depending on how it's used, this Apulian grape can yield simple, light reds or concentrated, muscular wines.

NERELLO MASCALESE AND NERELLO CAPPUCCIO Indigenous to the lava-streaked slopes of Sicily's Mount Etna, these varieties offer rich, firm reds edged in dusty minerality.

NERO D'AVOLA Sicilian winemakers prize this native grape for its lush, earthy flavors redolent of sweet blackberries and spice.

PRIMITIVO Plush tannins and rich, brambly red berry flavors are the hallmarks of this Zinfandel relative.

Producers/ Southern Italy

ABBAZIA SANTA ANASTASIA

Entrepreneur Francesco Lena created this stunning wine estate and hotel from a former abbey (*abbazia*) near Palermo. With single-variety wines based on native grapes, such as Nero d'Avola and Grillo, and new-wave blends using French grapes, Santa Anastasia is emblematic of Sicily's renewal (even as Lena's 2010 arrest for Mafia ties shows the island's struggle with its past).

● **Santa Anastasia Contempo Nero d'Avola / 2009 / Sicily / $$**
Sicily's premier grape variety, Nero d'Avola, yields this richly styled, violet-scented red.

● **Santa Anastasia Passomaggio / 2008 / Sicily / $$**
Combining earthy Nero d'Avola with plummy Merlot results in a juicy wine marked by sun-warmed red fruit and mint.

A MANO

California vintner Mark Shannon fell in love with Friulian Elvezia Sbalchiero when both were consulting at a winery in Sicily. The couple then fell hard for Apulia—its wines, food and people. Their label A Mano ("by hand") focuses chiefly on Apulian varieties and California-style technology (like thermo-controlled fermenting tanks); a juicy Primitivo is their runaway hit.

● **A Mano Primitivo / 2008 / Puglia / $**
At California's Bogle Vineyards, Mark Shannon made terrific Zinfandel. He applies that skill to this affordable old-vine Primitivo, Zinfandel's Italian sibling.

ARGIOLAS

Sardinia's most famous producer revitalized wine production on the island almost single-handedly. Longtime grape growers, the Argiolas family sold their fruit to bulk vintners before brothers Franco and Giuseppe decided to make wine themselves. In 1989 they hired Mariano Murru, who along with famed consultant Giacomo Tachis makes impressive wines from local grapes.

○ **Argiolas Costamolino / 2010 / Vermentino di Sardegna / $$**
A delicious, tropical-inflected Vermentino that exemplifies the zesty charms of Sardinia's signature white grape.

BOTROMAGNO

Botromagno is a poster child for Apulia's transformation: In its former life as a co-op, it churned out mediocre wine until the D'Agostino family bought it in 1991. Today brothers Alberto and Beniamino oversee a lineup of terrific, and terrifically affordable, reds and whites made mostly from native grapes. In-demand Tuscan winemaker Alberto Antonini lends a hand.

○ **Botromagno / 2010 / Gravina / $**
This blend of Greco and Malvasia is dry and subtly floral.

● **Botromagno Primitivo / 2009 / Puglia / $$**
Full-bodied and juicy, this Primitivo displays raisin-accented fruit that's nicely structured and not overripe.

COS

Few wineries succeed as brilliantly as COS at making benchmark renditions of Sicilian grapes. This biodynamic estate (its name is an acronym of the last names of its founders—Giambattista Cilia, enologist Giusto Occhipinti and Cirino Strano) is on the cutting edge of retro winemaking, with many grapes fermented in clay amphorae, a technique that's about as old as wine itself.

○ **COS Ramì / 2010 / Sicily / $$**
Fermented in concrete, this straw-yellow blend of two native grapes offers exotic notes of orange and ginger.

● **COS Frappato / 2010 / Sicily / $$**
Occhipinti endows the lightweight Frappato grape with unusual richness in this drinkable, strawberry-scented red.

● **COS Pithos / 2010 / Cerasuolo di Vittoria / $$$**
The amphora-aged Pithos—a blend of Frappato and Nero d'Avola—is a spicy, complex rendition of Cerasuolo di Vittoria, Sicily's most prestigious red (and first DOCG).

RARITIES & COLLECTIBLES

FATTORIA GALARDI The Galardi estate produces only one wine, Terra di Lavoro—one of the most extraordinary reds not only in Campania, but in all Italy. Based on the austere, powerful Aglianico variety, this blend is dark and smoky, with a seemingly endless, savory finish.

MONTEVETRANO Like Galardi, this Campanian estate has a single benchmark wine: a rare red made chiefly from Bordeaux grapes, created with the assistance of superstar consulting winemaker Riccardo Cotarella.

TENUTE DETTORI Naturalist winemaker Alessandro Dettori makes profound reds from ancient Cannonau vines in Sardinia, adhering to a philosophy that involves minimal yields from his old-vine vineyards and a biodynamic approach to grape-growing.

LEONE DE CASTRIS

This Apulian estate was founded in 1665 by a Spanish duke and Hapsburg viceroy who went native: He sold his family's property in Spain and bought vast tracts of Apulian farmland. These holdings form the core of the modern estate, owned by the de Castris family, the duke's descendants. Always reliable, the wines have improved greatly with the aid of consultant Riccardo Cotarella.

○ **Leone de Castris Messapia Verdeca / 2010 / Salento / $$**
The Verdeca grape makes a rich, citrusy, guava-scented white.

● **Leone de Castris Five Roses / 2011 / Salento / $$**
Made in a dry, fresh, fruit-forward style, Five Roses has long been one of Italy's best (and best-known) pink wines.

LIBRANDI

Calabria is a treasure trove of obscure native grapes, though not many wineries in this rustic region have Librandi's skill with them. A family firm that has bottled its own wines since the 1950s, Librandi crafts benchmark renditions of native grapes like Gaglioppo, Greco and Montonico, and uses French varieties too.

○ **Librandi Critone / 2010 / Val di Neto / $**
This unusual mix of Chardonnay and Sauvignon Blanc is both innovative and affordable, with lemon and stone-fruit notes.

● **Librandi / 2009 / Cirò Rosso Classico / $**
Made from the Gaglioppo grape, this well-crafted Cirò Rosso shows the peppery, herbal side of Calabria's hallmark red.

MARISA CUOMO

The Amalfi Coast estate of Marisa Cuomo and her husband, the talented winemaker Andrea Ferraioli, produces some red wine from the Aglianico and Piedirosso varieties, but it is Ferraioli's stunning whites that garner the loudest accolades. Ancient native grapes like Falanghina, Biancolella and Ginestra grown in these rocky soils make exotic wines like the white Fiorduva Furore Bianco blend.

○ **Marisa Cuomo Ravello Bianco / 2010 / Costa d'Amalfi / $$**
This blend of Biancolella and Falanghina, grown on a terraced vineyard more than 900 feet above sea level, shows off aromatic floral, honeysuckle and melon notes with a zesty kick of spice on the finish.

● **Furore Rosso / 2010 / Costa d'Amalfi / $$**
An especially lively red full of fresh ripe cherry flavors and black pepper highlights; only a few months spent in oak means that it's still bright and firm.

● **Furore Rosso Riserva / 2006 / Costa d'Amalfi / $$$**
Approachable sooner than most *riservas*, this 50/50 blend of Aglianico and Piedirosso is rich with black fruit and licorice, buoyed nicely by minerally acidity and chewy tannins.

MASTROBERARDINO

The dapper, charismatic Piero Mastroberardino is the latest in 10 generations of vintners to guide his family's Campania winery. Vast acreage, high-tech facilities and a commitment to native grapes make this quality-focused producer a go-to name for reds and whites up and down the price scale. Radici, a masterful Taurasi (a red wine made with Aglianico), tops the Mastroberardino portfolio, while less-expensive offerings make ideal introductions to Campania's wines.

○ **Mastroberardino / 2009 / Fiano di Avellino / $$**
Making this excellent Fiano entirely in stainless steel keeps its hazelnut aromas and bright pear fruit incredibly fresh.

○ **Mastroberardino Sannio / 2010 / Sannio / $$**
This is a reliably terrific example of the local Falanghina grape. The 2010 is crisp and mineral-rich, with compelling pear and herb notes.

● **Mastroberardino / 2010 / Lacryma Christi del Vesuvio / $$**
This minerally, peppery, ripe red from the slopes of Mount Vesuvius is made from the heirloom Piedirosso grape.

PLANETA

Francesca Planeta (daughter of Diego Planeta, president of Sicily's largest bulk-wine co-op) founded this winery with her cousins Alessio and Santi Planeta. From their first vintage in 1995, they built it into Sicily's largest and most dynamic brand. Originally known for well-made Chardonnay and Merlot, Planeta has helped pioneer wines made from native varieties such as Nero d'Avola, Frappato and Grecanico.

● **Planeta / 2010 / Cerasuolo di Vittoria / $$**
Beautifully fragrant spice and red-fruit notes define this juicy blend of Nero d'Avola and Frappato.

● **Planeta Santa Cecilia / 2007 / Sicily / $$$**
Winemaker Alessio Planeta coaxes the best out of Nero d'Avola in this spicy red with dense red-fruit flavors.

SELLA & MOSCA

Sella & Mosca boasts one of Italy's largest contiguous vineyards, and it's easily Sardinia's largest wine exporter. The estate produces some wines with international varieties like Sauvignon Blanc and Cabernet, but the most rewarding bottlings are made from indigenous grapes, like the hearty red Cannonau, zesty Vermentino and Terre Bianche Torbato.

○ **Sella & Mosca La Cala / 2010 / Vermentino di Sardegna / $**
This refreshing, seafood-friendly white is an amazing value.

● **Sella & Mosca Riserva / 2008 / Cannonau di Sardegna / $$**
Cannonau, the local name for Grenache, excels in Sardinia, as this enticing, raspberry-driven red clearly demonstrates.

VELENOSI

Angela Velenosi offers an eclectic array of wines from her ambitious Marche label, but those made from the region's native grapes stand out. Velenosi and husband Ercole established their winery in 1984 as young entrepreneurs; today it is a Marche star. Its most acclaimed offerings are the estate-grown Rosso Piceno reds; the basic Pecorino—a plump, juicy white—is a steal.

○ **Velenosi Pecorino Villa Angela / 2010 / Offida / $**
The unjustly obscure Pecorino grape is responsible for this white's zesty, full-bodied apricot and jasmine notes.

● **Velenosi Il Brecciarolo / 2008 / Rosso Piceno Superiore / $**
Burly Montepulciano and tangy Sangiovese come together in this wonderfully fresh, blackberry-edged red.

Spain

Wine Region

Spain is one of the most exciting—and disparate—wine-producing countries on the planet. It is influenced by the warm Mediterranean as well as the cool Atlantic; its winemaking can be very traditional or thrillingly avant-garde; and its bottles range from some of the greatest values in the world to some of the most expensive. Home to ancient vineyards and architecturally groundbreaking wineries, Spain offers an incredible variety of wine experiences.

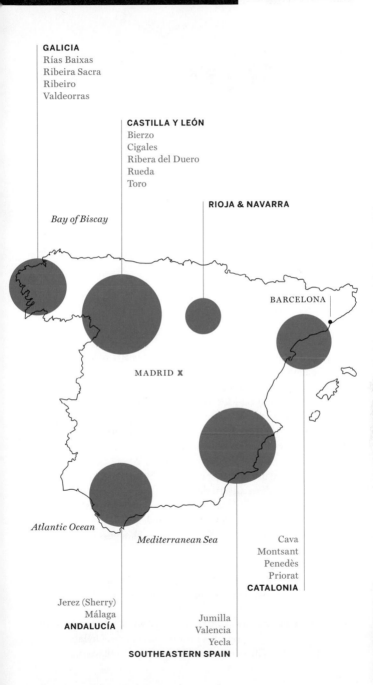

GALICIA
Rías Baixas
Ribeira Sacra
Ribeiro
Valdeorras

CASTILLA Y LEÓN
Bierzo
Cigales
Ribera del Duero
Rueda
Toro

RIOJA & NAVARRA

Bay of Biscay

BARCELONA

MADRID **X**

Atlantic Ocean

Mediterranean Sea

Cava
Montsant
Penedès
Priorat
CATALONIA

Jerez (Sherry)
Málaga
ANDALUCÍA

Jumilla
Valencia
Yecla
SOUTHEASTERN SPAIN

Spain

SPANISH WINE HAS a split personality. Mountain ranges divide Spain into distinct viticultural areas, some influenced mainly by the Mediterranean, others by the chillier Atlantic; in between are regions like Rioja, where vintages are identified as either Atlantic or Mediterranean. Albariño-based whites come from the cool Atlantic region of Rías Baixas, in Galicia. In Castilla y León, to the east, still within the Atlantic's grasp, Rueda produces zippier whites mostly from the Verdejo grape. Powerful reds come from Castilla y León's Ribera del Duero and Toro regions, while renowned Rioja, in north-central Spain, makes both modern and traditionally styled wines that can age for years. Catalonia, in Spain's Mediterranean northeast, is home to sparkling cavas, still wines from Penedès and Priorat's robust reds. Jerez, in the south, is famous for its sherries (see p. 297).

WINE TERMINOLOGY

VINO DE LA TIERRA (VDT) Like French *vins de pays*, basic regional VdT wines are often dull, but can offer great value, too.

VINO DE CALIDAD CON INDICACIÓN GEOGRAFICA A step up from VdT, this category recognizes improving regions. On labels, it's indicated with "Vino de Calidad" followed by a place name.

DENOMINACIÓN DE ORIGEN (DO) Spain's regional DOs set out legal standards for permitted grapes, harvest limits and vinification techniques, in addition to geographic sourcing requirements. Most quality wine belongs to this category.

DENOMINACIÓN DE ORIGEN CALIFICADA (DOCA) Just two areas, Rioja and Priorat, lay claim to the prestigious status of DOCa, the most rigorous regional wine designation.

DENOMINACIÓN DE ORIGEN DE PAGO/VINO DE PAGO Roughly equivalent to a French *grand cru,* the prestigious *vino de pago* classification is given to single, renowned estates; eleven *vinos de pago* have been approved since the category was introduced in 2003. Confusingly, many wines with *pago* on the label are not in this elite category (it's also a generic term for estate and/or vineyard), and some *vinos de pago* don't say *pago* at all, but list the name of the *pago* after "Denominación de Origen," as in "Denominación de Origen Finca Elez."

BODEGA & CELLER Both of these words mean "winery." The Catalan *celler* is used in Catalonia; the Spanish *bodega* is common throughout the rest of the country.

ROSADO Several regions in Spain produce superb *rosado* (rosé) wines, which are typically dry, with citrus and berry flavors.

VIÑA & VIÑEDO These terms for "vineyard" are often part of a winery's name. When not part of the winery name on a label, the words usually refer to a site from which the wine is sourced.

RIOJA & NAVARRA

CLAIM TO FAME

Though regions like Ribera del Duero and Priorat are now competing with Rioja for the title of Spain's greatest wine zone, this large region in the northeast still turns out an impressive percentage of the country's best reds. Many producers today strike a balance between earthy, old-school reds and superfruity modern versions. Meanwhile, up-and-coming neighbor Navarra has become a go-to source of value-priced reds and *rosados.*

REGIONS TO KNOW

RIOJA ALAVESA Distinctive chalky soils, an Atlantic-influenced climate and high elevation define this region. As a result, its wines are lighter and more rustic than those of Rioja Alta. While quality is not as consistent as in Rioja Alta, good values abound.

RIOJA ALTA The source of most of Rioja's greatest wines, the Alta ("high") subzone is located in the foothills of the Cantabrian mountains at the region's western end, where Atlantic-driven temperatures and limestone soils yield refined, ageworthy reds.

RIOJA BAJA Winemakers in Rioja Baja benefit from the warm, dry Mediterranean climate, and they rely more on Garnacha (rather than Tempranillo, dominant elsewhere). Their wines are softer, riper and less-structured reds made for early drinking.

KEY GRAPES: WHITE

VIURA Rioja's reputation rests on its reds, but both Rioja and Navarra produce lovely, vibrant whites based mostly on Viura, known elsewhere in Spain as Macabeo. By the 1990s, most white Riojas were made exclusively with Viura. Styles range from barrel-aged and often intentionally oxidized to fresh and bright.

KEY GRAPES: RED

GARNACHA Supple, sultry and loaded with fragrant red berry flavors, this variety is a key component of many Rioja reds and was, until recently, Navarra's dominant grape. Winemakers use its velvety tannins and plump body to soften Tempranillo's firm, earthy structure in blends. Internationally, it's better known by its French name, Grenache.

GRACIANO & MAZUELO Grown in small amounts, these minor grapes are native to northeast Spain. Graciano is increasingly prized by winemakers for its ability to add acidity and fragrance to a blend, while Mazuelo—called Carignane in France and Cariñena elsewhere in Spain—is a tough and tannic grape.

TEMPRANILLO Tempranillo's fragrant cherry flavors, tart acidity and firm tannins have long made it the top grape for Rioja's long-lived blends. Today it's also popular in Navarra, where it recently supplanted Garnacha as the most planted variety.

WINE TERMINOLOGY

While used widely throughout Spain, these terms are most closely associated with Rioja wines.

ALTA EXPRESIÓN An unofficial term for high-end reds typically aged in French (rather than American) oak for shorter than usual periods. These wines are darker, with bolder fruit flavors.

JOVEN Made to be drunk within a year or two of release, *joven* ("young") wines—also called *cosecha*—spend little time in oak, which keeps them fresh (and reasonably priced).

CRIANZA Matured at least two years, one in oak, *crianzas* are more complex than *jovens*. Rioja's top *crianzas* offer great value.

RESERVA Aged in barrel for at least 12 months and not released until at least three years after harvest, *reservas* showcase soft tannins, mellower fruit and oak-driven spicy vanilla.

GRAN RESERVA Only wine vinified from the best, most intense grapes can survive the five required years of aging—at least two of them in oak—and emerge more balanced and delicious.

Producers/ Rioja & Navarra

ARTAZU

When Rioja's outstanding Artadi winery expanded into neighboring Navarra in 1996, founder and winemaker Juan Carlos López zeroed in on the region's cooler, higher-altitude northern extreme, where grapes ripen more slowly. Today López makes three terrific Garnachas: a crisp *rosado* and a red wine under the Artazuri label, and the benchmark Artazu Santa Cruz.

- **Artazuri Tinto** / 2010 / Navarra / $
  Juicy and clean, marked by red fruit and a hint of spicy oak.
- **Santa Cruz de Artazu** / 2008 / Navarra / $$$
  One of Navarra's finest reds, this sturdy Garnacha is loaded with fresh black fruit bolstered by French oak aging.

CVNE

Unusual for Rioja, this venerable producer (CVNE is the Spanish acronym for Wine Company of Northern Spain) owns the the vineyards that supply about half of its grapes. Its labels include Viña Real, launched in the 1920s, which comes chiefly from Rioja Alavesa; as well as Cune and Imperial, sourced mostly from Rioja Alta. The affiliated Contino brand offers prestigious single-vineyard reds.

○ **Cune Monopole Blanco / 2010 / Rioja / $**
Made with Viura sourced from high-altitude vineyards, this fresh, floral-scented wine reveals subtle tropical notes.

● **Contino Graciano / 2007 / Rioja / $$$$**
This bright, juicy red may be Rioja's finest Graciano bottling.

LA RIOJA ALTA

This prestigious producer deftly straddles tradition and modernity even though it has been making high-quality wines for more than a century. Its lineup includes both classically mellowed, old-school bottlings such as the Gran Reserva 890 and powerful cuvées like the Viña Ardanza. The entry-level Alberdi is a perennial steal.

● **Viña Alberdi Crianza / 2005 / Rioja / $$**
An intensely complex, aromatic *reserva* with seductive wild berry, balsamic and vanilla notes that are pure and elegant.

● **Viña Ardanza Reserva Especial / 2001 / Rioja / $$**
Its 20 percent Garnacha content imparts a hint of spice to this earthy, orange peel–infused red, whose freshness belies its age.

MARQUÉS DE CÁCERES

When Enrique Forner founded this pioneering winery in the late 1960s, he received advice from famed French wine consultant Émile Peynaud. Today superstar winemaker Michel Rolland fills that role, helping to guide Marqués de Cáceres's terrific wines. While the Crianza is widely known and a reliable bet, don't overlook the whites and the *rosado*.

● **Marqués de Cáceres Rosado / 2011 / Rioja / $**
A Tempranillo-Garnacha rosé marked by bright strawberry and spice that make it a great summer sipper.

● **Marqués de Cáceres Crianza / 2008 / Rioja / $**
Matured in barrel for one year, this smooth, affordable Rioja is a great introduction to the region's reds.

MARQUÉS DE MURRIETA

The focused portfolio here—a mere four wines—remains largely faithful to Murrieta's roots in traditional-style Rioja production. Created by Peru native Luciano Francisco Ramón de Murrieta in 1852, the winery crafts two traditional reds and a white, Capellanía, using only estate fruit. The much more expensive Dalmau represents a modern departure for the winery, with its addition of Cabernet Sauvignon.

● **Marqués de Murrieta Castillo Ygay Gran Reserva Especial / 2004 / Rioja / $$$$** As traditional as they come, this *gran reserva* shows earthy cherry and plum flavors highlighted by spice notes (from American oak).

MARQUÉS DE RISCAL

Founded more than 150 years ago, this historic Rioja estate is a stalwart and one of the most successful wineries in Spain. In addition to three classically styled Riojas and a crisp *rosado*, it offers a bold, flavorful red under the Baron de Chirel label. A side project in Rueda turns out zesty Verdejos.

> **WINE INTEL**
> Riscal's glittering City of Wine complex in Elciego includes a Frank Gehry–designed luxury hotel, a pair of restaurants and a vinotherapy spa.

● **Marqués de Riscal Reserva / 2006 / Rioja / $$** In the traditional fashion, Riscal adds small amounts of Graciano and Mazuelo to this classic Rioja bottling.

MARQUÉS DE VARGAS

A new estate from an old Rioja family, Marqués de Vargas fulfills a long-held ambition of Hilario de la Mata and his son, Pelayo de la Mata, the current marquis (*marqués*) of Vargas. Founded in 1989 near Logroño, in Rioja Alta, the winery released its first vintage in 1991. Its three reds come from organically farmed estate vines and combine modern techniques (aging in French and Russian oak) with a traditional sensibility— meaning they're neither powerfully fruity nor austerely dry.

● **Marqués de Vargas Reserva Privada / 2005 / Rioja / $$$** Although it's eight years old, this firm, traditional-style Rioja Reserva is still tightly wound. Give it a few years more in bottle, or decant before serving.

● **Marqués de Vargas Hacienda Pradolagar / 2005 / Rioja / $$$$** Vargas's flagship red is bold but refined, with smoky red fruit that makes it a fantastic match for grilled lamb.

MONTECILLO

Montecillo makes reliably good—sometimes brilliant—wines on a grand scale, thanks to the three-decade tenure of winemaker María Martínez, as well as the deep pockets of its owners, the Osborne Group, which bought the winery in 1973. Martínez prefers classical reds (i.e., not too ripe), ages them in French (not American) oak and offers them for reasonable prices.

● **Montecillo Reserva / 2006 / Rioja / $$**
Rioja Alta, a subzone of Rioja, produces elegant, structured reds, which perfectly describes this juicy, old-school bottling.

MUGA

Like most Rioja producers, Muga has a passion for barrels, but its diverse cellar—which includes French, American, Hungarian, Russian and Spanish oak—reveals the winery's experimental streak. Founded in 1932, Muga has always excelled with traditional blends; prestige wines like Torre Muga and the more recently introduced Aro show its skill with a modern style.

● **Muga Selección Especial / 2005 / Rioja / $$$**
Muga's Selección Especial offers a taste of the complexity and polish of its *gran reservas,* but at a gentler price.

● **Muga Aro / 2006 / Rioja / $$$$**
This profound (and pricey) red offers herbs, spices and dark fruit, all layered with French oak that will mellow with time.

● **Muga Prado Enea Gran Reserva / 2004 / Rioja / $$$$**
Grapes for this *gran reserva* are the last to be picked at Muga each vintage, making its earthy fruit flavors especially deep.

PALACIOS REMONDO

After establishing world-renowned estates in Priorat and Bierzo, winegrower Alvaro Palacios is back at the helm of his family's winery in Rioja and carrying on his father's work. Alvaro's involvement has refreshed the already terrific Tempranillo- and Garnacha-based reds of Palacios Remondo.

○ **Plácet / 2008 / Rioja / $$$**
Palacios Remondo's white Rioja is a stellar example of the Viura grape, offering rich, exotic floral and papaya notes.

● **Propiedad / 2008 / Rioja / $$$**
A mixture of Garnacha and Tempranillo with red-fruit, herb and vanilla tones, this wine showcases Alvaro Palacios's great skill with blending.

REMELLURI

Remelluri is famous for helping kick-start the single-vineyard trend in Rioja in the 1970s. The estate has its roots in a 14th-century monastery, but its modern incarnation began in 1967 when Jaime Rodríguez Saliz bought it, attracted by vineyards that are among the highest in Rioja and hardscrabble soils that yield concentrated Tempranillo grapes, ideal for ageworthy reds. Son Telmo Rodríguez, now a celebrated winemaker in his own right, took charge of the cellar in 2010.

● **Remelluri / 2007 / Rioja / $$$**
Remulluri's introductory Rioja is made with the same techniques as its more expensive siblings and offers impressive layers of spicy red currant and cedar.

R. LÓPEZ DE HEREDIA VIÑA TONDONIA

This benchmark Rioja winery hasn't changed much since it was founded in 1877, turning out assured, graceful wines of remarkable consistency. Still family-run, the winery sources exclusively from hand-harvested estate vineyards and is one of the few in the world to maintain a working cooperage to craft its barrels. The stunning *reservas*—both red and white—are often released up to a decade later than most Rioja wines.

○ **R. López de Heredia Viña Tondonia Reserva Blanco / 1996 / Rioja / $$$** Tondonia's barrel-matured, late-released white wines are legendary for their unctuous, orange-laced flavors and incredible longevity.

● **R. López de Heredia Viña Cubillo / 2005 / Rioja / $$$**
Rioja's phenomenal 2005 vintage produced basic *crianza* reds like this one with far more depth and structure than usual.

GALICIA

CLAIM TO FAME

The green river valleys of Galicia, on the Atlantic coast of northwestern Spain, look more like Ireland than Iberia, with drizzly wet weather to match. But those valleys produce some of Spain's most outstanding white wines, especially the vibrant, mineral-laden offerings of Rías Baixas (*REE-ahs BYE-shus*), Galicia's top subzone. Based on the Albariño grape, Rías Baixas whites are fantastically fresh, with pronounced citrus flavors.

KEY GRAPES: WHITE

ALBARIÑO Most white grapes rot in weather as rainy as Galicia's, but this variety thrives in it. Crisp, citrusy and marked by a hint of sea-salt minerality, it's typically made into refreshing, unoaked wines that are best drunk young (preferably with any kind of seafood). That said, the handful of ambitious, high-end bottlings (some of which are aged partially in oak) deliver flavors that actually improve with a few years of bottle age.

GODELLO A few dedicated vintners rescued this once-rare grape (pronounced *go-DAY-yo*) from oblivion in the 1970s. Today it's increasingly popular as a single-variety wine, especially in the Valdeorras and Ribeira Sacra subregions, where it yields tangy, quince- and citrus-inflected whites.

TREIXADURA The chief grape of the Ribeiro DO (located along the Miño River and its tributaries), Treixadura creates wines with perky acidity and vibrant citrus and apple flavors.

KEY GRAPES: RED

MENCÍA It's rare to find a Galicia red wine in the U.S., but if you do, chances are it's made from this grape, most of which grows in the warmer, inland subregions of Valdeorras and Ribeira Sacra. There, it yields light reds with floral and licorice notes.

Producers/ Galicia

BODEGAS GODEVAL

One of the best-known wineries in the isolated Valdeorras region, Bodegas Godeval nearly single-handedly revived the rare Godello grape. Founded in 1986 by two grape researchers, Godeval bottled Galacia's first 100 percent Godello wines. Wine-maker and co-owner Horacio Fernández sources fruit from 42 acres of estate vines on the steep slopes of the Sil River valley.

○ **Viña Godeval / 2011 / Valdeorras / $$**
Aged in stainless steel, this seafood-loving white will instantly convert fans of zesty whites to the minerally Godello grape.

BODEGAS MARTÍN CÓDAX

Galicia's best cooperative winery, Martín Códax offers delicious Albariño masterminded by winemaking talent Luciano Amoedo. Its basic Albariño is among the most widely available and high-quality wines of its kind in the U.S., though visitors to Europe should look out for Amoedo's distinctive variations, including the lightly oaked Organistrum, and Lías, a modern, stainless steel–fermented interpretation.

○ **Martín Códax Albariño / 2011 / Rías Baixas / $**
Tangy and fresh, this makes a great introduction to Albariño's brisk, citrusy appeal.

DO FERREIRO

Gerardo Méndez fashions his wines from ancient family vines— some more than 200 years old—in the Salnés Valley, Galicia's coolest and wettest part. *Ferreiro* means "ironworker" (the profession of Méndez's grandfather), an appropriate name for an estate whose rocky, granite-based soils give its wines a steely strength. Méndez uses traditional techniques: farming organically, handpicking grapes and fermenting with wild yeasts.

○ **Do Ferreiro Albariño / 2010 / Rías Baixas / $$**
This white's crisp citrus and ripe peach flavors are a perfect match for fresh oysters.

○ **Do Ferreiro Rebisaca / 2010 / Rías Baixas / $$**
Treixadura grapes lend body and a silky texture to this zesty Albariño-led blend.

○ **Do Ferreiro Albariño Cepas Vellas / 2010 / Rías Baixas / $$$**
The rich, mineral- and lime-laced Cepas Vellas gets its intensity from vines that are more than 200 years old.

FILLABOA

While most wineries in Galicia rely at least in part on purchased grapes, this ambitious producer uses only estate-grown fruit. That means that quantities of its two wines—the flagship Albariño and the lees-aged, single-vineyard cuvée Selección Finca Monte Alto—are inherently limited. Exhibiting rare complexity for the Albariño grape, they are well worth hunting for.

○ **Fillaboa Albariño / 2011 / Rías Baixas / $$**
Fillaboa's Albariño shows remarkable depth of flavor, with zesty citrus and stone-fruit notes that are tailor-made for king crab or shellfish.

PAZO DE SEÑORÁNS

Rías Baixas was nowhere on the world's fine-wine radar when Marisol Bueno and her husband acquired Pazo de Señoráns in the Salnés Valley in 1979. She was instrumental in the campaign to gain DO status (granted in 1988) for the region, and her Albariños have long been a Rías Baixas standard-bearer. A rare second wine, Selección de Añada, is made only in great vintages.

○ **Pazo de Señoráns / 2011 / Rías Baixas / $$**
This is Albariño at its finest—racy and minerally, with juicy peach and pear flavors.

SANTIAGO RUIZ

Rosa Ruiz manages the winery in Rías Baixas's O Rosal subzone that her influential father, Santiago, brought to prominence. Though small, the label's impact in Rías Baixas has been important, thanks to the elder Ruiz's progressive winemaking and championing of once-obscure native grapes. To visit the quaint 19th-century estate, just follow the map on the bottle.

○ **Santiago Ruiz O Rosal / 2010 / Rías Baixas / $$**
Blending local varieties such as the floral Loureiro grape with Albariño gives this lighter-style white its signature taste.

SOUTHEASTERN SPAIN

CLAIM TO FAME
Ambitious winemakers have rediscovered Spain's warm Mediterranean coast. They're turning out terrific new offerings—sometimes from very old vines—and planting new vines that thrive in the region's hot, dry summers. Jumilla's and Yecla's Monastrells and the Bobal-based wines of Valencia are the region's brightest emerging stars, often delivering amazing value.

KEY GRAPES: RED
BOBAL This distinctive native grape creates dark, brooding reds (plus attractive *rosados*), and accounts for most of the production of the southeast's up-and-coming Utiel-Requena DO.

MONASTRELL The signature grape of Jumilla and of the adjacent Murcia region's only DO, Yecla, this makes spicy, inky, high-alcohol reds. It's the same grape as France's Mourvèdre.

RARITIES & COLLECTIBLES

DOMINIO DE PINGUS Danish winemaker Peter Sisseck arrived in Ribera del Duero in 1993, and by 1995 had located a parcel of ancient vines he believed could make one of Spain's greatest reds. That hunch proved prescient, and the first vintage of Pingus went on to receive international critical acclaim.

EMILIO ROJO A mere 50 cases come to the U.S. of this complex, granite-grown white, which sets the standard for Galicia's wines. Subtle and exotic, it's a blend of the local Ribeiro grape varieties Treixadura, Lado, Loureira Blanca, Albariño and Torrontés.

VEGA SICILIA This Ribera del Duero estate has been making world-class reds since 1864. It was planted primarily with Bordeaux varieties at a time when these grapes were virtually unknown in the region.

SYRAH, MERLOT & CABERNET SAUVIGNON After a pest destroyed its vineyards in the early 1990s, Jumilla led the region's adoption of these international grapes. Now they are steadily gaining ground throughout the southeast.

TEMPRANILLO The southeast's best examples of this cherry-inflected grape come from the Utiel-Requena DO.

Producers/ Southeastern Spain

BODEGAS CARCHELO

One reason Bodegas Carchelo turns out such reliably good wines is that it sells off half of its grapes, which means that winemaker Joaquín Gálvez Bauzá can be choosy about which fruit to keep. Another is that its vast Jumilla vineyards are located at an elevation of 2,300 feet, where cooler temperatures produce fresher wines. Carchelo's reds offer great quality, especially considering their reasonable prices.

● **Carchelo C / 2010 / Jumilla / $$**
This Monastrell-based red delivers loads of jammy, raspberry fruit typical of Jumilla, along with smoke and pepper notes.

BODEGAS CASTAÑO

The Castaño family sold its Yecla fruit in bulk for decades before patriarch Ramón Castaño Santa made the gutsy move to create an eponymous winery in 1980. Today his three sons run the vast estate, which spreads across 1,000 acres. The impressive age of some of their vines is one key to this dynamic winery's success; its Monastrell-based reds are perennial values.

● **Castaño Hécula Monastrell / 2009 / Yecla / $**
High-altitude vineyards (up to 2,400 feet) yielded the high-acid grapes for this tangy, fresh red.

● **Castaño Viñas Viejas Monastrell / 2010 / Yecla / $**
This brambly, supple Monastrell is one of Spain's best buys.

● **Castaño Solanera Viñas Viejas / 2009 / Yecla / $$**
Old vines contribute depth and a stony minerality to this blend of Monastrell, Cabernet and Tintorera.

CASA CASTILLO

Casa Castillo's adept and dashing José Maria Vicente has built this estate into one of Jumilla's stars. Working from a cache of Syrah and extremely old Monastrell vines planted in rugged, stony soils, the owner/winemaker crafts two single-vineyard reds and a more affordable, compulsively delicious Monastrell.

● **Casa Castillo Valtosca / 2009 / Jumilla / $$**
Notes of sage infuse this peppery, meaty—and excellent—red made entirely from Syrah.

● **Casa Castillo Las Gravas / 2008 / Jumilla / $$$**
This brilliant spicy blend of Monastrell, Cabernet and Syrah comes from a rocky, dry-farmed vineyard.

CASA DE LA ERMITA

Jumilla native Marcial Martínez Cruz made wine all over Spain before returning home in the late '90s to help create and serve as winemaker at this stellar estate. He selected a site in some of Jumilla's highest mountains, then planted French grapes such as Petit Verdot, Merlot, Syrah and Cabernet in addition to the region's signature Monastrell variety. His Monastrell, crushed mostly from organic grapes, is one of Jumilla's best.

● **Casa de la Ermita Crianza / 2009 / Jumilla / $$**
In this smooth red blend, Monastrell's spicy plum flavors get a boost of structure from Cabernet Sauvignon, and a perfumy, violet-like note from Petit Verdot.

OLIVARES

Having shifted from bulk to quality-driven, estate-bottled wine in 1998, Olivares is still realizing the full potential of its vineyards: over 300 acres of ancient vines in Jumilla's coolest area. While its main red, Altos de la Hoya, made the winery's reputation, its *rosado* and Panarroz bottlings are equally great value bets.

Olivares Rosado / 2011 / Jumilla / $

A juicy, hearty rosé with tangy cherry and strawberry flavors.

● **Panarroz / 2010 / Jumilla / $**

Jumilla is a source of delicious reds at fantastically low prices, as this spicy, unoaked blend demonstrates.

PRIMITIVO QUILES

One of the Alicante DO's oldest wineries, this Valencia estate has been a regional mainstay since 1780. While best known for its *fondillón*—a slightly sweet, oxidative red that's a Valencia specialty—Primitivo Quiles also produces two drier, Monastrell-based reds. Made from ancient vines, they're remarkably ripe.

● **Primitivo Quiles Cono 4 / 2009 / Spain / $**

The sunny climate of Valencia shines through in this medium-weight Monastrell's juicy raspberry and plum flavors.

CATALONIA

CLAIM TO FAME

In addition to sparkling cava (see p. 289), the northeast region of Catalonia produces the reds of Priorat, ranked among the world's most prized wines. Top bottles, like Álvaro Palacios's L'Ermita, sell for a small fortune; nearby DOs such as Montsant offer similar, if usually less ambitious, blends at a fraction of the price.

KEY GRAPES: RED

GARNACHA (GRENACHE) Catalonia's star grape, Garnacha grows best on old vines, preferably on hillsides, where lean soils concentrate its plush berry and cherry flavors. It's usually blended with such grapes as Cabernet, Syrah, Cariñena and Tempranillo.

CARIÑENA (CARIGNANE) A good companion to Garnacha, Cariñena delivers structure that boosts Garnacha's soft tannins, giving more power and increased longevity to the blend.

Producers/ Catalonia

ÁLVARO PALACIOS

Applying his Bordeaux training to Garnacha in the Priorat region, Álvaro Palacios created a wine in 1993 that would become a modern icon of Spain: L'Ermita. That, along with his first wine, Finca Dofí, established the backwater Priorat area as Spain's most exciting wine frontier and Palacios as one of the country's greatest stars. Today Palacios also crafts affordable high-quality wines, such as Camins del Priorat.

● **Camins del Priorat** / 2009 / Priorat / $$
Palacios's least costly red is spicy and taut, with ripe plum fruit.

● **L'Ermita** / 2009 / Priorat / $$$$
From a vineyard of nearly 100-year-old Garnacha vines, this is one of Spain's greatest wines—and priced accordingly.

CASTELL DEL REMEI

Despite its status as one of Catalonia's leading wineries (it was the first in Spain to plant French grapes, in the late 1800s), this venerable estate was hardly known in the international wine world until the 1980s. That's when the Cusiné family bought it and supertalented winemaker Tomàs Cusiné (he's since moved on) started crafting the polished blends that have made it famous.

● **Sicoris** / 2009 / Costers del Segre / $
This stylish, reasonably priced blend of Garnacha, Tempranillo and Cabernet is brimming with thyme and ripe cherries.

CELLER DE CAPÇANES

Five families came together to create this Montsant winery in 1933. Kosher bottlings have been an important part of their portfolio since 1995, when they began making wines for Barcelona's Jewish community. Today the co-op's range includes the entry-level Mas Donis and the powerful Cabrida wines, made only with Garnacha. The top red, Peraj Ha'Abib, is also kosher.

● **Capçanes Peraj Petita** / 2010 / Montsant / $$
The stewed-fruit aromas in this meaty, dark Garnacha-based blend open up in the glass, revealing red berry and herb notes.

CLOS ERASMUS

In 1989 Priorat champions Álvaro Palacios and René Barbier recommended that a friend, Swiss lawyer Daphne Glorian, buy an ancient Garnacha vineyard near the town of Gratallops. It was good advice: The resulting red, Clos Erasmus, became an instant cult classic that helped propel the then-obscure region into fine-wine fame. In addition to her premier cuvée, Glorian makes a more affordable (though still pricey) blend, Laurel.

● **Clos Erasmus / 2007 / Priorat / $$$$**
A spectacular expression of Priorat: intensely aromatic, with black cherry fruit supported by stony minerality.

LA CONRERIA D'SCALA DEI

Aptly named "Ladder of God," this 12th-century Priorat estate is home to steeply terraced slate vineyards. Winemaker Jordi Vidal produces concentrated red wines (Priorat's specialty) as well as a superb white Garnacha called Les Brugueres. Made from 100-year-old vines, this rare, viscous wine redefined Priorat whites from its very first vintage.

○ **La Conreria d'Scala Dei Les Brugueres / 2011 / Priorat / $$**
For such a scarce wine (just 300 cases make it to the U.S. each year), this intense, minerally white is reasonably priced.

SARA PÉREZ & RENÉ BARBIER, JR.

Two of Spain's brightest winemaking stars, Sara Pérez and René Barbier, Jr., are children of famous winemakers (their fathers, Luis Pérez and René Barbier, revolutionized the Priorat region). Each makes wines independently (Pérez at Mas Martinet, among others, and Barbier at his family's Clos Mogador estate), but the two join forces to create a handful of compelling Priorat and Montsant cuvées.

● **Mas Sorrer / 2010 / Montsant / $**
A plump, fruit-filled blend of Cabernet, Merlot and Syrah that offers a taste of *terroir* at a fabulous price.

● **Partida Bellvisos Gratallops / 2007 / Priorat / $$$$**
Made from a grape variety closely related to Grenache, this formidable village wine (*vi de vila*) comes from the hilltop town of Gratallops.

● **Venus La Universal Venus / 2007 / Montsant / $$$$**
Supple, floral Cariñena gets bolstered by blackberry-rich Syrah in this accomplished red.

TORRES

Although the newest Torres wines include Celeste (from Ribera del Duero) and Ibéricos (from Rioja), this venerable family winery is firmly rooted in Catalonia. Its Sangre de Toro line, with its famous plastic-bull bottle ornament, was launched in 1954; the Coronas label recently marked its centenary. Today the winery continues to expand its range under a fifth generation of the Torres family.

○ **Torres Viña Esmeralda** / 2011 / Catalunya / $$
For a Spanish spin on the Moscato craze, try this well-made bottling, which offers bright kaffir lime and nectarine flavors.

● **Torres Celeste** / 2009 / Ribera del Duero / $$
This rugged Tempranillo shows blackberry fruit accented with sage and spice notes.

● **Torres Mas La Plana** / 2008 / Penedès / $$$$
Mas La Plana is an ultra-premium Cabernet Sauvignon with beguiling black fruit, thyme and olive notes, and an undeniably Spanish personality.

CASTILLA Y LEÓN

CLAIM TO FAME

The Castilla y León region in north-central Spain is home to Vega Sicilia, a legendary winery that put the Ribera del Duero subregion on the fine-wine map nearly a century ago. Vega Sicilia's Unico—a Tempranillo-Cabernet blend renowned for its longevity—is among the world's most collectible reds. But not until the debut in the 1980s of Alejandro Fernández's Pesquera did interest in Ribera del Duero really take off. Today the nearby Toro region competes with Ribera reds in quality, while the Cigales DO is moving beyond its reputation for *rosados* and turning out more bold reds. The long-underrated Rueda zone—an anomaly in a region dominated by red wine—shines as a source of crisp whites, and in Bierzo, an influx of winemaking talent is turning out impressive reds from the local Mencía grape.

♛ KEY GRAPES: WHITE

VERDEJO Once nearly consigned to oblivion, Rueda's calling-card grape makes fragrant, citrusy whites that recall Sauvignon Blanc (a grape that Verdejo is frequently blended with).

♥ KEY GRAPES: RED

MENCÍA This red grape variety has become increasingly popular with winemakers in recent years. It is best known for giving the fragrant reds of Bierzo in northwestern León their alluring floral aromas and licorice tinge.

TEMPRANILLO Known locally under a handful of different aliases, including Tinto Fino, Tinta del País and Tinta de Toro, this is Castilla y León's star grape. Many of Ribera del Duero's savory, spicy, medium- to full-bodied wines are pure Tempranillo (although small amounts of other varieties are permitted). The Tempranillo-based wines of Toro are fuller-bodied and more concentrated than those of Ribera, and they're usually made to be consumed earlier.

Producers/ Castilla y León

BODEGAS ALEJANDRO FERNÁNDEZ/ TINTO PESQUERA

Until Alejandro Fernández's powerhouse Tempranillo, Pesquera, came along, the Ribera del Duero region had only one superstar winery—Vega Sicilia. Pesquera's instant acclaim helped galvanize the quality-wine revolution in Ribera, and Fernández went on to create a mini dynasty of four wineries in emerging areas throughout Spain: Pesquera and Condado de Haza in Ribera del Duero; Dehesa La Granja in Castilla y León; and El Vínculo in La Mancha.

● **Dehesa La Granja / 2005 / Vino de la Tierra de Castilla y León / $$** This supple, sunbaked Tempranillo is beautifully refined and approachably priced.

● **El Vínculo / 2005 / La Mancha / $$$**
This plummy red comes from the region of La Mancha, an up-and-coming area that until now has been best known for simple bulk wine.

● **Tinto Pesquera Crianza / 2009 / Ribera del Duero / $$$**
Always superb, Pesquera is a standard-bearer for Ribera, with layers of complex, herb-edged blackberry.

BODEGAS EMILIO MORO

This acclaimed, family-owned Ribera del Duero producer draws upon more than 200 acres of old family vineyards, the earliest dating back to 1932, to produce five Tempranillo wines. The collection reflects the breadth of vineyard age: The youngest fruit goes to the affordably priced Finca Resalso red, while the oldest vines are dedicated to the top-tier cuvées, including the revered Malleolus bottlings.

● **Finca Resalso / 2010 / Ribera del Duero / $**
Expertly farmed young vines yield a vivacious Tempranillo with fresh blackberry and mint notes.

● **Emilio Moro / 2008 / Ribera del Duero / $$**
A great everyday Ribera that exemplifies the fragrant charms of the Tempranillo grape.

● **Malleolus de Valderramiro / 2008 / Ribera del Duero / $$$$**
This powerhouse old-vine Tempranillo unfolds layer after layer of spicy and brooding blueberry flavors.

BODEGAS JOSÉ PARIENTE

Victoria Pariente created a stir when she and colleague Victoria Benavides fashioned a revelatory 1998 Verdejo from her father José's Rueda vineyards. That winery, called Dos Victorias, established the younger Pariente as one of Spain's rising stars. Today she's on her own and makes three wines that rank securely among the region's finest: two distinctive Verdejos and a rare Rueda Sauvignon Blanc.

○ **José Pariente Verdejo / 2011 / Rueda / $$**
A smooth, silky texture and zesty fresh grapefruit notes characterize this go-to white.

○ **José Pariente Fermentado en Barrica / 2009 / Rueda / $$$**
Old vines and barrel fermentation create a seductively creamy, vibrant Verdejo.

BODEGAS MAURO

For 30 years, Mariano García ran the cellar at Vega Sicilia, Spain's greatest estate, turning out legendary vintages and earning a reputation as the father of modern Spanish winemaking. Today he's the master of his own mini empire, of which this Ribera del Duero property is the flagship. His other enterprises include Bodegas Maurodos, in Toro, and a joint venture, Bodegas Leda, which produces two stunning Castilla y León reds.

- **Mauro / 2009 / Vino de la Tierra de Castilla y León / $$$**
This polished Tempranillo-Syrah blend costs just a little more than half the price of Mauro's famed Terreus and VS cuvées, making it a relative bargain.
- **Mauro VS / 2007 / Castilla y León / $$$$**
One of the hallmarks of this powerful wine is its long oak aging: This vintage saw 33 months in oak barrels.

CASTRO VENTOSA

The Pérez family is the largest owner of Mencía vines in the DO of Bierzo in northwestern Spain. More remarkable than the scale of the family's holdings are the quality and age of its vineyards, including several 100-year-old pre-phylloxera plantings, from which the estate makes some of the most profoundly layered Mencía wines in Spain.

- **El Castro de Valtuille Joven / 2009 / Bierzo / $**
Pérez's young, unoaked Mencía shows gamey ripe plum and brandied cherry flavors.
- **El Castro de Valtuille Mencía / 2007 / Bierzo / $$**
French oak adds a nice licorice note to the focused black cherry and plum of this Bierzo.
- **Valtuille Cepas Centenarias / 2009 / Bierzo / $$$$**
The family's oldest vines make unusually complex Mencía, with deep blackberry, black cherry and coffee nuances.

DOMINIO DE TARES

Part of a new breed of modern, quality-oriented wineries in Bierzo, Dominio de Tares harnesses old-vine Mencía to create some of the area's most interesting reds. Co-founder and original winemaker Amancio Fernández (formerly of Ribera's respected Bodegas Protos) demonstrated the grape's range with such complex bottlings as Bembibre and P3. Today Rafael Palacios makes the wines, which include phenomenal values as well as pricey, ambitious reds.

- **Dominio de Tares Baltos / 2009 / Bierzo / $$**
Baltos offers good Mencía character for the price, with tangy, slightly spicy red and black fruit.
- **Dominio de Tares Cepas Viejas / 2008 / Bierzo / $$$**
This fresh, peppery Mencía gets its impressive concentration from 60-year-old vines.

Portugal

Wine Region

If there's one wine that people associate with Portugal, it's port, the sweet, dark dessert wine of the Douro Valley. But the multicentury success of port has obscured Portugal's table wines— and that's a shame. Produced mostly from blends of native varieties and often from very old vines, Portuguese reds are spicy, sultry and full of character, and the country's whites are vibrant and incredibly refreshing.

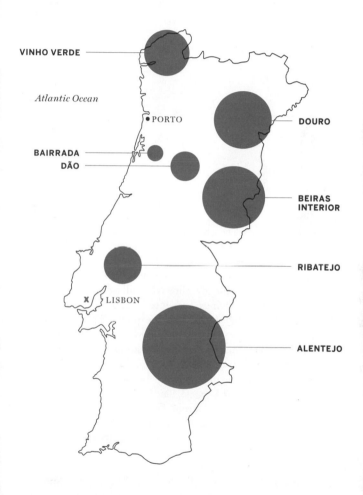

VINHO VERDE

Atlantic Ocean

● PORTO

DOURO

BAIRRADA
DÃO

BEIRAS
INTERIOR

RIBATEJO

X LISBON

ALENTEJO

Portugal

F OR CENTURIES, MOST of the grapes grown in Portugal's Douro Valley were used to make sweet, fortified ports—arguably the greatest dessert wines in the world, but loved by a limited audience. When Portugal entered the European Union in 1986, a change in the law allowed small producers to bottle and export their own wines, and since then, outside investment has enabled vintners to vastly improve quality. The results have been dramatic, particularly in the Douro, the country's premier wine region. Winemakers here now make compelling dry reds, nearly always with the same native grapes used to make port. There are regions to explore outside the Douro, though: Structured reds are made in Alentejo, Bairrada and Dão, while Lisboa (until recently known as Estremadura), Tejo and Península de Setúbal, all near the capital, Lisbon, make enjoyable value reds. Vinho Verde, in the northwest, is known for its zesty whites.

KEY GRAPES: WHITE

ALVARINHO This aromatic variety—called Albariño in Spain—helps give the wines of Vinho Verde their bright, citrus-driven flavors. Usually made into light-bodied, crisp whites that offer a slight prickle of effervescence, Alvarinho can create fuller-bodied, more complex wines, too.

LOUREIRO & TRAJADURA While both of these grapes are used as supporting players to Alvarinho in Vinho Verde, occasional single-varietal bottles of Loureiro are making their way to the U.S. Similar to Alvarinho, Loureiro offers mouthwatering acidity and floral aromatics.

❧ KEY GRAPES: RED

TINTA RORIZ (ARAGONEZ) In Spain, where it's called Tempranillo, this grape variety yields medium-bodied, cherry-rich red wines and is often blended with Garnacha. In Portugal, vintners more commonly combine it with native grapes like Touriga Nacional and Touriga Franca.

TOURIGA FRANCA The most widely planted grape in the Douro, Touriga Franca is rarely bottled on its own; instead it's valued for the fragrant aromas and firm, fine-grained tannins it contributes to red blends.

TOURIGA NACIONAL The country's star grape has a very thick skin that gives wines made from it their firm tannins. This factor, along with the grape's high acidity, also helps give these wines their ability to age—which is why Touriga Nacional forms the backbone of so many port wines and dry red blends. It offers spicy depth and juicy black currant, floral and licorice flavors and is increasingly gaining favor as a single-variety wine.

WINE TERMINOLOGY

DENOMINAÇÃO DI ORIGEM CONTROLADA (DOC) Portugal's "protected place of origin" labeling, sometimes abbreviated DOC to conform with the European Union system, applies only to wines produced in designated growing regions that have been vinified according to a strict set of rules designed to ensure quality. Regulations cover such factors as maximum yields, winemaking techniques and required aging periods.

RESERVA Wines labeled *reserva* must be at least half a percent higher in alcohol than wines at the DOC or IGP (similar to the French IGP; see p. 19) level, meaning that they have more body.

QUINTA A common term on many wine labels, this can mean farm, vineyard or estate.

Producers/ Portugal

ÁLVARO CASTRO

Vintner Álvaro Castro and his daughter Maria make some of the Dão's best wines, most labeled by vineyard or estate. Both the Quinta de Saes and the Quinta da Pellada tiers offer a range of great wines. Castro also collaborates with winemaking star Dirk Niepoort on a delicious cross-regional blend called Doda.

○ **Quinta de Saes Reserva** / 2010 / Dao / $$
A complex white with citrusy acidity and flinty minerality.

● **Quinta de Saes Reserva Estágio Prolongado** / 2008 / Dao / $$
Loaded with minerals, this lovely red is fresh and firm.

AVELEDA

The innovative Guedes family has helped set the standard for zesty Vinhos Verdes as far back as the 1880s. Their Aveleda estate produces around a million cases of wine a year—the eclectic range includes reds, a rosé, a sparkling wine made from grapes grown in Vinho Verde, and superb, single-variety whites.

○ **Aveleda Alvarinho** / 2011 / Minho / $
This bottling is 100 percent Alvarinho, a top grape that can be difficult to grow but yields focused, minerally whites.

○ **Casal Garcia** / NV / Vinho Verde / $
Aveleda's basic Vinho Verde offers tingly citrus flavors.

HERDADE DO ESPORÃO

Alentejo, in Portugal's south-central area, is one of Europe's most exciting emerging regions, and Herdade do Esporão is one of its leading producers. Australian vintner David Baverstock, in charge since 1992, deserves much of the credit: He makes modern, bold wines with Portuguese and French grapes.

○ **Herdade do Esporão Monte Velho** / 2010 / Alentejo / $
The Alentejo region yields particularly expressive whites, like this tangy, tropical-inflected blend.

● **Herdade do Esporão Quatro Castas** / 2010 / Alentejo / $$
Four *castas* (grape varieties), including Aragones—a.k.a. Tempranillo—are used to make this earthy, fruity red.

NIEPOORT

Although he's the descendant of a centuries-old Dutch port-producing family, Dirk Niepoort is one of today's most dynamic and forward-thinking vintners. His accomplishments include producing two of Portugal's greatest modern reds (Batuta and Charme) and creating the affordable Vertente offerings.

○ **Niepoort Dócil Loureiro / 2010 / Vinho Verde / $$**
A compulsively drinkable, lime-flavored Vinho Verde.

● **Niepoort Twisted / 2009 / Douro / $$**
Made from a traditional blend of local varieties, this minerally, black-fruit-infused red is unusually refined for its price.

POÇAS

Jorge Manuel Pintão studied winemaking in Bordeaux and interned at Château Giscours before returning in 1987 to take over the cellar at Poças, his family's port house. Three years later he produced its first dry red under the Coroa d'Ouro label, and while Poças's ports have achieved new heights, its table wines stand out for their consistency and value.

● **Poças Coroa d'Ouro / 2007 / Douro / $**
Jorge Pintão's original red remains a good value, with pure, polished red-fruit flavors.

● **Poças Vale de Cavalos / 2007 / Douro / $$**
This sexy, dark and fruity blend offers tremendous depth.

PRATS & SYMINGTON

This high-profile winery is a joint venture between Bruno Prats, formerly of Bordeaux's Château Cos d'Estournel, and the Symington family, owners of Graham's and Warre's. Prats and Charles Symington craft the acclaimed Chryseia red blend and a second wine, Post Scriptum. In 2009 they acquired Quinta de Roriz, adding the Prazo de Roriz red and a port to their lineup.

● **Post Scriptum de Chryseia / 2009 / Douro / $$**
This supple, ripe blend doesn't need aging to be enjoyable, though it does benefit from decanting.

● **Prazo de Roriz / 2009 / Douro / $$**
Despite an unusually hot summer, Quinta de Roriz's most affordable red is still balanced and delicious.

● **Chryseia / 2009 / Douro / $$$**
Living up to its reputation for power and finesse, this blend is brimming with refined black currant tones.

QUINTA DE SOALHEIRO

Located in an unusually warm and dry corner of Vinho Verde (*soalheiro* means "sunny"), this family-owned winery makes impressively lush, complex whites exclusively from the low-yielding Alvarinho variety. Siblings Luis and Maria João Cerdeira farm their vines organically and use estate-grown fruit. Small quantities and high demand mean that it can be challenging to find their wines in the U.S.

○ **Soalheiro Alvarinho / 2011 / Vinho Verde / $$**
Consistently one of Portugal's best Alvarinhos, this gets minerally intensity from granite soil.

QUINTA DO CRASTO

Perched on a steep mountain jutting over the banks of the Douro River, this well-known winery branched out from port to nonfortified wines in the early 1990s. Under the direction of the Roquette family, Crasto has had great success thanks to its focus on quality, plus a wealth of well-situated vineyards, many of them incredibly old (some of the best lots go into the winery's stunning, ageworthy *reserva*).

○ **Quinta do Crasto / 2010 / Douro / $$**
This refreshing, melony blend illustrates the Douro's potential for truly delicious whites.

● **Quinta do Crasto / 2009 / Douro / $$**
A velvety and affordable introduction to Crasto's stellar reds.

QUINTA DO VALE MEÃO

In 1994 Vito Olazabal, whose family had long been part of a large wine cooperative, purchased the entire Quinta do Vale Meão vineyard. This prime Douro site once contributed the majority of the fruit for Barca-Velha, Portugal's most esteemed red. Today its grapes—still trod by foot—go into a namesake port and a single, stellar dry red. Sister wine Meandro is similarly styled but with a gentler price tag.

WINE INTEL
Vale Meão's Xito Olazabal recently teamed up with two other Douro wine stars, Jorge Serôdio Borges and Jorge Moreira, to make wines from an old Dão estate, Quinta do Corujão.

● **Meandro / 2009 / Douro / $$**
Low yields boosted concentration in this fresh, powerful red.

● **Quinta do Vale Meão / 2009 / Douro / $$$$**
Vito's son, Francisco "Xito" Olazabal, now makes this benchmark single-vineyard cuvée.

QUINTA DO VALLADO

When Quinta do Vallado's sixth-generation owners and cousins Francisco and João Ferreira decided to make table wines from their family's port vineyards, they asked another cousin, Francisco "Xito" Olazabal, one of the Douro's best talents (see Quinta do Vale Meão, opposite), to head the cellar. The property also has one of the Douro region's few boutique hotels.

● **Quinta do Vallado Tinto / 2009 / Douro / $$**
Aging this blend chiefly in tank preserves the freshness of its earthy, supple red- and black-fruit flavors.

● **Quinta do Vallado Reserva / 2009 / Douro / $$$**
Vines averaging 80-plus years lent intensity to this serious—and seriously delicious—red blend.

SOGRAPE

Like many of Portugal's large wine companies, Sogrape has spent the past few decades reinventing itself. It made a fortune selling zillions of bottles of Mateus rosé and, more recently, Sandeman and Ferreira ports. But it now owns wineries across Portugal that produce terrific nonpink, nonfortified wines. These range from the low-priced Callabriga bottlings to prime Douro reds from Casa Ferreirinha and the iconic, $275 Barca-Velha.

● **Callabriga / 2009 / Alentejo / $**
Alentejo is a go-to region for spicy, deeply flavored blends that deliver super value—like this one.

● **Casa Ferreirinha Vinha Grande / 2008 / Douro / $$**
Masterful blending is the secret to this lively, intense red, which tastes much pricier than it is.

WINE & SOUL

Spouses and winemakers Sandra Tavares and Jorge Serôdio Borges rebuilt a tiny stone warehouse in the Douro's Vale de Mendiz, and named their first wine Pintas. Produced from a single vineyard, it caused a sensation and established the couple as rising stars. Their small-lot cuvées—two reds, a port and a white—are all made with grapes from very old vines.

● **Pintas Character / 2008 / Douro / $$$**
This second wine to the famous Pintas red offers intense, succulent dark berry fruit.

● **Pintas / 2008 / Douro / $$$$**
Eighty-year-old vines yield an elegant, very concentrated red.

Germany

Wine Region

Germany produces most of the world's greatest Rieslings. That, if nothing else, should make it indispensable to wine lovers. But Germany also makes a surprising number of other delicious and compelling wines at reasonable prices. Plus, the country's winemakers are increasingly releasing drier, fuller-bodied styles of Riesling, broadening the scope of Germany's already versatile and food-friendly wines.

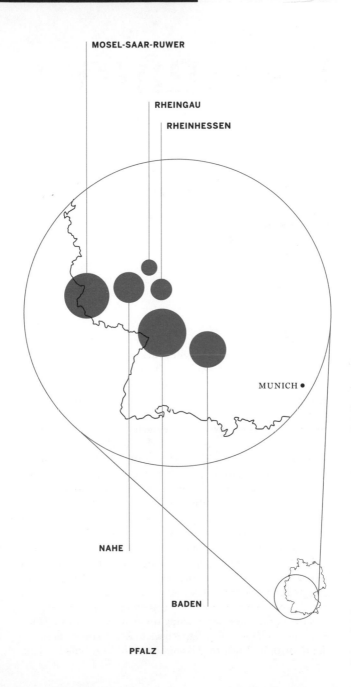

MOSEL-SAAR-RUWER

RHEINGAU

RHEINHESSEN

MUNICH •

NAHE

BADEN

PFALZ

Germany

THE KEY THING to know about Germany, when it comes to wine, is that it's cold. The country's northern climate makes it white wine territory, and here Riesling is king. Red grapes, particularly Pinot Noir, do grow in some parts of the country, but most varieties need more heat than the German climate provides. To maximize available sun, many of Germany's best vineyards cling to steep, south-facing slopes along the river valleys of the Rhine and Mosel, and the Mosel's Saar and Ruwer tributaries. The slate-soil vineyards of the Mosel-Saar-Ruwer and Rheingau regions produce intensely pure Rieslings. Mosel Rieslings tend to be delicate and minerally; Rheingau versions are drier and richer. The Rheinhessen makes many low-quality sweet wines, and some great bargains. Some of the best Scheurebes and Silvaners are made here, particularly in the Rheinterrasse subregion. The warmer Pfalz, Nahe and Baden regions yield lusher Rieslings, as well as Pinot Gris (Grauburgunder) and Gewürztraminer. Some of Germany's best Pinot Blancs (Weiss-burgunder) come from Baden and Pfalz. Baden also produces most of the country's Pinot Noir (Spätburgunder).

Most of Germany's winemaking sites have been cultivated for centuries, with the oldest dating back to Roman times. Battered in the 1970s and '80s by the dominance of large bulk bottlers,

Germany's wine industry has strengthened over the past 20 years, stoked by an energetic new generation of vintners. All over Germany, *Jungwinzer* ("young winemaker") associations have popped up, fostering a sense of community and contributing to a renewed focus on quality. Germany also has benefited from a string of exceptionally warm vintages; on average, Germany's vineyards have warmed up by an estimated 2 degrees Fahrenheit over the past 25 years. The impact has been dramatic for both red and white grapes.

❖ KEY GRAPES: WHITE

GEWÜRZTRAMINER & MUSCAT (MUSKATELLER) Marked by floral, intensely fragrant aromas, these white grapes thrive in Germany's cool climate.

MÜLLER-THURGAU (RIVANER) & SILVANER Wines made with these grapes rarely make it to the U.S., mainly because there's not much worth importing. Typically used for refreshing, simple table wines, these popular varieties can sometimes yield sleek, exciting whites when grown for quality rather than quantity.

PINOT GRIS & PINOT BLANC Members of the Pinot family, these whites come in both sweet and dry versions, with Pinot Blanc generally dry. Pinot Gris is called Grauburgunder when made in a crisp style; sweeter versions are often named Ruländer.

RIESLING Germany's most widely planted and prestigious grape is made into a vast range of wine styles, from bracingly dry to unctuously sweet, from fruity and floral to searingly mineral.

SCHEUREBE Often used for dessert wines, this unusual white variety displays black currant aromas and citrusy flavors.

❖ KEY GRAPES: RED

DORNFELDER First cultivated in 1979, this new grape yields juicy, deeply colored reds that are catching on in Germany.

PINOT NOIR Germany is now the world's third-largest producer of Pinot Noir. Spätburgunder, as it's called in Germany, is still far from a household name in the U.S., but these wines are worth seeking out for their delicate, fresh cherry flavors.

WINE TERMINOLOGY

The exacting specificity of German wine labels can make them hard to decipher, yet it's incredibly helpful once you've cracked the code. The two primary quality categories are QbA and QmP. German labels offer more information than most, including producer and geographic origin as well as winemaking details like grape ripeness. Grapes are usually listed, though in regions like the Rheingau, Riesling is assumed.

QUALITÄTSWEIN OR QUALITÄTSWEIN BESTIMMTER ANBAUGE-BIETE (QBA) This basic category includes most German wine, meaning it's the designation used on everything from bulk wines such as Liebfraumilch, the sweet blend that tarnished Germany's reputation in the 1980s, to solidly made value bottlings.

QUALITÄTSWEIN MIT PRÄDIKAT (QMP) A big step up from QbAs, wines labeled QmP are held to higher quality standards; they are ranked by the grapes' sugar levels, or ripeness, at the time of harvest (see below).

RIPENESS LEVELS & SWEETNESS In theory, grapes with higher sugar levels have the potential to make sweeter wines. Yet in practice, perceived sweetness depends more on the balance between acidity and sugar or the amount of natural grape sugar allowed to ferment into alcohol. So, while wines in less-ripe categories are usually drier than those made from riper grapes, there are no guarantees. The least-ripe category is Kabinett and these wines can taste dry or have a hint of sweetness. Spätlese is the next designation up and wines in this category range from dry to sweet but have more concentrated flavors than Kabinett; they are a fantastic match for spicy foods. Richer and typically sweeter than Spätleses, Auslese wines come from handpicked grapes that ripen on the vine long after most fruit is picked. The sweetest designations are Beerenauslese (BA) and Trockenbeer-enauslese (TBA). Made with superripe grapes, they are opulent dessert wines famous for aging beautifully for many decades.

TROCKEN & HALBTROCKEN *Trocken* wines taste dry, while *halb-trocken* ("half-dry") bottlings have a very subtle sweetness. *Spät-lese trocken* means the wine is dry in style yet made from grapes picked at Spätlese levels of ripeness.

CLASSIC & SELECTION These terms denote wines that are high quality and dry. Classic wines are usually made with a single variety and bear the name of the producer but not the vineyard. Selection wines are higher in quality; they must be made from hand-harvested grapes and list the producer and vineyard.

ERSTES GEWÄCHS, GROSSES GEWÄCHS & ERSTE LAGE These relatively new, elite designations are reserved for top-quality wines sourced from specific vineyards recognized as superior. Erstes Gewächs and Grosses Gewächs denote (relatively) dry wines, with the former used exclusively in the Rheingau and the latter abbreviated "GG" on labels. Erste Lage (comparable to the French *premier cru*) wines are identified by an icon—the number 1 next to a bunch of grapes—placed after the vineyard name.

Producers/ Germany

DR. BÜRKLIN-WOLF

Known for producing some of the best Rieslings in Pfalz, this 416-year-old winery is also one of the largest family-owned estates in Germany. (Though, at 210 acres, it is pocket-sized compared to many U.S. counterparts.) Under Bettina Bürklin-von Guradze and winemaker Fritz Knorr, the winery has shifted its focus to dry Rieslings. Inspired by Burgundy's *grand cru* and *premier cru* designations, it identifies its best vineyards with the initials "G.C." and "P.C." Entry-level wines offer excellent value.

○ **Dr. Bürklin-Wolf Estate Riesling / 2011 / Pfalz / $$**
This wine beautifully showcases the fantastic 2011 vintage: It provides expressive fruit flavors and terrific balance for a surprisingly low price.

○ **Dr. Bürklin-Wolf Ruppertsberger Gaisböhl G.C. / 2009 / Pfalz / $$$** This estate's luscious flagship cuvée comes from a prime site owned entirely by Bürklin-Wolf.

○ **Dr. Bürklin-Wolf Wachenheimer Rechbächel P.C. / 2009 / Pfalz / $$$** The south-facing slopes of the esteemed Rechbächel vineyard yielded a perfectly ripe, peach-infused Riesling that is dry and crisp.

DR. LOOSEN

Every wine region needs someone like Ernst Loosen, a charismatic risk-taker who helped revolutionize German winemaking. Loosen intended to become an archaeologist but in 1988 took over his family's Mosel estate, where he has concentrated his efforts on old, ungrafted vines and low yields. His powerful Rieslings epitomize site-specific winemaking; his more affordable wines carry the Dr. L label.

○ **Dr. L Riesling / 2010 / Mosel / $**
The 2010 vintage of this widely available, exotically fragrant white is a great value.

○ **Dr. Loosen Red Slate Dry Riesling / 2010 / Mosel / $$**
Made with grapes grown in red slate soils, this fruity, bright Riesling features notes of candied apple and grapefruit.

○ **Dr. Loosen Wehlener Sonnenuhr Riesling Spätlese / 2010 / Mosel / $$$** The Wehlen "sundial" (*sonnenuhr*) vineyard produces delicate Rieslings, like this sleek, delicious bottling.

FRITZ HAAG

This esteemed Mosel winery did not seem in need of rejuvenating when young Oliver Haag took over from his father in 2005: Its wines have been admired for centuries. Yet the younger Haag's first vintages instantly earned new acclaim for the Fritz Haag estate, making its top Rieslings even more coveted.

○ **Fritz Haag Brauneberger Juffer Sonnenuhr Riesling Spätlese / 2010 / Mosel / $$$** From an especially warm and steep section of the Juffer vineyard, this opulent, off-dry Riesling will age beautifully.

JOH. JOS. PRÜM

The eldest of three daughters, 33-year-old Katharina Prüm has been apprenticing with her famous winemaker father, Manfred, for a decade and will soon become the latest in a line of Prüms to helm this renowned Mosel estate. The family's Rieslings are built for the long haul, with mineral flavors that expand with time and continue to gain complexity for decades after release.

○ **Joh. Jos. Prüm Wehlener Sonnenuhr Riesling Spätlese / 2010 / Mosel / $$$** A Mosel classic, with a stunning mix of rich, honeyed apricot and apple flavors and minerally acidity.

MAXIMIN GRÜNHAUS/SCHLOSSKELLEREI C. VON SCHUBERT

The Maximin Grünhaus estate consists of a trio of exalted, ancient vineyards in the tiny Ruwer Valley region. Romans first planted grapes here; the vines were later farmed by monks and finally acquired by ancestors of the current owner, Dr. Carl von Schubert, in 1882. Today von Schubert farms without pesticides or herbicides, and vintner Stefan Kraml, who arrived in 2004, turns the estate's grapes into gorgeously expressive Rieslings.

○ **Maximin Grünhäuser Riesling / 2010 / Mosel / $$**
This Qualitätswein Riesling offers graceful layers of spicy fruit.

○ **Maximin Grünhäuser Riesling Trocken / 2010 / Mosel / $$**
A boost of minerality and depth differentiates this Trocken from the winery's entry-level bottling.

○ **Maximin Grünhäuser Herrenberg Kabinett / 2010 / Mosel / $$$** Wines from the 46-acre Herrenberg vineyard have been recognized for quality since the 16th century.

REICHSRAT VON BUHL

The Reichsrat von Buhl estate landed in good hands when businessman Achim Niederberger bought it in 2005, a lucky break for one of the most historic wineries in Pfalz. Niederberger hired a skilled team that is making the most of von Buhl's 128 acres under vine, which include some of the best sites in Pfalz. Now biodynamically farmed, they yield superb Riesling.

○ **Reichsrat von Buhl Armand Riesling Kabinett / 2011 / Pfalz / $$** At just 8.5 percent alcohol, this succulent, lightly peachy Riesling is built for sipping while it's young and fresh.

SCHLOSSGUT DIEL

Though their Nahe winery is small, Caroline Diel and her father, Armin, make an array of wines, including Pinot Noir, Pinot Gris (Grauburgunder) and Scheurebe, in addition to sweet and dry Rieslings. The winery's stellar reputation has been built on its Rieslings, which come from a trio of top *grand cru* vineyards.

○ **Diel Eierfels Riesling Trocken / 2010 / Nahe / $$$**
Two *grand cru* sites contribute fruit to this exhilarating, stony Riesling, which explains its nuanced complexity.

● **Diel Caroline Pinot Noir / 2009 / Nahe / $$$$**
This silky, cherry- and earth-inflected red is easily one of the best German Pinot Noirs to hit the U.S.

WEINGUT KARTHÄUSERHOF

Packaged in distinctive, mostly bare green bottles with small neck labels, Karthäuserhof wines come from an ancient estate along the Ruwer River, farmed for centuries by Carthusian monks and owned more recently by generations of the Tyrell family. Christof Tyrell oversees a portfolio of compelling Rieslings sourced from a single impressive vineyard on the right bank of the Ruwer near the town of Eitelsbach.

○ **Karthäuserhof Eitelsbacher Karthäuserhofberg Riesling Kabinett Feinherb / 2010 / Mosel-Saar-Ruwer / $$$** Feinherb Rieslings have a touch of sweetness; this one is light-bodied and marked by pineapple, honeysuckle and citrus tones.

WEINGUT LEITZ

Josef Leitz got his winemaking start working out of a cellar attached to his family's home in suburban Rüdesheim (an old Rheingau wine town). His stunning Rieslings quickly made him one of the brightest stars of the modern German wine industry— a legacy son Johannes now continues. With the addition of a new facility, Leitz turns out a range of dry and sweet Rheingau Rieslings offering terrific value (the Leitz Out bottling, for starters) and extraordinary quality.

○ **Leitz Out Riesling / 2010 / Rheingau / $**
The easiest to find of Leitz's wines, this low-priced offering has a touch of sweetness to its peach and apple flavors.

○ **Leitz Eins Zwei Dry 3 Riesling / 2010 / Rheingau / $$**
Most famous for his sweeter style Rieslings, Leitz also makes this refreshing, food-friendly dry version.

○ **Weingut Leitz Rüdesheimer Berg Rottland Hinterhaus Riesling Trocken / 2010 / Rheingau / $$$** From one of the most famous vineyards in Germany, this shows stunning purity and balance.

WEINGUT ROBERT WEIL

Star Rheingau winemaker Wilhelm Weil made many radical changes when he took over his family's estate in 1987, such as picking a vineyard 17 separate times in order to harvest only perfectly ripe grapes. The resulting wines are some of Germany's most prized. The finest come from three premier vineyard sites near the town of Kiedrich; grapes from other locations go into Weil's two entry-level blends.

○ **Robert Weil Estate Dry Riesling / 2010 / Rheingau / $$**
This displays a peachy richness that complements the
vintage's signature acidity.
○ **Robert Weil Tradition Riesling / 2010 / Rheingau / $$**
A hint of sweetness and citrusy freshness makes this out-
standing white incredibly food-friendly.

WEINGUT SELBACH-OSTER

The Selbach family has been making wine since the 1600s. In
1961, Hans Selbach joined his family's well-known *négociant*
firm and three years later established the tiny Selbach-Oster
estate winery, which initially relied only on a historic five-acre
vineyard. Today his son Johannes continues to work on a small
scale, making masterful Rieslings with fruit sourced from nearly
50 acres of superlative, steeply terraced estate vines.
○ **Selbach Incline Riesling / 2010 / Mosel / $**
Selbach collaborated with importer Terry Theise to introduce
this juicy, refined—and affordable—Mosel white.
○ **Selbach-Oster Graacher Domprobst Riesling Spätlese /
2010 / Mosel / $$$** A single-vineyard star of the vintage, with
effortless intensity and lightly sweet guava and mineral notes.
○ **Selbach-Oster Rotlay Zeltinger Sonnenuhr Riesling / 2010 /
Mosel / $$$** This tightly coiled, monumentally structured
Riesling comes from a tiny parcel within one of the world's
most famous vineyards.

WEINGUT WITTMANN

While still in his teens, Rheinhessen dynamo Philipp Wittmann
created dry Rieslings and dessert wines that won over critics
and drew new attention to the region. In the 20 years since,
Wittmann has gone from talented newcomer to established
leader (and married another celebrated young winemaker, Eva
Clüsserath). At his family's 1663 estate, he farms biodynamically
and fashions cuvées (like the obscure white Albalonga) that are
at the cutting edge of Rheinhessen wine.
○ **Wittmann 100 Hills Dry Riesling / 2010 / Rheinhessen / $$**
Wittmann's most affordable wine bristles with tangy green
apple and white peach.
○ **Wittmann Westhofener Riesling Trocken / 2010 /
Rheinhessen / $$$** Limestone soil around the village of
Westhofen gives a minerally edge to this white's exotic fruit.

Austria

Wine Region

Wine buyers at top U.S. restaurants have helped introduce Americans to Austrian wines. Before sommeliers fell in love with Austria's signature grape, Grüner Veltliner, the country's gorgeous white wines were largely an afterthought in America. Austria's finest reds, Zweigelt and Blaufränkisch, are more obscure but worth the hunt. Supple and fruity, they are much easier to drink than they are to pronounce.

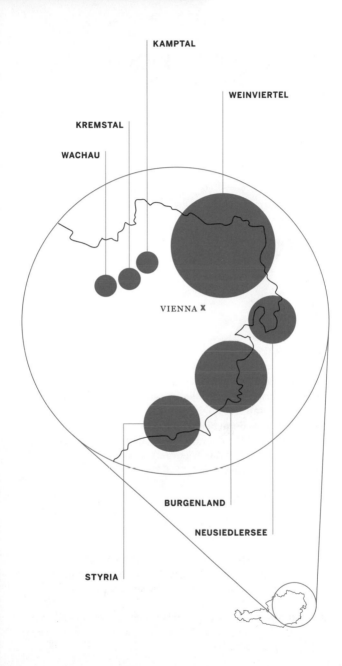

KAMPTAL

WEINVIERTEL

KREMSTAL

WACHAU

VIENNA X

BURGENLAND

NEUSIEDLERSEE

STYRIA

Austria

USTRIA'S GREAT WHITE wines come mainly from the large province of Lower Austria (Niederöster-reich), north of Vienna, where vineyards line the Danube River. The small Wachau region there is responsible for many of the country's richest Grüner Veltliners and Rieslings; the neighboring Kremstal and Kamptal areas also make stellar examples. South of Vienna, Burgenland, one of Austria's warmest areas, produces most of the country's reds, along with a number of great dessert wines. Styria (Steiermark) makes vivid whites from Sauvignon Blanc, Chardonnay and Welschriesling.

KEY GRAPES: WHITE

GELBER MUSKATELLER U.S. sommeliers have championed this rare grape, which yields delicate, floral-scented whites.

GRÜNER VELTLINER Austria's signature grape is a crisp, peppery white bursting with mineral and apple flavors. Top Grüners improve over time, gaining notes of honey and smoke.

RIESLING Austrian versions of this minerally white tend to be drier and fuller-bodied than Rieslings from Germany and fruitier than Alsace examples.

SAUVIGNON BLANC (MUSKAT-SYLVANER) & CHARDONNAY (MORILLON) These international whites are gaining ground in Austria; Sauvignon Blanc from Steiermark is the finest.

WEISSBURGUNDER The most famous examples of this grape variety (a.k.a. Pinot Blanc) come from Burgenland, where it is the basis of superb dessert wines and many dry whites; southern regions, such as Sudsteiermark, are also good sources of dry Weissburgunder wines.

WELSCHRIESLING & MÜLLER-THURGAU (RIVANER) These high-yielding varieties are responsible for much of Austria's simple, everyday whites, though a handful of excellent sweet Welschrieslings can be found.

 KEY GRAPES: RED

BLAUFRÄNKISCH This spicy red grape yields medium-bodied wines that are exceptionally food-friendly.

ST. LAURENT Though rarely imported, this local variety may be Austria's most seductive red, with lush, smoky flavors and exuberant aromas reminiscent of Pinot Noir.

ZWEIGELT Fresh cherry and licorice tinges and juicy acidity define Zweigelt, Austria's most popular red.

WINE TERMINOLOGY
Austrian wine labels list grape and region, and, except for simple table wines, use rankings similar to Germany's Qualitätswein designations, which define the ripeness of grapes for quality wines and hence the finished wine's potential alcohol and sweetness (see p. 142). In 2002 Austria introduced the Districtus Austriae Controllatus (DAC) regional wine classification system.

DISTRICTUS AUSTRIAE CONTROLLATUS (DAC) Similar to the French AOC and Italian DOC systems, DAC wine categories have rules that cover yields, permitted grapes, winemaking requirements and geographic limits for sourcing. The wines must also adhere to a certain taste profile. DAC terms are intended to ensure that wines represent quality examples of the country's most important styles; today there are seven appellations.

FEDERSPIEL A Wachau term for wines made from riper grapes that are then fermented into medium-bodied dry wines similar to those made in a Kabinett style (see p. 142).

GEMISCHTER SATZ A wine made from a traditional "field blend" of different grape varieties. For these bottlings, winemakers grow and ferment the grape varieties together, rather than blending them after fermentation.

SMARAGD Used only in the Wachau, this term applies to wines made from grapes that were picked later than those for Feder-spiel wines (see above). The extra hang time on the vine gives Smaragd wines exceptional richness and body, and occasionally a touch of sweetness.

STEINFEDER A term used in the Wachau to define light, low-alcohol wines that are made for drinking young (and perfect for picnics and parties).

Producers/ Austria

DOMÄNE WACHAU

The members of this huge Wachau cooperative farm one-third of the vineyards in the region (nearly 1,100 acres), yet its wines deliver the consistency and quality more typical of a far smaller operation. Prime grapes go into the higher-end Terrassen and Einzellagen tiers, yet even these bottlings are accessibly priced, and the best of them can be poured alongside Wachau's finest.

O **Domäne Wachau Terrassen Grüner Veltliner Federspiel** / 2011 / Wachau / $ At around $15, this exhilaratingly juicy and lush Grüner is a total steal.

O **Domäne Wachau Terrassen Grüner Veltliner Smaragd** / 2010 / Wachau / $$ Smaragd wines are ripe, richly textured and full; this one offers silky citrus and honey notes.

O **Domäne Wachau Terrassen Riesling Federspiel** / 2011 / Wachau / $$ An intensely fragrant Riesling, with succulent stony apple and floral tones.

NIKOLAIHOF-WACHAU

Few wineries can boast a legacy as ancient as that of this famous Wachau estate. It was officially founded in 985, and its wine cellar was once a Roman crypt. The Saahs family's methods have changed little in the two centuries or so since they purchased Nikolaihof from the Catholic Church. They make small amounts of estate-grown wines using traditional, biodynamic techniques, and the resulting cuvées display rare purity.

○ **Nikolaihof Vom Stein Riesling Federspiel / 2009 / Wachau / $$$** Grapes achieve extra ripeness in the stony Vom Stein vineyard; this expressive, beautifully made Riesling offers fragrant lemon and flower notes.

○ **Nikolaihof Im Weingebirge Grüner Veltliner Smaragd / 2009 / Wachau / $$$$** About as captivating as Grüner gets, this shows off gorgeous harmony between delicate spice and firm mineral flavors.

SCHLOSS GOBELSBURG

In 1996 Michael Moosbrugger was an obsessive young wine collector with a burning desire to make his own wine. Then Willi Bründlmayer (see p. 154) gave him the opportunity of a lifetime: to lease the vineyards at Schloss Gobelsburg, a 12th-century monastery with grapevines growing in some of Kamptal's finest *terroir* (Bründlmayer acts as a consultant to the winery). Since then, quality has soared, and Moosbrugger's gone from winemaking novice to established star.

WINE INTEL
Visitors to the Schloss Gobelsburg and Bründlmayer wineries can stay at the Wine & Spa Resort Loisium, a sleek, wine-themed hotel and spa whose 900-year-old cellar houses a modern wine museum.

○ **Gobelsburger Reserve Riesling / 2011 / Kamptal / $$** Perfumed with apple and mineral notes, this introductory Riesling is incredibly succulent.

○ **Schloss Gobelsburg Steinsetz Reserve Grüner Veltliner / 2010 / Kamptal / $$** Hailing from a vineyard south of the monastery, this dense, energetic Grüner Veltliner is loaded with juicy melon flavors.

○ **Schloss Gobelsburg Heiligenstein Erste Lage Riesling / 2009 / Kamptal Reserve / $$$** Summer heat supposedly earned the Heiligenstein ("saints' rock") site its original name—Hellenstein ("hell's rock")—and makes it a famous source of opulent, ageworthy Riesling.

WEINGUT ALZINGER

In just 25 years, the Alzinger family climbed into Wachau's top ranks, thanks to Rieslings and Grüner Veltliners of compelling precision. Leo Alzinger's parents founded the vineyard in 1925 and sold grapes to the local cooperative for six decades; today Leo and his grown son (also called Leo) fashion estate-grown whites that are as celebrated as they are scarce.

○ **Alzinger Dürnsteiner Riesling Federspiel / 2010 / Wachau / $$$** This shows the tangy, juicy freshness that's a hallmark of the 2010 vintage, along with silky apple and citrus flavors.

WEINGUT BERNHARD OTT

This estate in Wagram, a region located northwest of Vienna, has built its reputation on rivetingly pure, unoaked examples of Grüner Veltliner. Bernhard Ott took over the family cellars from his father in 1995 and inherited a swath of vineyards that he has steadily improved, the latest step being a conversion to labor-intensive biodynamic farming.

○ **Ott Am Berg Grüner Veltliner / 2010 / Wagram / $$** Ott's introductory bottling is reliably crisp, zesty and buoyant.

WEINGUT BRÜNDLMAYER

Willi Bründlmayer has run this organically farmed 200-acre Kamptal winery for the past three decades. Seven Grüners and five Rieslings form the core of the magnificent portfolio; some of Bründlmayer's reds are aged in acacia, a traditional practice championed by him that is becoming increasingly common.

○ **Weingut Bründlmayer Kamptaler Terrassen Grüner Veltliner / 2010 / Kamptal Reserve / $$** Bright and focused, with clear, juicy mineral and stone-fruit flavors.

○ **Weingut Bründlmayer Kamptaler Terrassen Riesling / 2010 / Kamptal / $$** Like all of Bründlmayer's wines, this crisp, bone-dry Riesling comes from organically farmed vines.

WEINGUT EMMERICH KNOLL

It's debatable whether Emmerich Knoll makes better Riesling or Grüner—this Wachau winemaker excels at both. A leading figure in Austria's wine renaissance of the 1980s, Knoll and son Emmerich III own 37 acres of steep vineyards along the warmer, eastern stretch of the Wachau Valley. Their wines expertly combine freshness and power, and can improve for decades.

○ **Weingut Knoll Ried Loibenberg Loibner Riesling Smaragd /
2010 / Wachau / $$$** Grapes from the famous Loibenberg
vineyard yield exceptionally dense, ageworthy whites, like this
gorgeous, multifaceted Riesling.

WEINGUT FRANZ HIRTZBERGER

At harvest, Franz and son Franzi Hirtzberger make several
passes through their Wachau vineyards, picking only the ripest
grapes each time around. It's easier said than done: Their fruit
grows on some of the region's steepest terraces, situated high
over the Danube. This obsession with perfect ripeness means
that even their Federspiel (lighter) wines are among the weight-
iest of their kind, and the rest are opulent and ageworthy, and
coveted by collectors.

○ **Franz Hirtzberger Rotes Tor Grüner Veltliner Federspiel /
2010 / Wachau / $$$** This Grüner is loaded with spicy,
herb-edged fruit flavors. Although it has just 12.5 percent
alcohol, it tastes much richer.

○ **Franz Hirtzberger Hochrain Riesling Smaragd / 2010 /
Wachau / $$$$** A small crop meant that Hirtzberger made
even less of this rare Riesling than usual in 2010; marked by
apricot and lemon, it will age well for many years.

WEINGUT HIEDLER

Creating wines that are equal parts crisp and rich is not easy.
But that is clearly the forte of Kamptal winemaker Ludwig
Hiedler, who specializes in succulent, showy Grüner Veltliners,
Rieslings and Weissburgunders (Pinot Blancs). Hiedler makes
his wines exclusively with estate-grown grapes from small vineyards around the town of Langenlois and uses no chemical
fertilizers or pesticides.

○ **Hiedler Löss Grüner Veltliner / 2010 / Kamptal / $$**
Silty loess (*löss*) soils yield especially fruity Grüner, such as
this mouthwatering, savory bottling, which combines ripe
melon and subtle herb notes.

○ **Hiedler Urgestein Riesling / 2010 / Kamptal / $$**
This flinty Riesling's minerally backbone comes from vines
planted in extremely rocky soil.

○ **Hiedler Maximum Weissburgunder / 2009 / Kamptal / $$$**
One of the best Pinot Blancs made anywhere, this nutty, lush
white stops just short of being too rich.

WEINGUT HIRSCH

Johannes Hirsch began to help run his family's Kamptal winery when he was in his 20s. He promptly ripped out every red variety growing in their vineyards—never mind that Hirsch's reds were among the region's best. He converted to biodynamic farming and was the first Austrian to use screw-caps for all his wines, a lineup of outstanding Grüners and Rieslings.

O **Hirsch Zöbing Riesling / 2010 / Kamptal / $$**
A racy, dry Riesling from vineyards near the town of Zöbing.

O **Hirsch Heiligenstein Erste Lage Riesling / 2009 / Kamptal / $$$** Picked by hand from steep slopes, this shows the intensity that's characteristic of the Heiligenstein site.

WEINGUT JAMEK

While many of his fellow vintners were churning out sweetened innocuous wines for the export market in the 1950s, Wachau's Josef Jamek was creating (then unheard of) single-vineyard Rieslings and naturally dry cuvées that helped galvanize a quality wine revolution. His daughter Jutta and her husband, Hans Altmann, today run what has become an iconic estate, with Riesling and Grüner Veltliner its chief varieties.

O **Jamek Ried Achleiten Grüner Veltliner Federspiel / 2010 / Wachau / $$** Although it comes from a famous vineyard, this high-toned, citrusy white is relatively affordable.

WEINGUT NIGL

Rising star Martin Nigl makes Rieslings and Grüner Veltliners on his Kremstal estate that compete with those of the more prestigious (and expensive) Wachau region. Grapes from the estate's oldest vineyards go into the Privat line. Though layered with complex flavors, even Nigl's top wines retain a sense of delicacy, partly a result of his reliance on primarily steel tanks (rather than barrels) to mature them.

O **Nigl Freiheit Grüner Veltliner / 2010 / Kremstal / $$**
Tangy lime and herb flavors define this dry, zesty white.

O **Nigl Alte Reben Reserve Grüner Veltliner / 2010 / Kremstal / $$$** Old vines (*alte reben*) give this reserve wine its bright, expansive palate and stony depth.

O **Nigl Privat Pellingen Erste Lage Reserve Riesling / 2010 / Kremstal / $$$$** An exceptionally pure, silky and racy Riesling from a first-growth (*erste lage*) vineyard.

WEINGUT PRAGER

Ilse Prager's husband, Vienna-born biologist turned winemaker Toni Bodenstein, has made Prager into one of the Wachau's most sought-after names. The estate's top bottlings come from the Achleiten vineyard, a revered ancient site planted with Riesling and Grüner Veltliner. But its newest vineyards are in far cooler high-elevation sites—conditions that help preserve the wines' bright flavors and acidity in the face of Austria's increasingly warm summers.

○ **Prager Achleiten Grüner Veltliner Smaragd / 2010 / Wachau / $$$$** In contrast to many Smaragd wines, this bright, ageworthy Grüner Veltliner is restrained, with medium-bodied mineral and citrus tones.

○ **Prager Wachstum Bodenstein Grüner Veltliner Smaragd / 2010 / Wachau / $$$$** Very low yields in 2010 gave this spicy, substantial Grüner its full body and focused fruit.

○ **Prager Wachstum Bodenstein Riesling Smaragd / 2010 / Wachau / $$$$** Extra-ripe grapes from a cool vineyard create a fantastically fresh, citrus- and quince-driven Riesling.

WEINGUT RAINER WESS

Rainer Wess marketed wine for years—including a stint as a sales manager for Robert Mondavi in Europe—before he realized a long-held dream of making his own. Starting in 2003 with purchased grapes from the famous Loibenberg vineyard, Wess quickly developed a reputation for particularly refined Riesling and Grüner Veltliner. His basic Wachau wines are nearly always terrific bargains.

○ **Rainer Wess Wachauer Grüner Veltliner / 2010 / Wachau / $$** Sourced from several vineyards, this affordable Grüner makes a terrific introduction to Wess's sleek, elegant style.

Greece

Wine Region

Wine has been made in Greece for millennia—grape presses dating back to 1600 BC have been found on Crete. But in all those years, there has never been as much excitement about Greek wine as there is now. Radical quality improvements in the past few decades have propelled Greece's citrusy, mineral-laden whites and food-friendly reds—most made with indigenous grape varieties—to newfound international popularity.

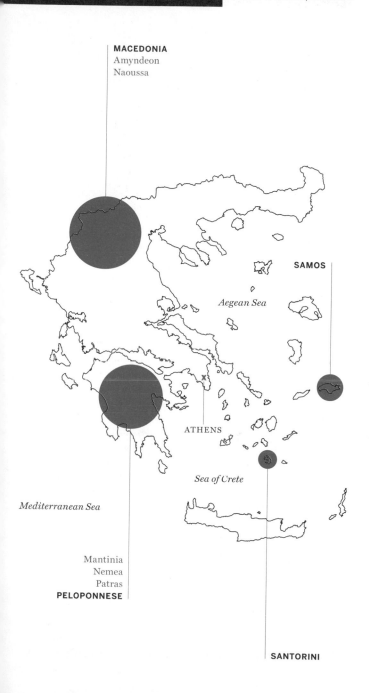

MACEDONIA
Amyndeon
Naoussa

SAMOS

Aegean Sea

ATHENS

Sea of Crete

Mediterranean Sea

Mantinia
Nemea
Patras
PELOPONNESE

SANTORINI

Greece

GREECE HAS BEEN producing wine for 4,000 years. Unfortunately, its modern reputation was tainted by decades of churning out resin-flavored plonk. But the country's admission to the European Union in 1981, coupled with a burst of winemaking creativity, transformed its wine industry. Today, despite economic woes, Greece is making remarkably good wine.

The go-to zone for aromatic reds and fresh, floral whites is the Peloponnese and its top subregions, Nemea and Mantinia. The volcanic island of Santorini makes the nation's finest whites, based on the Assyrtiko grape. In northern Greece, Macedonia produces young, fruity reds as well as tannic, ageworthy ones; the best come from Naoussa and neighboring Amyndeon.

KEY GRAPES: WHITE

ASSYRTIKO A Santorini specialty, Assyrtiko yields exhilarating, mineral-laden whites capable of improving for decades.

ATHIRI This ancient white grape, often blended with Assyrtiko, is the source of succulent, citrusy whites.

MALAGOUSIA A satiny texture and lush, full-bodied stone-fruit flavors define wines made from this recently revived grape.

MOSCHOFILERO This pink-skinned Peloponnesian native produces crisp, floral, low-alcohol white and rosé wines.

ROBOLA Known as Ribolla Gialla in Friuli, Robola is responsible for the minerally, lemon-inflected whites of Cephalonia.

RODITIS This bulk wine staple also produces charming, floral whites in the Peloponnese's Patras appellation.

SAVATIANO The common Savatiano grape is the usual basis for retsina, a simple, ubiquitous white wine flavored with pine resin.

KEY GRAPES: RED

AGIORGITIKO A lush texture and juicy cherry flavors are this grape's hallmarks, whether it's made into fresh rosés or rich reds.

XINOMAVRO Macedonia's signature grape yields bold, ageworthy reds marked by savory black olive and herb notes.

WINE TERMINOLOGY

Greek wine labels typically feature regions rather than grapes, as a wine's region tends to determine the main grape from which it is made. Naoussa reds are required to be made from Xinomavro; Nemea reds, from Agiorgitiko. Mantinia wines are mostly Moschofilero; Assyrtiko dominates Santorini's wines.

Producers/ Greece

ALPHA ESTATE

At a remote winery in Amyndeon, near the Albanian border, vintner Angelos Iatridis and vine guru Makis Mavridis craft powerful, fruity wines that are as modern as the computer-controlled tanks used to ferment them. Amyndeon's cool climate means that these wines retain vibrant acidity despite their ripeness.

● Alpha Estate Syrah-Merlot-Xinomavro / 2008 / Florina / $$$
Spicy Syrah, plummy Merlot and juicy Xinomavro combine in this dense, fruit-forward blend.

BOUTARI

Boutari's portfolio, which features wines from the best regions all over Greece, offers a snapshot of the country's phenomenal diversity. Family-owned since its founding in Naoussa in 1879, Boutari produces Greece's most famous example of the Xinomavro grape with its flagship bottling, the Grande Reserve Naoussa. Also look for its fresh, sunny Santorini white and its supple Nemea red, among others.

○ Boutari Moschofilero / 2010 / Mantinia / $$
This showcases Moschofilero's floral and mineral sides, with a lovely touch of zesty citrus.

● Boutari / 2008 / Naoussa / $$
Boutari's Grande Reserve sells out quickly, but its basic Naoussa red is widely available and beautifully refined.

DOMAINE SIGALAS

Santorini vintner Paris Sigalas, a mathematician, started his winery as a hobby in 1992. It's now one of the country's leading estates, acclaimed for expertly crafted, minerally Assyrtikos and elegant red wines made from indigenous grapes. Domaine Sigalas boasts very old vines, all of which are organically farmed and woven into round tangles resembling birds' nests; the shape protects the vines from the island's high winds.

○ Sigalas Asirtiko-Athiri / 2011 / Santorini / $$
The addition of some Athiri softens the more austere Assyrtiko grape in this succulent, tightly wound white.

○ Sigalas Fermented in Oak Barrel / 2010 / Santorini / $$
Even the anti-oak purists are likely to be seduced by this seamless, oak barrel–aged Assyrtiko, which delivers generous citrus, cream and spice.

DOMAINE TSELEPOS

Yiannis Tselepos, one of the central figures of the Greek wine renaissance, started his Peloponnesian winery with his wife, Amalia, in 1989, after studying enology in Dijon, France, and working for several wineries in Burgundy. Known for his fragrant, mineral-tinged Moschofilero, he also makes a world-class Gewürztraminer and wines from three French grapes: Chardonnay, Merlot and Cabernet Sauvignon.

○ **Tselepos Moschofilero** / 2010 / Mantinia / $$
Textbook Moschofilero, this is both vibrant and delicate, with pure, fresh mineral, citrus and floral tones.

● **Tselepos Agiorgitiko** / 2007 / Nemea / $$
Mature and round with a lingering earthiness, this appealing red is made from the indigenous St. George variety.

GAIA WINES

When Bordeaux-trained vintner Yiannis Paraskevopoulos worked for Boutari, he was sent to Santorini to research vineyards. What he saw inspired him to found his own winery, Gaia, with another vineyard expert, Leon Karatsalos. Their pure, razor-sharp Assyrtiko made the brand an instant success. Today they're even better known for refined Agiorgitikos from the semi-mountainous Nemea region.

○ **Thalassitis** / 2010 / Santorini / $$
First released in 1994, this has become one of Greece's best-known white wines, thanks to its flinty minerality and refreshing citrus notes.

● **No'tios Agiorgitiko** / 2010 / Peloponnese / $
Terrific acidity upholds ripe, velvety raspberry and cherry flavors in this delicious red.

KIR-YIANNI

Yiannis Boutaris founded Kir-Yianni in 1997 after leaving Boutari, the company his grandfather founded in 1879. Since then, the Naoussa-based Kir-Yianni has become one of Greece's top producers, known for some of the country's most exceptional Xinomavro, the peppery native red that's the winery's signature grape. Son Stellios now oversees the cellar, making wine with native grapes, plus some skillful modern-style blends.

○ **Kir-Yianni Petra** / 2010 / Florina / $
Lavishing care on the humble Roditis grape—harvesting low yields and using careful winemaking—results in a white brimming with bright, citrusy charm.

● **Kir-Yianni Paranga** / 2009 / Macedonia / $$
A modern blend of Xinomavro, Merlot and Syrah, this is aged in steel tanks, which keeps its dark-fruit flavors at the forefront.

NEW
WOR

United
States/
Australia/
New
Zealand/
Argentina/
Chile/
South
Africa

166
UNITED
STATES

254
ARGENTINA

LD

226 AUSTRALIA

244 NEW ZEALAND

262 CHILE

272 SOUTH AFRICA

United States

/ **Wine Region**

Three years ago, the United States surpassed France as the world's largest consumer of wine. That's especially significant for American winemakers, since more than 65 percent of what we drink in the U.S. comes from our own vineyards. California accounts for the vast majority of that volume, but these days wine lovers are discovering bottlings from many other wine-producing states as well.

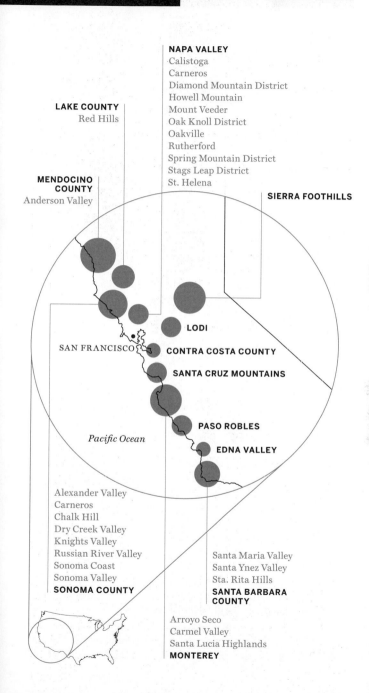

NAPA VALLEY
Calistoga
Carneros
Diamond Mountain District
Howell Mountain
Mount Veeder
Oak Knoll District
Oakville
Rutherford
Spring Mountain District
Stags Leap District
St. Helena

LAKE COUNTY
Red Hills

SIERRA FOOTHILLS

**MENDOCINO
COUNTY**
Anderson Valley

LODI

SAN FRANCISCO

CONTRA COSTA COUNTY

SANTA CRUZ MOUNTAINS

PASO ROBLES

Pacific Ocean

EDNA VALLEY

Alexander Valley
Carneros
Chalk Hill
Dry Creek Valley
Knights Valley
Russian River Valley
Sonoma Coast
Sonoma Valley
SONOMA COUNTY

Santa Maria Valley
Santa Ynez Valley
Sta. Rita Hills
**SANTA BARBARA
COUNTY**

Arroyo Seco
Carmel Valley
Santa Lucia Highlands
MONTEREY

United States

W HEN IT COMES to U.S. wine, there's California, and then there's everyone else. California is America's viticultural powerhouse, producing about 90 percent of the nation's wine, with Washington, New York and Oregon accounting for most of the rest. The temperate West Coast makes fine wine from European *Vitis vinifera* varieties (grapes such as Chardonnay, Sauvignon Blanc, Cabernet Sauvignon and Pinot Noir). Other parts of the country with cold, harsh winters once grew only the hardy native American *Vitis labrusca* varieties but have since switched to European varieties and hybrids, with winemakers in New York and Virginia leading the way. The classic American style, which sometimes emphasizes bold flavors over subtlety and is known for its ripe fruit and generous use of oak, is also changing: Many of today's American wines are exhibiting more nuance and *terroir*.

WINE TERMINOLOGY

AMERICAN VITICULTURAL AREA (AVA) Most U.S. labels carry an AVA, the legally defined region from which the wine comes. Unlike many European designations, AVAs don't stipulate how a wine must be produced, which grapes may be used or the maximum yields allowed per vineyard. Rather, U.S. law dictates that a wine labeled with an AVA must contain at least 85 percent grapes from that region. If an AVA wine lists a vintage date, 95 percent of the fruit is required to be from that year's harvest. Wines with the name of one grape, often called varietal wines, must contain 75 percent of that grape variety. Some states go beyond these requirements. Oregon, for example, mandates a higher minimum percentage for most varietal wines and for geographic designations.

MERITAGE Pronounced like "heritage," this category recognizes multivariety blends made from traditional Bordeaux grapes—chiefly Cabernet Sauvignon and Merlot in reds and Sauvignon Blanc and Sémillon in whites. Many producers use proprietary names for these wines—for instance, Mondavi's Opus One.

OLD VINES The U.S. government does not regulate the phrase *old vines* on labels, meaning that vintners can define it however they like. Many vintners agree that vines older than 35 years qualify as old, though some believe only those a half-century or older make the cut.

RESERVE Another term that has no legal definition, *reserve* can be used on any wine regardless of its age or how it was made; how much the word is worth depends entirely on the brand.

CALIFORNIA

CLAIM TO FAME
Compared with Europe, which has had millennia to figure out how to match grape to place, California is just getting started. While it boasts a winemaking history dating back to the late 1700s, the state became one of the world's top wine zones in just the past 40 years. Many of California's best regions hug the coast: Vines depend on ocean-driven wind and fog to chill grapes nightly and help create thick-skinned, complexly flavored fruit. Still, vineyards grow in nearly every corner of the state. And while plantings are dominated by international varieties like Cabernet Sauvignon and Chardonnay, California's experimental winemakers work with a vast array of other grapes, producing wines of every type and style.

REGIONS TO KNOW

CARNEROS Straddling the southern ends of Napa and Sonoma counties, Carneros has a blustery climate that's perfect for Chardonnay and Pinot Noir; sparkling versions are a specialty.

CENTRAL COAST Not to be confused with the scorching-hot Central Valley (which is bulk-wine central), this stretch of Pacific Coast is a premium growing region that stretches between San Francisco and Santa Barbara. Of its 32 subregions, a few stand out. **MONTEREY** occupies a peninsula south of San Francisco and specializes in Chardonnay and Pinot Noir (though it successfully grows aromatic whites like Sauvignon Blanc and Riesling, too). Halfway to Los Angeles, **PASO ROBLES** offers terrific bold, fruity reds, especially Zinfandel, Rhône varietals (Syrah, Grenache, Mourvèdre) and Cabernet Sauvignon. Southern California's **SANTA BARBARA COUNTY** owes its success with cool-climate wines (notably Chardonnay, Syrah and Pinot Noir) to a geological oddity: coastal valleys that run east–west and act as superhighways for chilly ocean air. Subregions include the **SANTA MARIA** and **SANTA YNEZ** valleys and **STA. RITA HILLS.**

LAKE COUNTY This district has long been a top source of delicious Sauvignon Blanc; now its **RED HILLS** subzone is gaining fame for Napa-like Cabernets at refreshingly gentle prices.
LODI & THE SIERRA FOOTHILLS Located inland and east of San Francisco Bay, Lodi, in the Central Valley, and the Sierra Foothills region are famous for old-vine Zinfandels.

MENDOCINO COUNTY Home to an unlikely mix of loggers, liberals and vintners, this rugged North Coast region grows an equally unlikely mix of grapes ranging from Charbono to Carignane. Easier to find are its fantastic old-vine Zinfandels and cherry-driven Pinot Noirs. The cool, rainy subregion of **ANDERSON VALLEY** has emerged as an excellent source of silky Pinot Noirs, crisp Chardonnays and refined sparkling wines.

NAPA VALLEY California's most prestigious wine region produces benchmark Cabernets that are among the world's finest reds. (It produces great Merlot and Cabernet Franc, too, but they're less fashionable at the moment.) Northeast of San Francisco, Napa, which includes 15 subregions, is blocked from the Pacific by the Mayacamas Mountains, making it warmer than its western neighbor, Sonoma County. The most tannic, powerful Cabernets come from hillside vineyards on famous slopes such as **HOWELL, SPRING** and **DIAMOND** mountains; more restrained versions are made from grapes grown on the valley floor or benchlands, like **OAK KNOLL DISTRICT, STAGS LEAP DISTRICT** and **ST. HELENA.**

NORTH COAST This large umbrella region encompasses all of Northern California's best-known AVAs, including those in Napa, Sonoma, Mendocino and Lake counties. It's typically used for larger-production blends from multiple vineyards.

SANTA CRUZ MOUNTAINS Though it's home to Ridge Vineyards, one of the U.S.'s best producers, this forested district south of San Francisco remains under the radar. That's slowly changing, though, as boutique vintners discover its superb terrain.

SONOMA COUNTY Thanks to its patchwork quilt of varied soils and microclimates, Sonoma's million-plus acres grow heat-seeking Cabernet and Merlot as easily as they do heat-shy grapes like Sauvignon Blanc and Pinot Noir. Located an hour north of San Francisco, the county is hemmed in between the Pacific and the Mayacamas Mountains, which funnel ocean-driven fog. The prestigious **RUSSIAN RIVER VALLEY** turns out world-class Pinot Noir and Chardonnay, as does the newer **SONOMA COAST,** which offers elegant wines from Sonoma's western extreme. Warmer regions such as parts of the **ALEXANDER VALLEY** and **KNIGHTS VALLEY** turn out polished Cabernet and Merlot, along with some lush Chardonnays. **DRY CREEK VALLEY** is one of Sonoma's warmer subregions and an ideal spot for Zinfandel, as well as Cabernet and Syrah. **SONOMA VALLEY** produces perhaps the most diverse wines, with firm reds coming from hillside vines and cool-climate grapes thriving in the valley's southern end.

❧ KEY GRAPES: WHITE

CHARDONNAY The state's most planted variety makes wines that range from rich and heavily oaked to minerally and crisp.

PINOT GRIGIO Most California Pinot Grigio used to be pretty bad, but today winemakers are crafting some delicious, citrusy wines with the grape, particularly from cooler regions.

RIESLING The popularity of this crisp white has risen in recent years. Though a handful of wineries have been making ambitious, small-lot Rieslings for decades, today they are joined by many larger wineries that are producing fresh, fruity and often lightly sweet bottlings, many of which come from Monterey.

SAUVIGNON BLANC California versions of this zippy white variety display succulent tropical fruit and citrus flavors; these distinguish it from grassier New Zealand versions and minerally white Bordeaux.

VIOGNIER, MARSANNE & ROUSSANNE Often blended to create lush, stone-fruit- and apple-inflected white wines, these Rhône Valley grape varieties are most associated with the Paso Robles and Santa Barbara regions.

 KEY GRAPES: RED

CABERNET SAUVIGNON The grape that put California on the international map back in the 1970s, Cabernet remains the state's iconic wine. Complex, ageworthy examples from Napa Valley still set the standard.

MERLOT Though its reputation suffered as a result of overproduction in the 1990s, Merlot has bounced back in quality and, less quickly, prestige—which means shrewd shoppers can find great Merlots that are much less expensive than Cabernets.

PETITE SIRAH Winemakers use this spicy grape primarily to add color and tannin to blends. Planted in pockets up and down the state, Petite Sirah has a small but passionate following.

PINOT NOIR A cool climate is essential for good Pinot, and the state's best bottles come from coastal regions, including western Sonoma, the Anderson Valley and Santa Barbara County.

SYRAH Syrah is the most important Rhône red in California. Often blended with Grenache and/or Mourvèdre, it thrives in the California sun, particularly in the so-called Rhône Zone around Paso Robles. Syrahs made in warm regions like Paso Robles are lush and fruity, while taut, elegant bottlings are made in cooler areas like Santa Barbara.

ZINFANDEL Although Zinfandel is not a native (it's an obscure Croatian grape related to Italy's Primitivo), California winemakers have been cultivating it for some time, giving it a distinctive American identity. Sonoma's Dry Creek Valley, Paso Robles, Mendocino and Contra Costa County are top spots for the grape.

Producers/ California

ALTA MARIA VINEYARDS

By day James Ontiveros manages sales for the famed Bien Nacido Vineyards, located on a swath of land in Santa Barbara's Santa Maria district. On the side, Ontiveros moonlights with college buddy and winemaker Paul Wilkins on their boutique Alta Maria label. The duo's four wines reflect Ontiveros's knack for selecting top grapes and Wilkins's delicate touch in the cellar.

○ **Alta Maria Vineyards Chardonnay** / 2009 / **Santa Maria Valley** / $$ Aging just part of this Chardonnay in barrel gives it a lovely balance of citrusy acidity and subtle, creamy oak.

○ **Alta Maria Vineyards Sauvignon Blanc** / 2010 / **Santa Ynez Valley** / $$ Ontiveros scored fruit from the well-known La Presa Vineyard to make this mouthwatering, melony white.

● **Alta Maria Vineyards Pinot Noir** / 2009 / **Santa Maria Valley** / $$ With more elegance than its price suggests, this is lithe and full of tea-inflected berry tones.

ALYSIAN

Gary Farrell sold his namesake Russian River winery in 2004 with the intention of slowing down. But this meticulous Pinot wizard can't seem to help himself: Three years later he debuted Alysian, which delivers benchmark Russian River Pinot Noir and Chardonnay sourced from a handful of stellar vineyards.

● **Alysian Russian River Selection Pinot Noir** / 2009 / **Russian River Valley** / $$$ Farrell's only multivineyard red is fragrant, layered and seamlessly balanced.

● **Alysian Rochioli Vineyard Allen-Rochioli Blocks Pinot Noir** / 2009 / **Russian River Valley** / $$$$ This stunning Pinot from a legendary site offers a seductive mix of spice and cherry.

BEAULIEU VINEYARD

First made in 1936, Beaulieu's iconic Georges de Latour Private Reserve helped define world-class Napa Valley Cabernet Sauvignon. Quality wavered over the years, but it's once again among the greats, thanks to renewed attention to high-end wines at this large brand. Beaulieu's Reserve and Napa Valley wines have improved, too; they offer reliably good quality at reasonable prices.

● **Beaulieu Vineyard Cabernet Sauvignon / 2009 / Napa Valley / $$** Blending fruit from different microclimates creates a complex, blackberry-inflected red.

● **Beaulieu Vineyard Cabernet Sauvignon / 2009 / Rutherford / $$$** An excellent value from a prestigious Napa subregion, this red is loaded with vanilla-edged cassis.

● **Beaulieu Vineyard Georges de Latour Private Reserve Cabernet Sauvignon / 2008 / Napa Valley / $$$$** The ripest, richest (and priciest) BV red, this standard-setting Cabernet bursts with roasted black cherry, spice and vanilla character.

BEDROCK WINE CO.

Morgan Twain-Peterson crushed his first wine at the age of five, with some help from his famous winemaker dad, Ravenswood founder Joel Peterson. His early training paid off: Today the 32-year-old has an expert hand with grapes that include Zinfandel, Syrah, Cabernet Sauvignon and Pinot Noir. Look for both of his fine labels: the value-driven Sherman & Hooker's and the boutique Bedrock Wine Co.

WINE INTEL
In 2010 Bedrock's Morgan Twain-Peterson helped create the Historic Vineyard Society, a non-profit group dedicated to the preservation of California's heritage vines.

● **Bedrock Wine Co. The Bedrock Heirloom Red Wine / 2010 / Sonoma Valley / $$$** General William Tecumseh Sherman was an early owner of the 125-year-old Bedrock vineyard, the source of this seamless field blend of 22 varieties.

● **Bedrock Wine Co. Hudson Vineyard South T'n'S Blocks Syrah / 2010 / Carneros / $$$** More than a third of the grapes for this beautifully structured, ageworthy Syrah were crushed traditionally, by foot.

● **Bedrock Wine Co. Monte Rosso Zinfandel / 2010 / Sonoma Valley / $$$** Monte Rosso's famous vines, dating to the 1880s, have long yielded some of America's greatest Zinfandels, including this exuberant, beautifully refined bottling.

BENOVIA

Joe Anderson and Mary Dewane purchased an established vineyard along Sonoma's Westside Road (the Park Avenue of Pinot addresses) to create this ambitious Russian River winery (they've since accumulated other vineyard sites). Their second savvy move was partnering with talented Hartford Court veteran Mike Sullivan; he crushed Benovia's first vintage in 2006.

● **Benovia Winery Pinot Noir / 2010 / Russian River Valley / $$$** Benovia works its Pinot Noir by hand during fermentation, resulting in especially supple tannins and focused flavors.

● **Benovia Winery Pinot Noir / 2010 / Sonoma Coast / $$$** Sullivan's restrained style suits the cool 2010 vintage, which showcases this Pinot's juicy, zesty red fruit.

● **Benovia Winery Cohn Vineyard Pinot Noir / 2009 / Sonoma County / $$$$** Aromatic and lightly spicy, the winery's flagship cuvée comes from one of Sonoma's oldest Pinot vineyards.

BERINGER VINEYARDS

The best-known wines from this historic Napa producer straddle both ends of the price spectrum: a huge-volume, lightly sweet blush Zinfandel and a $115 Private Reserve Cabernet. Winemaker Laurie Hook, a 27-year veteran of Beringer, masterminds the broad portfolio. Best bets include affordable Sauvignon Blancs and richly styled Cabernets and Chardonnays.

○ **Beringer Private Reserve Chardonnay / 2010 / Napa Valley / $$$** The winery's buttery, generously oaked top white is more vibrant than usual, thanks to a cool summer in 2010.

● **Beringer Private Reserve Cabernet Sauvignon / 2008 / Napa Valley / $$$$** Stash this firm, black-fruited Cabernet away for a few years to give it time to soften.

BLACKBIRD VINEYARDS

Michael Polenske abandoned a financial career to follow his passion for wine, restaurants and antiques. Blackbird, his Napa label, takes inspiration from Bordeaux's Pomerol region, with two Merlot-based wines anchoring a portfolio of blends. Aaron Pott, formerly of Bordeaux's Château Troplong Mondot and Napa's Quintessa, crafts the bold wines.

● **Blackbird Vineyards Arise / 2009 / Napa Valley / $$$** At $50, this is the least expensive red in the pricey Blackbird collection, offering dense berry flavors and a firm structure.

BOGLE VINEYARDS

The Bogle family has been farming in California's Clarksburg region since the late 1800s but only ventured into grape growing in 1968. Generations of accumulated expertise, plus a location in the prime but overlooked Sacramento Delta region, enables Bogle to produce some of the state's best value wines, including its portfolio stars: Petite Sirah and Old Vine Zinfandel.

● **Bogle Vineyards Old Vine Zinfandel** / 2009 / California / $
Old vines yield a tiny amount of fruit with concentrated flavors, which makes this juicy red's sticker price pretty amazing.

● **Bogle Vineyards Petite Sirah** / 2009 / California / $
This red is always tasty, with loads of inky, berry notes.

BONNY DOON VINEYARD

Iconoclastic, pun-loving Central Coast vintner Randall Grahm plays up his role as the industry's outrageous jester, but since selling his high-volume brands in 2006, he's gotten serious about his small-lot cuvées. His eclectic, *terroir*-driven lineup features mostly Rhône and lesser-known Italian and Spanish grapes.

○ **Bonny Doon Vineyard Le Cigare Blanc** / 2010 / Arroyo Seco / $$ Grahm's flagship white is a captivating, mineral-tinged blend of Grenache Blanc and Roussanne.

● **Bonny Doon Vineyard Contra** / 2010 / California / $
This plummy, rich blend includes Carignane from 100-year-old vines in Contra Costa County.

● **Clos de Gilroy Grenache** / 2010 / Central Coast / $$
Flat-out delicious, with exuberant, spicy red and black fruit.

BRANDER VINEYARD

This smallish Santa Barbara County winery is a rare breed in California: a Sauvignon Blanc specialist. Fred Brander planted some of the region's first Sauvignon Blanc vines in 1975; early success encouraged Brander to plant more. Today he makes eight versions, each showcasing a distinctive style or site.

○ **Brander Sauvignon Blanc** / 2010 / Santa Ynez Valley / $
The winery's entry-level Sauvignon is citrusy and floral.

○ **Brander Cuvée Nicolas Sauvignon** / 2010 / Santa Ynez Valley / $$ Pungent grass and lime tones are crisp and food-friendly.

○ **Brander Sauvignon au Naturel** / 2010 / Santa Ynez Valley / $$$ Soaking crushed grapes and skins together for a day gives this refined, melony white its silky texture.

BREGGO

Famous for refined Pinot Noir and Pinot Gris, Breggo sources grapes from the fog-prone Anderson Valley, whose cool temperatures yield elegant wines. (It's also the home of Boontling, a local dialect that inspired the winery's name: *Breggo* is Boontling for "sheep.") Quality-focused Napa vintner Cliff Lede acquired the winery in 2009 and has retained its Pinot-centric lineup.

○ Breggo Wiley Vineyard Pinot Gris / 2010 / Anderson Valley / $$ Alsace varietals like Pinot Gris thrive in Anderson Valley, as this lush, apple-inflected white illustrates.

● Breggo Pinot Noir / 2010 / Anderson Valley / $$$
This is elegant and crisp, marked by cherries and spice.

● Breggo Savoy Vineyard Pinot Noir / 2009 / Anderson Valley / $$$ Dark fruit is up front in this impressively structured yet graceful red, typical of the Savoy vineyard.

BUEHLER VINEYARDS

John and Helen Buehler purchased this remote property on a Napa Valley hillside in 1971, before local real estate prices skyrocketed. That helps explain how the Buehlers (John, Jr., now runs the winery) keep prices so reasonable for their terrific estate wines. Yet even their non-estate Russian River Chardonnay is a steal, thanks to longtime winemaker David Cronin.

○ Buehler Vineyards Chardonnay / 2010 / Russian River Valley / $$ Enjoy a creamy texture, juicy acidity and ripe peach tones at half the price of similar wines.

● Buehler Vineyards Zinfandel / 2010 / Napa Valley / $$
Dry-farmed (i.e., unirrigated) vines are part of the secret to this terrific Zin's bright, berry-rich intensity.

BUENA VISTA WINERY

Founded in 1857 by a Hungarian nobleman, California's oldest premium winery has had its ups and downs over the years. But Buena Vista is on an upswing now, with a range of quality single-vineyard Chardonnays and Pinot Noirs from the cool Carneros region and an ambitious new owner, Boisset Family Estates.

○ Buena Vista Chardonnay / 2009 / Carneros / $$
Former winemaker Jeff Stewart fermented and aged this in French oak, which accounts for its creamy vanilla notes.

● Buena Vista Pinot Noir / 2009 / Carneros / $$
Estate-grown grapes impart cherry-driven juiciness and spice.

CALERA WINE COMPANY

Established 40 miles southeast of Santa Cruz in 1975, Josh Jensen's Calera was named for the remnants of a limestone kiln (*calera* in Spanish) in the vineyard. Limestone-loving Burgundian grapes and Viognier are Calera's specialties; its (not inexpensive) Mount Harlan Chardonnays and Pinots have made Jensen one of California's most respected vintners. His Central Coast wines, made with purchased fruit, offer great value.

○ **Calera Chardonnay / 2010 / Central Coast / $$**
Jensen is a master of oak aging, meaning that the fruit in this lithe, citrusy Chardonnay takes center stage.

● **Calera Ryan Pinot Noir / 2009 / Mount Harlan / $$$**
The organically farmed Ryan Vineyard yields fragrant, midweight Pinots with bright berry notes.

CAMBRIA ESTATE WINERY

Cambria's vast 1,600-acre estate is located in the Santa Maria Valley, which funnels cool ocean breezes inland. This makes it perfect for growing high-acid Chardonnay, the grape that accounts for about 65 percent of Cambria's production. Winemaker Denise Shurtleff excels with other varieties, too, turning out smaller-production Pinot Noir, Syrah and Pinot Gris.

○ **Cambria Katherine's Vineyard Chardonnay / 2010 / Santa Maria Valley / $$** Of Cambria's many Chardonnays, this rich, tangerine-edged bottling is the most affordable.

○ **Cambria Bench Break Vineyard Chardonnay / 2010 / Santa Maria Valley / $$$** This is made in a lush, oak-edged style, with pear and lemon tones.

● **Cambria Julia's Vineyard Pinot Noir / 2009 / Santa Maria Valley / $$** This reasonably priced Pinot is finessed and smoky.

CAYMUS VINEYARDS

Both Cabernets made by this family estate rank among Napa's finest: the dense Special Selection Cabernet, which helped create the California cult wine phenomenon in the 1970s, and a less pricey (though still expensive) sibling Cabernet. The secret to their seamless power? Winemaker Chuck Wagner combines sturdy mountain grapes with suppler fruit from the valley floor.

● **Caymus Vineyards Cabernet Sauvignon / 2009 / Napa Valley / $$$$** Made in a similarly rich, firm and boldly fruity style as Special Selection, but at about half its price.

RARITIES & COLLECTIBLES

KISTLER VINEYARDS Sold chiefly through its mailing list, Kistler's sumptuous whites are some of Sonoma's most sought-after and remarkable Chardonnays. That's been true since 1978, when Steve Kistler and Mark Bixler founded the winery.

LITTORAI Winemaker and proprietor Ted Lemon once worked at Domaine Guy Roulot, where at the age of 24 he became the first American ever to manage a Burgundy estate. Nowadays, his single-vineyard Sonoma Chardonnays are as coveted as his dazzling Pinot Noirs.

STONY HILL VINEYARD Minerally, vividly etched Chardonnays with the structure to age gracefully have made this producer a reference point since the 1950s; even vintages from the 1970s are still drinking well.

CHATEAU MONTELENA WINERY

Chateau Montelena's 1973 Napa Chardonnay helped validate the ambitions of the entire California wine industry by famously besting prestigious white Burgundies at a Paris tasting in 1976. The winery was bought and rehabilitated in 1972 by Jim Barrett, who runs it today with his son Bo Barrett. They continue to craft restrained, ageworthy Chardonnay and Cabernet.

○ **Chateau Montelena Chardonnay** / 2009 / Napa Valley / $$$ Fresh and refined, this is full of bold pineapple and lemon.

● **Chateau Montelena Cabernet Sauvignon** / 2009 / Calistoga Napa Valley / $$$ At about one-third the price of the estate-grown Cabernet, this cassis-inflected red is a relative bargain.

CLOS DU VAL

A pioneer of Napa's Stags Leap District in the early 1970s, Clos Du Val grows heat-loving red grapes such as Cabernet at its original home ranch and heat-shy varieties on its property in Carneros, Napa's cooler, southern zone. What all Clos Du Val wines have in common, though, is a restrained style that balances ripe fruit flavors with bright, food-friendly acidity.

● **Clos Du Val Cabernet Sauvignon** / 2009 / Napa Valley / $$$ An elegant red with savory currant notes and firm tannins.

● **Clos Du Val Cabernet Sauvignon** / 2007 / Stags Leap District / $$$$ Co-founder Bernard Portet grew up in a Bordeaux wine family—an influence seen in this sleek, earthy flagship red.

CLOS LACHANCE

Bill and Brenda Murphy started out as hobby winemakers, but they have built Clos LaChance into one of the most respected wineries of the Central Coast. Located just 600 feet shy of the Santa Cruz Mountains appellation, Clos LaChance crafts an exquisite Chardonnay and terrific Rhône-inspired blends from younger vineyards farther inland, in warmer San Martin.

○ **Clos LaChance Chardonnay / 2009 / Santa Cruz Mountains / $$** This barrel-aged Chardonnay is rich, tangy and creamy.

● **Clos LaChance Lila's Cuvée / 2008 / California Central Coast / $$$** A hefty portion of Petite Sirah gives this high-end Rhône-style blend its brawny structure.

● **Clos LaChance Pinot Noir / 2009 / Santa Cruz Mountains / $$$** This crisp, fruity, minerally Pinot benefits from hot days and cool mountain nights.

CLOS PEGASE

There are 1,000 works of museum-quality art on display at this modernist Calistoga winery. But Clos Pegase's wines are worth the stop in their own right. Visitors will find a boldly styled collection of estate-grown Napa wines, made by winemaker Richard Sowalsky with the help of consulting star Paul Hobbs.

○ **Clos Pegase Mitsuko's Vineyard Chardonnay / 2009 / Carneros / $$** Grapes from cooler Carneros endow this white with lemony acidity and creamy peach tones.

● **Clos Pegase Cabernet Sauvignon / 2008 / Napa Valley / $$$** Rich but not over-the-top, this is sourced from vineyards in two very different subregions: Calistoga and Carneros.

CORISON

Cathy Corison lent her winemaking talents to such star producers as Staglin Family Vineyard and Long Meadow Ranch before devoting her time to her own boutique Napa label. Making just four cuvées—two Cabernets, a Gewürztraminer and a Cabernet Franc—Corison crafts expertly balanced, assured wines that aim for finesse and harmony over sheer strength.

● **Corison Cabernet Sauvignon / 2009 / Napa Valley / $$$$** Blackberry and cedar notes define this sleek, vivid red.

● **Corison Kronos Cabernet Sauvignon / 2008 / Napa Valley / $$$$** From old vines surrounding the winery in St. Helena, this offers impressively vibrant black cherry and spice flavors.

COVENANT

Not much kosher Cabernet is made in California, which is exactly why Jeff Morgan and partner Leslie Rudd decided to create one. Morgan makes two top-tier Cabernets from prime Napa vineyards under the Covenant name. A second label, Red C, includes a Cabernet, a Chardonnay and a Sauvignon Blanc.

● **Red C Cabernet Sauvignon** / 2009 / Napa Valley / $$$
There's an alluring violet edge to this dark, big-boned Cabernet, a baby brother to the Covenant red.

● **Covenant Cabernet Sauvignon** / 2009 / Napa Valley / $$$$
Sourced from an old three-acre vineyard, this 100 percent Cabernet is deeply concentrated with refined tannins.

DOMINUS ESTATE

This luxury winery's stunning yet simple façade (designed by Swiss architects Herzog & de Meuron) contrasts with a legion of faux-Tuscan and faux-French neighbors in Napa Valley's high-rent districts. Dominus owner Christian Moueix is one of Bordeaux's leading winemakers. His U.S. outpost produces just two Cabernet-based wines—a famed top red and a second bottling called Napanook.

● **Napanook Cabernet Sauvignon** / 2008 / Napa Valley / $$$
The historic Napanook Vineyard delivers a particularly suave, plum- and tobacco-driven Cabernet.

● **Dominus Cabernet Sauvignon** / 2008 / Napa Valley / $$$$
This multilayered, world-class red improves for days after opening—if you can wait that long to polish it off.

DUCKHORN VINEYARDS

Duckhorn rode to fame on the wave of Merlot's popularity by making some of the best Napa versions of the grape, but proved it could deliver superb Cabernet, too. Dan and Margaret Duckhorn have since created spin-off labels such as Goldeneye and Migration (focused primarily on Pinot Noir and Chardonnay), Paraduxx (unique red blends) and the affordable Decoy wines.

○ **Decoy Sauvignon Blanc** / 2010 / Napa Valley / $$
This offers a quality similar to Duckhorn's zesty premier Sauvignon Blanc, but for about $10 less.

● **Duckhorn Vineyards Merlot** / 2009 / Napa Valley / $$$
Adding a bit of Cabernet and Cabernet Franc gives extra structure and weight to this black currant–infused Merlot.

DUTTON-GOLDFIELD WINERY

Steve Dutton's late father was one of Sonoma's best-known grape growers, supplying fruit to many of the region's most esteemed wineries from the family's Dutton Ranch. While the Dutton family still sells most of its grapes, Steve and winemaker Dan Goldfield (Hartford Court, La Crema) cherry-pick some of the top Chardonnay and Pinot lots for their joint venture.

● **Dutton-Goldfield Emerald Ridge Vineyard Pinot Noir / 2010 / Green Valley of Russian River Valley / $$$** This refined, lightly spicy Pinot shows why Dutton Ranch grapes are so coveted.

● **Dutton-Goldfield Freestone Hill Vineyard Pinot Noir / 2009 / Russian River Valley / $$$** Hailing from a vineyard 10 miles from the coast, this displays supple cherry and cola flavors.

ELYSE WINERY

Ray Coursen and his wife, Nancy, left Cape Cod in 1983 and eventually became Napa vintners. Ray started at the bottom—taking a job as a cellar rat and attending whatever classes he could—and gradually worked his way up to winemaker at the well-regarded Whitehall Lane. Today the Coursens' Elyse label consists of a range of richly styled (and under the radar) wines.

● **Elyse C'est Si Bon / 2008 / Sierra Foothills / $$** The Coursens looked to inland vineyards to create this generously fruity Rhône blend.

● **Elyse York Creek Vineyard Petite Sirah / 2010 / Napa Valley / $$$** An inky, mocha-accented red from the Spring Mountain District that showcases the powerful tannins of Petite Sirah.

● **Elyse Morisoli Vineyard Cabernet Sauvignon / 2007 / Rutherford / $$$$** Cabernets from this Napa zone are renowned for their firm structure and intense fruit, which characterize this red perfectly.

FAR NIENTE

The late Gil Nickel and his wife, Beth, bought this run-down pre-Prohibition Napa winery in 1979 and beautifully restored it. Lavish gardens and vintage cars offer pleasant distractions, but the wines are the real draw. Far Niente's Chardonnays and Cabernets always earn high marks—and command high prices.

● **Far Niente Cabernet Sauvignon / 2009 / Oakville / $$$$** Oakville's tendency toward luscious richness is fully expressed in this blackberry-scented, ripe and tannic red.

FLORA SPRINGS

Centenarian matriarch Flora Komes and her late husband, Jerry, revived this abandoned winery in Napa's Rutherford district in the 1970s. They soon turned into serious producers, owning more than 600 acres of Napa vines. Grandchildren Nat Komes and Sean Garvey are preparing to run this Cabernet-focused winery, which also makes terrific lower-profile whites.

○ **Flora Springs Barrel Fermented Chardonnay / 2010 / Napa Valley / \$\$\$** Rich quince and apple star in this oaked white.

● **Flora Springs Trilogy / 2009 / Napa Valley / \$\$\$\$**
Merlot and Malbec soften Cabernet in this well-known blend, marked by supple tannins and deep, brambly fruit.

FLOWERS VINEYARD & WINERY

Walt and Joan Flowers planted their first Chardonnay and Pinot Noir in 1991 on the foggy Sonoma Coast. They were among the first to see the area's potential for great vineyards—especially on high ridges on the fog line. Their lush Chardonnays and refined Pinots gave the district credibility and remain among its stars.

○ **Flowers Camp Meeting Ridge Chardonnay / 2009 / Sonoma Coast / \$\$\$\$** Delicate spice and cream notes inflect this full, yet fresh and alluring, barrel-fermented white.

● **Flowers Sea View Ridge Pinot Noir / 2009 / Sonoma Coast / \$\$\$\$** This spectacular Pinot is loaded with fragrant wild berry and mineral tones framed by silky tannins.

FOXGLOVE

Foxglove co-owners and twins Bob and Jim Varner make tiny quantities of their cult-worthy Santa Cruz Mountains Chardonnay and Pinot Noir under their prestigious Varner and Neely labels, respectively. The brothers' deft touch is also evident in the Foxglove line, which offers a taste of their refined style at extremely affordable prices.

○ **Foxglove Chardonnay / 2010 / Central Coast / \$**
A secret to this tropical-inflected Chardonnay's lively, juicy flavors—and its low price—is no oak aging.

● **Foxglove Cabernet Sauvignon / 2010 / Paso Robles / \$**
This defines exactly what you want in an affordable Cabernet: lots of juicy, slightly savory black fruit.

● **Foxglove Zinfandel / 2010 / Paso Robles / \$**
A fantastically bright, fruit-driven Zinfandel.

FREEMARK ABBEY

As you might expect of a Napa Valley winery that dates back more than 125 years, Freemark Abbey has seen a lot of history—although it's never actually been an abbey. Founded in 1886 by the first woman on record as owning a winery in Napa, Freemark Abbey helped pioneer the release of single-vineyard Cabernet Sauvignons in the 1970s. These remain a focus, though other varieties also excel.

○ **Freemark Abbey Chardonnay** / 2010 / Napa Valley / $$
A refreshing antidote to buttery, heavy Chardonnays, this one features vibrant pear and spice notes.

● **Freemark Abbey Merlot** / 2009 / Napa Valley / $$
Combining grapes from valley floor and mountain vineyards creates a balanced, firm wine with savory red fruit.

● **Freemark Abbey Cabernet Sauvignon** / 2008 / Napa Valley / $$$ This reasonably priced Napa Cabernet highlights dense cedar and black currant flavors.

FROG'S LEAP

New York State native and former Stag's Leap Wine Cellars winemaker John Williams started his own Napa venture on a site that was once a frog farm, hence the brand's playful name. Since the 1980s, Frog's Leap has set a high bar for eco-friendly farming, forgoing chemicals, pesticides and even irrigation in its vineyards. The sophisticated wines reflect a similar conviction, holding to a restrained, food-friendly style that has come increasingly back in vogue.

● **Frog's Leap Zinfandel** / 2009 / Napa Valley / $$
A departure from blockbuster Zins, this one offers refined, midweight berry and spice.

● **Frog's Leap Merlot** / 2009 / Rutherford / $$$
Here's a seamless, red-fruited Merlot from Napa's prestigious Rutherford district, where the winery is located.

GALLO FAMILY VINEYARDS

Gifted winemaker Gina Gallo and her vineyard manager brother Matt redefined global giant E. & J. Gallo by teaming up to create this higher-end Sonoma label. Anchored by the Sonoma Reserve tier, which features bottlings from every key Sonoma subregion, the portfolio gains luster from three single-vineyard wines and, at the top, two acclaimed estate cuvées.

RARITIES & COLLECTIBLES

COLGIN CELLARS Colgin produces five wines—two Cabernets, two Cabernet blends and a Syrah—all of them stratospherically priced and extremely hard to find. But tasting the wines' blend of power and subtlety makes it clear why collectors go to such lengths to acquire them.

DIAMOND CREEK VINEYARDS Founder Al Brounstein was the first to bottle single-vineyard Cabernets in Napa, making structured wines that take years to soften, then improve for decades. Today his wife, Boots, and stepson Phil Ross keep his legacy alive.

HARLAN ESTATE One of the greatest names in Cabernet, Harlan sources its extraordinary flagship red from a rocky vineyard above Oakville, producing only 2,000 cases annually. Collectors snap them up the moment they're released.

○ **Gallo Signature Series Chardonnay / 2009 / Russian River Valley / \$\$** Grapes from the prestigious Russian River Valley subzone are key to this ripe, apple-inflected white's quality.

● **Gallo Family Vineyards Frei Ranch Vineyard Cabernet Sauvignon / 2006 / Dry Creek Valley / \$\$\$** A few years of bottle age have helped soften this meaty, firm red.

● **Gallo Signature Series Cabernet Sauvignon / 2008 / Napa Valley / \$\$\$** Though the label focuses on Sonoma, this Napa offering is rich, dark and beautifully balanced.

GRGICH HILLS ESTATE

After clobbering the French with his 1973 Chateau Montelena Chardonnay at a famous 1976 Paris tasting, Mike Grgich might have been happy to remain a Napa legend. Yet he has since raised funds to replace minefields with vineyards in his native Croatia, converted his estate to biodynamic farming, and resisted the trend toward supersize wines, staying true to his balanced style.

○ **Grgich Hills Estate Fumé Blanc / 2010 / Napa Valley / \$\$** Fumé Blancs are Sauvignon Blancs typically aged in oak; this creamy example highlights crisp, herbaceous flavors.

○ **Grgich Hills Estate Chardonnay / 2009 / Napa Valley / \$\$\$** A bright, melony white from the Chardonnay expert.

● **Grgich Hills Estate Cabernet Sauvignon / 2008 / Napa Valley / \$\$\$** Grgich's best-known red is especially intense in 2008, thanks to a dry growing season.

GROTH VINEYARDS & WINERY

This boutique Napa winery first gained fame in the 1980s for its Reserve Cabernet, an estate-grown red from 28 acres in Oakville. But the vineyards required replanting in 2000, and the Groth family was unable to make Reserve Cabernet until 2005, when the new vines came into their own. Its reappearance sparked new interest in all of Groth's sustainably farmed wines.

○ **Groth Sauvignon Blanc** / 2011 / **Napa Valley** / **$$**
Aging on its lees adds a lush, silky texture to this citrusy white.

● **Groth Cabernet Sauvignon** / 2009 / **Oakville** / **$$$**
Instead of shelling out $125 for the Reserve Cabernet, try this ageworthy, firmly structured sibling.

HANDLEY CELLARS

After a stint at Arrowood Winery, Milla Handley moved to the Anderson Valley in the late '70s, when the idea of making world-class Pinot in Mendocino County was unheard of. In 1982 Handley established her own winery, where she pioneered the cultivation of Burgundian and Alsace grapes in the region. Her rose petal–scented Gewürztraminer is outstanding.

○ **Handley Gewürztraminer** / 2011 / **Anderson Valley** / **$$**
With incredibly fragrant citrus and floral notes, this makes a terrific introduction to Gewürztraminer.

● **Handley Pinot Noir** / 2009 / **Anderson Valley** / **$$$**
An affordable, compelling Pinot with crisp strawberry tones.

● **Handley RSM Vineyard Pinot Noir** / 2009 / **Anderson Valley** / **$$$** Released only in superb vintages, this lithe, spicy cuvée comes from a vineyard named for Handley's late husband.

HANZELL VINEYARDS

Though a lot of California Chardonnays and Pinots are all about instant gratification—i.e., they offer loads of sweet fruit and oak but fade quickly—Hanzell's wines start to bloom only after many years in bottle. Shy when released, these long-lived, Sonoma-grown wines, made since 1957, reward those with patience.

○ **Hanzell Chardonnay** / 2009 / **Sonoma** / **$$$$**
Hanzell's taut and polished '09 Chardonnay reveals its floral and citrus complexity after an hour or so in a decanter.

● **Hanzell Pinot Noir** / 2009 / **Sonoma** / **$$$$**
From a great vintage for Sonoma Pinot Noir, this exhibits layer after layer of red fruit, citrus and spice.

HIRSCH VINEYARDS

Before he got into the wine business for himself, in 2002, David Hirsch sold his grapes to a notable list of Sonoma's top winemakers. He has spent nearly three decades decoding the wild jumble of different soils in his extraordinary Sonoma Coast vineyard, and the expertise he gained in the process made the winery's site-specific cuvées—sumptuous Pinot Noirs and a Chardonnay—instantly famous.

> **WINE INTEL**
> Hirsch Vineyards is in the new Ft. Ross-Seaview AVA, a western slice of the Sonoma Coast that's mostly above the fog line—a key factor in this extreme region.

○ **Hirsch Vineyards Chardonnay / 2009 / Sonoma Coast / $$$** Minerality, freshness and intense, apricot-tinged fruit combine brilliantly in this exquisite white.

● **Hirsch Vineyards The Bohan-Dillon Pinot Noir / 2010 / Sonoma Coast / $$$** Made to drink sooner than Hirsch's other Pinots, this bottling offers juicy, brisk red fruit indicative of the cool 2010 summer.

HOURGLASS

Talk about serendipity: When a vine pest ravaged the Zinfandel vines in Jeff and Carolyn Smith's Hourglass Vineyard, they replanted with Cabernet Sauvignon, just in time to catch Napa's heralded 1997 vintage. Praise for the sleek, *terroir*-driven wine came immediately, and a second site, Blueline Vineyard, debuted with the 2006 vintage. Hourglass also produces excellent Cabernet Franc and Merlot, verifying that there's more to this cult producer than beginner's luck.

● **Hourglass Blueline Vineyard Merlot / 2009 / Napa Valley / $$$$** High-profile winemaking consultant Bob Foley lent finesse to this expressive, bright, fruit-filled red.

HUNDRED ACRE WINERY/LAYER CAKE WINES

Jayson Woodbridge's fearless confidence made him a successful investment banker. That trait also allowed him to plunge into the wine business in 2000 with zero experience. Woodbridge's Hundred Acre reds—a handful of Napa Cabernets and a Barossa Shiraz—are expensive cult classics. Fortunately, he also applies his skills to the affordable and tasty Layer Cake wines.

● **Layer Cake Pinot Noir / 2010 / Central Coast / $$** Woodbridge is famous for his big, bold reds; this Pinot shows his skill with a more delicate grape.

JORDAN VINEYARD & WINERY

Jordan produces just two wines each year. Winemaker Rob Davis worked with the legendary André Tchelistcheff to craft the Sonoma estate's first Cabernet in 1976; more than 30 years later, he still favors a muscular, old-school style. Meanwhile, the Chardonnay has taken on a brighter, more elegant cast, thanks to a recent move to Russian River Valley fruit.

○ Jordan Chardonnay / 2010 / Russian River Valley / $$
Davis has changed how he makes this wine, not just its sourcing; this vintage is the most refined and aromatic yet.

● Jordan Cabernet Sauvignon / 2008 / Alexander Valley / $$$
A wine built for food, this features crisp acidity, firm tannins and savory herbal notes.

JOSEPH PHELPS VINEYARDS

First made in 1974, Joe Phelps's seamless Insignia red helped bring Bordeaux-style blends to prominence in California, and remains a standard-bearer for the entire state. Led today by the founder's son Bill Phelps and winemakers Damian Parker and Ashley Hepworth, Phelps still specializes in Bordeaux grapes.

● Joseph Phelps Cabernet Sauvignon / 2009 / Napa Valley / $$$ Generous amounts of seductive cherry flavors define this red, though it has the structure to improve with age.

● Joseph Phelps Insignia / 2008 / Napa Valley / $$$$
This benchmark, Cabernet-based red testifies to the virtues of blending different grape varieties: It's always extraordinary, showcasing equal parts grace and power.

KENDALL-JACKSON

This Sonoma-based megabrand maintains impressive standards despite its size. Almost all grapes come from 15,000 acres of estate vines amassed by the company's late founder, Jess Jackson, which gives winemaster Randy Ullom unusual control over quality. Best known for its Vintner's Reserve Chardonnay, the KJ portfolio includes many great single-vineyard offerings.

○ Kendall-Jackson Avant Chardonnay / 2010 / California / $
Prime grapes from coastal vineyards and minimal aging only in neutral oak are the secrets to this sleek white's freshness.

● Kendall-Jackson Grand Reserve Cabernet Sauvignon / 2008 / Sonoma County / $$ More structured than most Sonoma Cabs, with firm tannins and succulent dark berry notes.

LA CREMA

Elizabeth Grant-Douglas was apprenticed to Melissa Stackhouse for years before taking over her boss's job as La Crema's wine-maker in 2010. Under Stackhouse, La Crema rebuilt its reputation for superb Chardonnay and Pinot, while turning out large quantities of each. Grant-Douglas continues to source from cool-climate vineyards, a key to La Crema's continued resurgence.

○ **La Crema Chardonnay** / 2010 / Sonoma Coast / $$
Grant-Douglas aged this in oak for just seven months, which keeps the spotlight on its vibrant apricot fruit.

● **La Crema Pinot Noir** / 2010 / Sonoma Coast / $$
It's tough to find good Sonoma Coast Pinot for less than $25; this delicious, red-fruit-infused bottling delivers.

LADERA VINEYARDS

When a movie company wanted to use Anne and Pat Stotesbury's vast Montana ranch for filming one summer, the couple decamped to Napa and got into the wine business. In the mid-'90s they bought a spectacular vineyard in Mount Veeder's Lone Canyon and, later, a Howell Mountain site. Their stunning estate-grown wines reflect their grapes' mountain origins.

● **Ladera Cabernet Sauvignon** / 2008 / Napa Valley / $$$
Though it comes from estate vineyards primarily in the pricey Howell Mountain subzone, this red carries a friendlier price.

● **Ladera Cabernet Sauvignon** / 2007 / Howell Mountain / $$$$
Always 100 percent Cabernet, this flagship bottling showcases firm Howell Mountain tannins and layers of rich black fruit.

LA JOTA VINEYARD CO.

In a valley saturated with inky, dense Cabernets, this Howell Mountain estate offers an alternative: perfumed Napa reds that possess elegance and are built to age extraordinarily well. Chris Carpenter still makes the wines—two Cabernets, a Merlot and a Cabernet Franc—in Frederick Hess's historic 1898 fieldstone winery, located in the northeast corner of Napa Valley.

● **La Jota Cabernet Franc** / 2009 / Howell Mountain / $$$$
Thirty-some-year-old mountain vines give this red its ripe, minerally intensity and unusual depth.

● **La Jota Cabernet Sauvignon** / 2009 / Howell Mountain / $$$$
Here's a beautifully polished, blackberry-flavored version of a typically tannic and brawny Howell Mountain Cabernet.

LANG & REED WINE COMPANY

John Skupny is obsessed with Cabernet Franc, Bordeaux's underdog grape, which gets blended into many Napa wines but rarely takes center stage. The winemaker works tirelessly to determine the greatest Cabernet Franc clones and the best sites in Napa to grow them. The resulting reds show off the variety's seductive side, brimming with blueberry and spice notes.

● **Lang & Reed Cabernet Franc** / 2010 / North Coast / $$
Some of the fruit for this expressive, cherry-inflected red comes from a 1970s-era vineyard in Lake County, north of Napa.

● **Lang & Reed Cabernet Franc Two-Fourteen** / 2009 / Napa Valley / $$$ L&R's top cuvée takes its name from the rare clone that yielded grapes for this plush, single-vineyard red.

LAUREL GLEN VINEYARD

In the 1980s, Patrick Campbell's structured Sonoma Mountain wines helped prove that Napa's neighbor could produce top-tier Cabernet, too. In 2011, Campbell sold Laurel Glen to Bettina Sichel, who enlisted star consultant David Ramey and organic viticulture guru Phil Coturri to put their stamp on the wines, which are made from grapes grown on a single 16-acre estate.

● **Laurel Glen Counterpoint** / 2008 / Sonoma Mountain / $$
Mountain vineyards give this rich yet supremely balanced Cabernet its sturdy tannins.

LIOCO

Buddies Kevin O'Connor (former sommelier) and Matt Licklider (ex-wine importer) launched this Chardonnay- and Pinot-focused project in 2005. Their LIOCO wines (the moniker is a mash-up of their surnames) are sourced from premier vineyards in places like Anderson Valley and the Sonoma Coast, and reflect the duo's shared passion for minimalist winemaking (low to no barrel aging, wild yeasts) and old vines.

○ **LIOCO Chardonnay** / 2010 / Sonoma County / $$
The LIOCO team took advantage of the cool 2010 vintage to create this tangy, citrusy, mineral-driven white.

❀ **LIOCO Indica Rosé** / 2011 / Mendocino County / $$
A citrusy, invigorating rosé crafted by winemaker John Raytek.

● **LIOCO Hirsch Vineyard Pinot Noir** / 2009 / Sonoma Coast / $$$ This vibrant Pinot expresses the Hirsch Vineyard trademarks: bright red berry fruit and floral highlights.

LOUIS M. MARTINI WINERY

This Sonoma producer started out making jug wines in 1933, with quality rising over the years. The biggest jump occurred after Gallo bought the winery in 2002, leaving Michael Martini in charge of winemaking. Thanks to his talent and Gallo's deep pockets, the wines are rock solid, and top cuvées—such as the Lot No. 1 and Monte Rosso Cabernets—are world-class.

● **Louis M. Martini Cabernet Sauvignon** / 2009 / Napa Valley / $$ A Cabernet specialist, Michael Martini highlights the warmly fruity, hedonistic side of the grape in this bottling.

● **Louis M. Martini Cabernet Sauvignon** / 2009 / Sonoma County / $$ Here's a great house Cabernet, with plenty of polish and complexity.

● **Louis M. Martini Lot No. 1 Cabernet Sauvignon** / 2008 / Napa Valley / $$$$ Just 20 barrels of this impressively structured red were made, all fermented in a micro-winery annex.

LUNA VINEYARDS

Although initially known for championing the Italian Sangiovese grape, and, more recently, for powerful versions of Cabernet and Merlot, this midsize Napa label actually produces more Pinot Grigio than all of its other wines combined. Founded by industry execs George Vare and Mike Moone, Luna Vineyards also makes golfer Arnold Palmer's eponymous wines.

○ **Luna Pinot Grigio Napa Valley** / 2010 / Napa Valley / $$ The winery aims for a straightforward, ripely fruity style in its workhorse white.

LYNMAR ESTATE

Lynn Fritz grew grapes for other Sonoma wineries before founding Lynmar Estate in 1990. But it wasn't until winemaker Hugh Chappelle arrived in 2004 that this Russian River label broke into the ranks of the region's top producers. Chappelle left in 2010, yet Lynmar's cool-climate wines continue to possess the same expressive flavors and elegance that made them famous.

○ **Lynmar Estate Chardonnay** / 2009 / Russian River Valley / $$ Four Russian River vineyards contribute fruit to this boldly styled, full-flavored white.

● **Lynmar Estate Quail Hill Vineyard Pinot Noir** / 2009 / Russian River Valley / $$$ Consulting winemaker Paul Hobbs had a hand in this forceful, lusciously ripe Pinot.

MACMURRAY RANCH

MacMurray Ranch takes its name from a stunning western swath of the Russian River Valley that was once owned by actor Fred MacMurray (of *My Three Sons* fame). The ranch, now owned by Gallo, provides a portion of the grapes for MacMurray's Pinot-focused portfolio, which includes bottlings from some of California's top Pinot regions and Oregon's Willamette Valley, along with some cool-climate whites.

● **MacMurray Ranch Pinot Noir / 2009 / Sonoma Coast / $$**
Bright acidity gives a lift to this red's earthy berry flavors.

● **MacMurray Ranch Winemaker's Block Selection Pinot Noir / 2009 / Russian River Valley / $$$** A top cuvée with seamless dark fruit and a long, minerally finish.

MACROSTIE WINERY & VINEYARDS

Steve MacRostie's wines come from a prestigious region (Sonoma Coast) and get all of the TLC associated with high-profile labels—yet they remain under the radar. MacRostie started making Sonoma Coast Pinot and Chardonnay with purchased fruit; in 1997 he planted his own vines on Wildcat Mountain and added Syrah to the mix. Although MacRostie sold the winery in 2011, winemaker Kevin Holt remains.

○ **MacRostie Chardonnay / 2009 / Sonoma Coast / $$**
Elegant and intense, this white offers spicy, satiny pear tones.

● **MacRostie Wildcat Mountain Vineyard Pinot Noir / 2008 / Sonoma Coast / $$$** Low yields and ruthless barrel selection give this reserve-style red lovely weight and richness.

MAYACAMAS VINEYARDS

Bob and Elinor Travers purchased this venerable, remote Mount Veeder estate in 1968 and still produce the kind of old-school Cabernets that made Napa famous: firm reds with moderate alcohol levels and earthy, herb notes. Tight and sometimes lean on release like traditional Bordeaux reds, Mayacamas wines soften with time, and the best age beautifully for decades.

○ **Mayacamas Vineyards Sauvignon Blanc / 2010 / Mount Veeder-Napa Valley / $$** A Bordeaux-like Sauvignon Blanc redolent of bracing, fresh-squeezed limes.

● **Mayacamas Vineyards Merlot / 2007 / Mount Veeder-Napa Valley / $$$** The firm herb and black currant in this red would be perfect with a juicy steak.

MELVILLE VINEYARDS AND WINERY

All of the fruit for the Melville family's wines comes from its 139-acre estate in the Santa Rita Hills area of Santa Barbara County (the setting for the hit indie film *Sideways*). This is prime territory for Pinot Noir, and with Greg Brewer of Brewer-Clifton in charge of the cellar, the hits just keep coming.

- Melville Estate Verna's Syrah / 2010 / Santa Barbara County / $$ A super-fragrant and flavorful Syrah, with layers of spice, black fig and sandalwood.
- Melville Estate Pinot Noir / 2010 / Sta. Rita Hills / $$$ Sixteen different Pinot Noir clones lend complexity to this heady, superripe Pinot.

MERRY EDWARDS WINERY

Merry Edwards first made wine under her own name in 1997, focusing on small quantities of cool-climate Pinot Noir, plus a Sauvignon Blanc and Chardonnay. Edwards has honed her craft for nearly 40 California vintages, with early experience at pioneering wineries such as Mount Eden and Matanzas Creek. Her background shows in her bold, supremely balanced wines.

- Merry Edwards Pinot Noir / 2009 / Russian River Valley / $$$ Warmer inland vineyards yield the lusciously ripe, dark fruit and opulent texture that typify the Merry Edwards style.
- Merry Edwards Pinot Noir / 2009 / Sonoma Coast / $$$ A multivineyard blend full of crushed-berry and truffle notes.
- Merry Edwards Pinot Noir Flax Vineyard / 2009 / Russian River Valley / $$$ Minuscule yields from this young vineyard produced an especially dense, dark Pinot.

MERRYVALE

Located in a 1930s building along a narrow stretch of Napa Valley's famed Highway 29, this lauded winery has been owned by the Schlatter family since the mid-'90s. Merryvale's affordable Starmont label became so successful that it's now its own brand, produced at a newish facility in Carneros. The winery's prestigious Profile bottling remains the portfolio's star.

- Merryvale Pinot Noir Carneros / 2010 / Carneros / $$$ This complex Pinot offers delicate floral and berry tones.
- Merryvale Cabernet Sauvignon / 2008 / Napa Valley / $$$$ A forceful, concentrated red bolstered by meaty tannins and pronounced black currant flavors.

MORLET FAMILY VINEYARDS

Luc Morlet could easily have taken over his family's Champagne domaine. Instead, he fell in love with an American, settled in California and ended up becoming one of the state's most vaunted artisan winemakers. A veteran of cult producers Peter Michael Winery and Staglin Family Vineyard, Morlet created his own, instantly coveted label in 2006, with his wife, Jodie.

○ **Morlet Family Vineyards La Proportion Dorée** / 2010 / Sonoma County / $$$$ Modeled on the great whites of Bordeaux, this seductively layered, Sémillon-based blend is profound.

● **Morlet Family Vineyards Mon Chevalier** / 2009 / Knights Valley / $$$$ Massive, mineral-edged and potent, this Cabernet blend should develop for decades in the cellar.

MOUNT EDEN VINEYARDS

Brilliant winemaker and proprietor Jeffrey Patterson runs the cellar at this Santa Cruz Mountain estate, which was founded in the 1940s in the hills overlooking what is now Silicon Valley. Mount Eden's long-respected wines are gaining new cachet as buyers seek out more restrained styles. Patterson crafts outstanding Cabernet and Pinot Noir, though they have been overshadowed by the winery's crisp, refined Chardonnays.

○ **Mount Eden Vineyards Estate Chardonnay** / 2009 / Santa Cruz Mountains / $$$ This famous, formidable white offers a minerally intensity that can take years to unwind.

● **Domaine Eden Pinot Noir** / 2010 / Santa Cruz Mountains / $$$ A recently acquired vineyard provides fruit for the new Domaine wines, like this buoyant, raspberry-flavored Pinot.

MURPHY-GOODE

Though Murphy-Goode has been part of Jackson Family Wines since 2006, the Murphy family still maintains the vineyards, and David Ready, Jr., son of an original partner, makes these tasty, large-volume wines. The portfolio contained just white wines in the pre-Jackson years; now some reds are in the mix.

● **Murphy-Goode All In Claret** / 2007 / Alexander Valley / $$ Cabernet, Merlot and Petit Verdot all thrive in Sonoma's Alexander Valley, the source of this herb-accented blend.

● **Murphy-Goode Liar's Dice Zinfandel** / 2009 / Sonoma County / $$ Winemaker and dice-game enthusiast Dave Ready, Jr., named this superripe red, which tastes of blackberry jam.

RARITIES & COLLECTIBLES

AUBERT Mark Aubert is so revered for his masterful single-vineyard Chardonnays that his lush Pinot Noirs can get overlooked (though not by the collectors on his always-full mailing list).

DEHLINGER WINERY Tom Dehlinger's experience and talent are evident in his exquisite Russian River Pinot Noirs, which have been examples of the region's capacity for nuance and grace for almost four decades.

KOSTA BROWNE WINERY California's newest Pinot Noir star was the brainchild of two Sonoma sommeliers, Dan Kosta and Michael Browne, who presciently saved up their tip money for eight months back in 1997 in order to purchase their first half-ton of Pinot Noir grapes.

THE OJAI VINEYARD

Instead of owning vineyards, winemaker Adam Tolmach and his wife, Helen, contract with some of the Central Coast's best growers to buy grapes by the acre, an arrangement that encourages quality, not quantity. Tolmach makes as many as 20 wines each vintage, a mix of outstanding reds and refined whites.

○ **The Ojai Vineyard Chardonnay / 2010 / Santa Barbara County / $$** A pure, refreshing Chardonnay that's very food-friendly.

○ **The Ojai Vineyard McGinley Vineyard Sauvignon Blanc / 2010 / Santa Ynez Valley / $$** Incredibly concentrated grapes give this melony, oak-aged Sauvignon Blanc rare intensity.

● **The Ojai Vineyard Bien Nacido Vineyard Pinot Noir / 2009 / Santa Maria Valley / $$$** Redolent of crushed cherries, earth and spice, this fragrant Pinot comes from a famous vineyard.

OPUS ONE

Robert Mondavi boosted California wine's prestige 34 years ago when he partnered with the late Baron Philippe de Rothschild—proprietor of Bordeaux's Château Mouton Rothschild, among others—to create the one-wine brand Opus One. Though quality sometimes has fallen short of its hefty price tag, the Cabernet-dominated blend regained firmer footing in the last decade.

● **Opus One / 2008 / Napa Valley / $$$$**
This vintage favors elegance over sheer power, with delicate spice and floral notes highlighting its deep black fruit.

PEAY VINEYARDS

There's just one Peay vineyard, a 51-acre site spreading over a dramatic ridge at Sonoma's northwestern edge. Its cool, windy climate makes ripening grapes a nail-biting exercise for winemaker Vanessa Wong and the Peay brothers, Nick and Andy, who planted their vines in the late '90s. The payoff comes in vibrant, expressive wines with an emphatic sense of place.

○ **Peay Vineyards Estate Chardonnay / 2010 / Sonoma Coast / $$$** Sleek, high-toned yellow fruits (apples, pears, citrus) and firm minerality evoke a comparison to Burgundy's whites.

● **Peay Vineyards Les Titans Estate Syrah / 2009 / Sonoma Coast / $$$** Ultra-slow-ripening grapes result in aromatic flavors of fresh-cracked pepper and violets.

● **Peay Vineyards Pinot Noir / 2010 / Sonoma Coast / $$$** Top-quality purchased grapes yield this refined intro Pinot.

PISONI VINEYARDS & WINERY

Burgundy fanatic Gary Pisoni created one of California's most praised Pinot Noir vineyards in the rugged Santa Lucia Mountains in 1982. Along with his sons—winemaker Jeff and business manager/grape grower Mark—he later created the much-coveted Pisoni label (and sister brand, Lucia Vineyards).

● **Lucia Garys' Vineyard Pinot Noir / 2010 / Santa Lucia Highlands / $$$** Even in a cool vintage, Jeff Pisoni is able to create a full-bodied, lushly styled red.

● **Pisoni Estate Pinot Noir / 2009 / Santa Lucia Highlands / $$$$** Pisoni's mountain-grown vines catch morning sun and avoid fog, giving this Pinot its bold fruit and firm tannins.

PRIDE MOUNTAIN VINEYARDS

A brick stripe on the crush pad at Pride Mountain traces the Napa/Sonoma county line, which runs through this hilltop Spring Mountain estate. Pride is known for dense reds and oak-kissed whites. It's a style made famous under former winemaker Bob Foley and brilliantly executed today by Sally Johnson.

○ **Pride Mountain Vineyards Chardonnay / 2010 / Napa Valley / $$$** The Pride family sources this wine from cool Carneros; its bright, lemony style contrasts with the rich estate bottling.

● **Pride Mountain Vineyards Vintner Select Merlot / 2009 / Sonoma County / $$$$** Pride's top Merlot is bigger, richer and more structured than even some Cabernets.

QUPÉ

A Rhône fanatic, Bob Lindquist is one of the country's most renowned interpreters of Syrah, as well as of the unjustly obscure Rhône whites Roussanne and Marsanne. Based in Santa Barbara's famed Bien Nacido Vineyards, Lindquist sources grapes from some of the most prized Central Coast sites, then turns them into refreshingly balanced wines.

○ **Qupé Bien Nacido Hillside Estate Roussanne / 2009 / Santa Maria Valley / $$$** A white of dazzling strength and poise that shows why Qupé is a reference point for Rhône varietals.

● **Qupé Syrah / 2010 / Central Coast / $$**
One of the region's most consistently delicious and affordable Syrahs, this offers exuberant, racy red berry fruit.

RAMEY WINE CELLARS

As winemaker for boutique producers like Chalk Hill, Matanzas Creek and Rudd, David Ramey wowed both critics and his peers. For the past 17 years he has run his own Sonoma outfit. His exceptional single-vineyard Chardonnays have become collectors' favorites; his Cabernet and Syrahs show equal finesse.

○ **Ramey Chardonnay / 2009 / Sonoma Coast / $$$**
This complex white compares well with wines twice its price.

○ **Ramey Hyde Vineyard Chardonnay / 2009 / Napa Valley-Carneros / $$$** An ageworthy, tightly wound bottling from one of California's top sites for Chardonnay.

● **Ramey Pedregal Vineyard Cabernet Sauvignon / 2009 / Oakville / $$$$** This full-bodied, solidly built and outstanding red justifies its very hefty price.

RAVENSWOOD

When Joel Peterson started making Zinfandel in the 1970s, most Americans knew it only as a sweet pink (a.k.a. blush) pour called White Zinfandel. Peterson's evangelism for bold, full-throttle Zin helped sway a generation of wine drinkers and created a wildly successful megabrand, now owned by wine giant Constellation. Site-specific Zins top the broad portfolio.

● **Ravenswood Old Vine Zinfandel / 2009 / Lodi / $**
Lodi is a great source of old vines and value reds like this one.

● **Ravenswood Old Vine Zinfandel / 2009 / Sonoma County / $$**
Complementary varieties—like Petite Sirah, Carignane and Syrah—boost Zin's softer structure in this blend.

RIDGE VINEYARDS

One of the most celebrated names in American wine, Ridge makes its legendary Cabernet blend, Monte Bello, from Santa Cruz Mountain grapes. Winemaker Paul Draper, who joined Ridge less than a decade after its 1962 founding, credits superb vineyards and a minimalist approach for the wines' success. Don't overlook Ridge's accessibly priced old-vine Sonoma Zins.

● **Ridge Estate Monte Bello Vineyard Cabernet Sauvignon / 2009 / Santa Cruz Mountains / $$$** Only the most ageworthy Cabernet from Monte Bello makes the cut for the flagship blend described below; the rest goes into this muscular red.

● **Ridge Monte Bello / 2009 / Santa Cruz Mountains / $$$$** A brilliant, powerful Cabernet, Merlot and Petit Verdot blend.

ROBERT CRAIG WINERY

Robert Craig built his eponymous winery and planted one of his estate vineyards at the end of a winding, rugged road nearly 2,300 feet up Napa Valley's Howell Mountain. It's a perch that suits Craig well, given his passion for mountain-grown grapes. Craig makes always excellent, firmly structured Cabernets and Cab blends, and small amounts of Chardonnay and Zinfandel.

● **Robert Craig Affinity Cabernet Sauvignon / 2009 / Napa Valley / $$$** Tasting of black cherries, smoke and creamy oak, this red gets complexity from five different Bordeaux grapes.

● **Robert Craig Cabernet Sauvignon / 2009 / Howell Mountain / $$$$** Craig's mountain-grown grapes have thick skins that give his wines their chewy tannins, on display in this fine red.

ROBERT MONDAVI WINERY

After a series of shake-ups in the mid-2000s, Robert Mondavi's industry-transforming winery found stable footing under its current owner, Constellation Wines. Refocused on its Napa roots, Mondavi is led by winemaker Genevieve Janssens, who is steadily restoring luster to high-end bottlings like the Reserve Cabernet and adding finesse to entry-level offerings.

● **Robert Mondavi Winery Cabernet Sauvignon / 2009 / Napa Valley / $$** Blending fruit from Napa's cooler and warmer regions keeps this Cabernet consistent regardless of vintage.

● **Robert Mondavi Winery Cabernet Sauvignon Reserve / 2008 / Napa Valley / $$$$** One of America's benchmark reds, this comes chiefly from the historic To Kalon vineyard.

ROCHIOLI VINEYARDS & WINERY

The Rochioli family had been farming for decades when they began making wine under this Sonoma Valley label in the mid-'80s. Joe, Jr., and Tom Rochioli now run the show. It can take years to get on the winery's mailing list for their Burgundy-inspired single-vineyard reds and whites, but luckily their other offerings are more widely available.

○ **Rochioli Chardonnay** / 2010 / **Russian River Valley** / $$$
The finish of this lush Chardonnay is long and harmonious, with apple and spice notes.

○ **Rochioli Sauvignon Blanc** / 2011 / **Russian River Valley** / $$$
Rocchioli's succulent estate-grown Sauvignon Blanc comes chiefly from a vineyard planted in 1959.

● **Rochioli Pinot Noir** / 2010 / **Russian River Valley** / $$$
Beautifully perfumed, this wine shows the coolness of the vintage in its vibrant, midweight red fruit and herb tones.

ROSENBLUM CELLARS

Veterinarian turned vintner Kent Rosenblum never owned any vines, but built his namesake label into an incredibly successful brand through the strength and unmatched breadth of his Zinfandel portfolio. Though the winery's current owner, drinks giant Diageo, has cut back on Rosenblum's vineyard-specific Zins, the label remains a go-to choice for juicy, exuberant reds.

● **Rosenblum Vintner's Cuvée Cabernet Sauvignon** / 2009 / **California** / $ Grapes from cooler coastal vineyards give this Cabernet its lively red-fruit flavors.

● **Rosenblum Cellars Maggie's Reserve Zinfandel** / 2009 / **Sonoma Valley** / $$$ Here's a brawny, powerful Zinfandel from a vineyard planted in 1901.

ROY ESTATE

Star winemaker Philippe Melka has a hand in the two Bordeaux-style reds that Napa Valley's Roy Estate offers each year. Always based on Cabernet Sauvignon, with smaller amounts of Merlot and Petit Verdot, Roy's hedonistic wines come from a stony, 17-acre vineyard site in the valley's southeast section, in the foothills of Atlas Peak.

● **Roy Estate Proprietary Red Wine** / 2009 / **Napa Valley** / $$$$
An opulently fruity and ripe blend of Cabernet, Merlot and Petit Verdot with sweet, substantial tannins.

SAINTSBURY

A trailblazer in the Carneros region, Saintsbury helped prove that this southern slice of Napa and Sonoma counties, with warm afternoons and cool breezes, is an ideal territory for Pinot and Chardonnay. Long known for delivering quality at fair prices, Saintsbury is gaining new luster under winemaker Jerome Chery, an alumnus of cult producer Littorai.

● Saintsbury Pinot Noir / 2010 / Carneros / $$
Expertly blending fruit from over a dozen vineyards resulted in a bright, spicy Pinot with black tea and cherry notes.

● Saintsbury Stanly Ranch Pinot Noir / 2010 / Carneros / $$$
The Stanly Ranch provides such superb fruit that this bottling has replaced the winery's reserve cuvée.

SEBASTIANI VINEYARDS & WINERY

Although the Sebastiani family sold its Sonoma winery back in 2008, winemaker Mark Lyon stayed on. His wines showcase the region's diversity, as he specializes in matching grape to place. Sebastiani's Zinfandel from Dry Creek, Chardonnay from Alexander Valley and Pinot from the temperate Russian River region offer high quality at wallet-friendly prices.

● Sebastiani Secolo / 2007 / Sonoma County / $$$
Although it's a Bordeaux-style blend with an Italian name, this ripe dark red tastes unabashedly Californian.

● Sebastiani Cherryblock Cabernet Sauvignon / 2008 / Sonoma Valley / $$$$ The winery's top bottling is decadent, with violet and earth tones accenting sweet dark fruit.

SEQUOIA GROVE

In recent years Sequoia Grove's wines, especially the Napa Cabs, have gone from good to formidable, a leap coinciding with the arrival of winemaker Molly Hill, who joined director Michael Trujillo at the Rutherford winery in 2003. With a tasting room on Highway 29, Sequoia Grove is on its way to joining Napa's elite.

○ Sequoia Grove Napa Valley Chardonnay / 2010 / Carneros / $$ Napa's coolest subzone produced especially fresh, vivacious whites in 2010, like this citrusy offering.

● Sequoia Grove Vintner Select Cabernet Sauvignon Stagecoach Vineyard / 2007 / Atlas Peak Napa Valley / $$$$ This is a blockbuster mountain Cabernet, with huge tannins, blackberry fruit and plenty of oak.

SHAFER VINEYARDS

Shafer's beautifully made wines enjoy near-universal acclaim. Chalk that up to winemaker Elias Fernandez's skills and the estate's prime vineyards, which include 79 acres in Napa's Stags Leap District. Though the Hillside Select Cabernet is an age-worthy classic, the less famous One Point Five is a savvy choice.

● **Shafer Merlot / 2009 / Napa Valley / $$$**
A sophisticated bottling that features Merlot's most winning attributes: velvety, deep plum flavors and savory complexity.

● **Shafer One Point Five Cabernet Sauvignon / 2009 / Napa Valley Stags Leap District / $$$$** Almost delicate in comparison to many Napa Cabs, with seductive cherry and violet.

SIDURI WINES/NOVY FAMILY WINERY

A winemaker with a devoted following but no vineyards, Adam Lee sources Pinot Noir from all over California and even Oregon for his Siduri label. Under his Novy brand, he makes mostly cool-climate Syrah and a bit of Gewürztraminer, among other varieties, from regions like the Russian River and Bennett valleys.

● **Novy Family Winery Syrah / 2009 / Santa Lucia Highlands / $$** Windy Monterey brings out Syrah's fragrant, spicy side.

● **Siduri Wines Pinot Noir / 2010 / Santa Lucia Highlands / $$**
A relatively approachable price makes this cherry-driven bottling one of Lee's most popular.

● **Siduri Wines Keefer Ranch Vineyard Pinot Noir / 2010 / Russian River Valley / $$$** Sonoma's Keefer Ranch produces concentrated Pinot with deep, dark fruit.

SIGNORELLO ESTATE

Ray Signorello, Sr., never intended to become a vintner. In the mid-1970s, he planted grapevines on his Napa Valley retreat, planning to sell the fruit. But a bumper crop in 1985 left the oil and gas executive with unsold grapes, and a family brand was born. Today Ray, Jr., with an assist from winemaking genius Luc Morlet, makes very fine wines, all estate-grown.

○ **Signorello Vieilles Vignes Chardonnay / 2009 / Napa Valley / $$$$** Strictly for fans of rich Chardonnays, this offers lavish tiers of candied pineapple and butterscotch flavors.

● **Signorello Padrone Proprietary Red Wine / 2007 / Napa Valley / $$$$** Fruit from two prime, steep vineyard sections went into this brawny, Cabernet-based blend.

SIMI WINERY

Although other Sonoma wineries are older than Simi, none of them kept operating straight through Prohibition, as Simi did, thanks to a legal loophole. Today its entry-level Chardonnay and Cabernet Sauvignon make two reliable, well-priced choices, and Simi's excellent small-production wines (crafted by skilled winemaker Steve Reeder) are well worth the step up in price.

○ **Simi Chardonnay / 2010 / Sonoma County / $$**
Combining grapes from Sonoma's cooler and warmer zones is the secret to this fresh, apricot-inflected white's consistency.

● **Simi Landslide Cabernet Sauvignon / 2008 / Alexander Valley / $$$** This packs an impressive amount of deep, dark fruit and structure for the price.

SMITH-MADRONE

Spring Mountain is one of the best zones in Napa for Cabernet, and while Smith-Madrone's full-bodied, herb-inflected reds represent the AVA well, its whites are equally outstanding. Brothers Stu and Charles Smith have been making their mountaintop wines since the early '70s; their minerally Rieslings and Chardonnays are long-lived—and unjustly under the radar.

○ **Smith-Madrone Riesling / 2010 / Spring Mountain District / $$** Not much Riesling still grows in Napa; this tangy apple and floral version makes a case for planting more.

○ **Smith-Madrone Chardonnay / 2009 / Spring Mountain District / $$$** Unusually cold growing conditions preserved the lemony acidity in this cedar-edged Chardonnay.

SOBON ESTATE

Headed by second-generation winemaker Paul Sobon, this estate is one of the top family-owned wineries in the Sierra Foothills. The clan's enthusiasms include everything from juicy Zinfandels to opulent Rhône whites to the Italian Sangiovese grape. Paul also takes charge of the wine for Sobon Estate's sister label, Shenandoah Vineyards.

● **Sobon Estate Old Vines Zinfandel / 2010 / Amador County / $** Tame this red's rustic berry flavors and gripping tannins with grilled or barbecued meat.

● **Sobon Estate ReZerve Primitivo / 2009 / Amador County / $$** The Italian Primitivo variety is genetically related to Zinfandel; here it yields a Zin-like red with berry and earth notes.

SPOTTSWOODE ESTATE VINEYARD & WINERY

This charity-minded Napa Valley winery, owned by Mary Novak, donates 1 percent of its profit to environmental causes. But there's another reason to buy its wines: Winemaker Jennifer Williams, with consultation from Rosemary Cakebread, produces superb, ageworthy Cabernet from organic grapes and a terrific Sauvignon Blanc, among other wines.

○ **Spottswoode Sauvignon Blanc / 2010 / Napa Valley and Sonoma Mountain / $$$** Spottswoode's less-well-known Sauvignon Blanc is reliably delicious and well-priced.

● **Spottswoode Cabernet Sauvignon / 2009 / Napa Valley / $$$$** Spottswoode produces one of the country's best Cabernets from America's defining Cabernet region, Napa.

STAGLIN FAMILY VINEYARD

This estate is such a cornerstone of Napa's Rutherford District that it's hard to believe it was established only in 1985. Managed by Shari Staglin and her dream team of talent—winemaker Fredrik Johansson, viticulturist David Abreu and consultant Michel Rolland—Staglin produces Cabernets that are among the most sought-after in Napa (and priced accordingly).

○ **Staglin Family Vineyard Estate Chardonnay / 2010 / Rutherford, Napa Valley / $$$$** Ultra-low crop yields account for the concentrated flavors of this hedonistic yet balanced white.

● **Staglin Family Vineyard Estate Cabernet Sauvignon / 2008 / Rutherford, Napa Valley / $$$$** A definitive Rutherford Cabernet, with dense, caramel-laced cherry and olive flavors.

STAG'S LEAP WINE CELLARS

In 2007 Warren Winiarski sold his landmark Napa winery to Chateau Ste. Michelle and Tuscan vintner Piero Antinori, who hired star consultant Renzo Cotarella. Quality, already good, has notched up even further: It's easy to imagine current vintages competing with marquee Bordeaux, the way a Stag's Leap Cabernet famously did at a legendary Paris tasting in 1976.

● **Stag's Leap Wine Cellars Cabernet Sauvignon Artemis / 2009 / Napa Valley / $$$** Sourced from vineyards throughout Napa, this red gets its plush texture from a bit of Merlot.

● **Stag's Leap Wine Cellars Fay Estate Cabernet Sauvignon / 2008 / Napa Valley / $$$$** A polished, violet-tinged wine from the first Cabernet vineyard planted in the Stags Leap District.

ST. CLEMENT VINEYARDS

Sometimes making great wine is about whom you know. Despite having few vines of its own, Napa Valley's St. Clement is extremely well-connected, holding long-standing relationships with esteemed small growers like the Armstrongs and O'Shaughnessys. Up-and-coming winemaker Danielle Cyrot (a Californian with Burgundy winemakers in her family tree) took the cellar's helm in 2005. She's since proved herself a savvy leader to steer St. Clement's portfolio.

○ **St. Clement Sauvignon Blanc / 2010 / Napa Valley / $$**
The coolness of the 2010 vintage comes across clearly in this fresh, lightly tropical and grassy white.

● **St. Clement Merlot / 2009 / Napa Valley / $$**
Cyrot aims for a style straight down the middle for this Merlot, which features ideally ripe plum flavors set against supple tannins and a dash of spice.

STELTZNER VINEYARDS

Pioneering Napa Valley grape grower Dick Steltzner released his first wine in 1977. With the help of his children and skilled winemaker Tom Dolven, Steltzner has continued to produce remarkably sleek wines in the Stags Leap District. In 2012, the Steltzners sold the estate and winery to the Plumpjack Group (which makes Plumpjack and Cade brands), and the winery's name is likely to be changed soon.

● **Steltzner Vineyards Pool Block Cabernet Sauvignon / 2009 / Stags Leap District / $$$** Vines planted right by the family pool yield the Steltzner's favorite Cabernet, marked by earth, blackberry and coal notes.

STORYBOOK MOUNTAIN VINEYARDS

Jerry and Sigrid Seps make distinctive and extraordinary Zinfandels from their old, high-elevation vineyards located in the rugged Mayacamas Mountains of northern Napa Valley. Compared to most fleshy, superripe Zinfandels produced in Sonoma Valley or Paso Robles, Storybook Mountain's versions have a muscular, pleasingly austere edge, exhibiting equal parts elegance, power and structure.

● **Storybook Mountain Vineyards Eastern Exposures Zinfandel / 2009 / Napa / $$$** A small amount of Viognier gives this refined Zinfandel a floral note.

SWANSON VINEYARDS

Napa's Swanson Vineyards began when Clarke Swanson, Jr., purchased 100 acres near Oakville in 1985. Swanson—an heir to his family's frozen-dinner fortune—then enlisted renowned grape guru André Tchelistcheff, who advised planting Merlot. That variety remains Swanson's flagship, though its small-lot wines—especially Cabernet—can outshine its leading grape.

● Swanson Vineyards Instant Napa Cabernet Sauvignon / 2009 / Napa Valley / $$$ For fans of soft, warmly fruity Cabernets, Swanson's bold new red hits the mark.

● Swanson Vineyards Merlot / 2008 / Oakville / $$$ Winemaker Chris Phelps adds a bit of Petit Verdot, a very fragrant Bordeaux varietal, to boost this luscious red's aromas.

TABLAS CREEK VINEYARD

Launched in 1987, this joint venture between importer Robert Haas and the Perrin family of Châteauneuf-du-Pape is arguably California's most influential producer of Rhône-style wines. By importing vine cuttings from the Perrin's Château de Beaucastel and selling them to other local growers, Tablas Creek contributed to an explosion of Rhône-style wines on the Central Coast.

○ Côtes de Tablas Blanc / 2010 / Paso Robles / $$
A minerally, honeydew-scented blend of white Rhône grapes.

● Patelin de Tablas / 2010 / Paso Robles / $$
The first vintage of this new entry-level red offers ripe, bright and juicy berry flavors for an affordable price.

● Tablas Creek Esprit de Beaucastel / 2009 / Paso Robles / $$$
A top Rhône blend, this is based on spicy, dark Mourvèdre.

TALLEY VINEYARDS

Brian Talley's family has been farming the Central Coast since 1948, although his kin's crop originally was chiefly vegetables, not grapes. Yet Talley's deep familiarity with the local *terroir* is one secret to his winery's success. His thrilling Pinots and Chardonnays have made Talley Vineyards a Central Coast superstar.

○ Talley Vineyards Rincon Vineyard Chardonnay / 2010 / Arroyo Grande Valley / $$$ There's a sneaky power to this masterful Chardonnay, which unfurls rich peach and caramel flavors.

● Talley Vineyards Rosemary's Vineyard Pinot Noir / 2010 / Arroyo Grande Valley / $$$$ Talley made just 18 barrels of this alluring, plum- and blackberry-infused cuvée.

TREFETHEN FAMILY VINEYARDS

The Trefethen family can claim the largest contiguous single-owner vineyard in Napa Valley—a sprawling 500-plus acres in the Oak Knoll District. The subzone's cooler temperatures mean that a wider range of grape varieties thrive here, and Trefethen succeeds at everything from Cabernet Sauvignon to Riesling. Best of all, its substantial acreage means higher volumes and wines that are relatively easy to find.

○ **Trefethen Family Vineyards Dry Riesling / 2011 / Oak Knoll District of Napa Valley / $$** Unusually cold weather heightened the vibrancy of intense green apple and lime tones in this beautifully made Riesling.

○ **Trefethen Family Vineyards Harmony Chardonnay / 2009 / Oak Knoll District of Napa Valley / $$$** A relatively mild growing season preserved the freshness of this stylish, judiciously oaked Chardonnay.

TRINCHERO NAPA VALLEY

Bob Trinchero jump-started the blush wine megatrend of the 1980s by inventing White Zinfandel for his family's Sutter Home brand. The Trinchero's Napa Valley venture shifts gears entirely: By purchasing prime Napa Valley vineyards and hiring winemaker Mario Monticelli, they've created a spare-no-expense estate winery responsible for head-turning Cabernets, Merlots and other Bordeaux varietals.

○ **Trinchero Napa Valley Mary's Vineyard Sauvignon Blanc / 2011 / Napa Valley / $$** Made in a lush, exotic style, this white gets extra richness from a dollop of Sémillon.

● **Trinchero Napa Valley Mario's Vineyard Cabernet Sauvignon / 2008 / St. Helena / $$$** Named for Bob Trinchero's father, this heady, concentrated red is made with grapes from vineyards surrounding the winery.

TRUCHARD VINEYARDS

Though Carneros is better known now for Burgundian varietals such as Chardonnay and Pinot Noir, Truchard Vineyards—one of the region's original labels—proves that grapes like Cabernet Sauvignon and Syrah can succeed here, too. Tony and Jo Ann Truchard started out with 20 acres in 1974; today they farm 270, keeping a portion of the grapes to craft their own wines and selling off the rest.

- ○ **Truchard Vineyards Estate Chardonnay** / 2010 / Carneros / $$
  Loads of crisp, bright acidity keep this exuberant Chardonnay
  refreshingly vibrant.
- ● **Truchard Vineyards Estate Pinot Noir** / 2009 / Carneros / $$
  Seven different clones of Pinot Noir go into this lithe red,
  which is defined by wild strawberries and herbs.
- ● **Truchard Vineyards Estate Cabernet Sauvignon** / 2009 /
  Carneros / $$$ The antithesis of a hulking Napa Cabernet,
  this medium-weight offering has zesty, food-friendly red
  currant and herb flavors.

WALTER HANSEL WINERY

Reasonably priced Russian River Pinot Noir and Chardonnay
might seem like a contradiction, but that's only because wine-
maker Stephen Hansel's wines aren't better known. While not
cheap, his fragrant, expressive cuvées sell for significantly less
than is typical for wines that are crafted so luxuriously (hand-
picked grapes, French oak barrels). Their style is inspired by
Burgundy, which means that fans of buttery, sweetly ripe wines
should look elsewhere.

- ○ **Walter Hansel Estate Chardonnay** / 2010 / Russian River
  Valley / $$ Hansel's vineyard-specific wines often sell out soon
  after release, so look for his slightly more available Estate
  Pinot Noir and Chardonnay.

WENTE VINEYARDS

One of California's oldest family-owned wineries, Wente is the
most important winery in the Livermore Valley, located an
hour's drive east of San Francisco. C.H. Wente founded the
estate in 1883, and its wines are now produced by his fifth-
generation descendant, winemaker Karl Wente. Forays into
cooler climates like Monterey, and ambitious new cuvées such
as the Nth Degree and Small Lot tiers, are gaining new fans for
this under-the-radar producer.

- ○ **Morning Fog Chardonnay** / 2010 / Livermore Valley / $
  Chilly fog and winds from San Francisco Bay are the reason
  this affordable, pear-driven white is so vibrant.
- ○ **Nth Degree Chardonnay** / 2010 / Livermore Valley / $$$
  Packed with compelling quince and spice tones, Wente's top
  white puts the often-overlooked Livermore Valley in an
  elegant new light.

WILLIAMS SELYEM

Only the most determined (and deep-pocketed) fans are able to get their hands on one of Williams Selyem's single-vineyard Pinot Noirs, old-vine Zinfandels or Chardonnays—these coveted bottlings show up mostly at auction or on posh restaurants' wine lists. Happily, the Russian River Valley estate's winemaker, Bob Cabral, produces five more-accessible, multivineyard wines.

○ **Williams Selyem Unoaked Chardonnay / 2010 / Russian River Valley / $$$** Fermentation in stainless steel emphasizes this Chardonnay's invigorating lime and nectarine notes.

● **Williams Selyem Forchini Vineyard South Knoll Zinfandel / 2009 / Russian River Valley / $$$** Hundred-year-old vines give extra concentration to ripe blackberry and plum flavors.

● **Williams Selyem Pinot Noir / 2010 / Russian River Valley / $$$** A noteworthy success from a challenging growing season, this Pinot is perfumed and spicy.

WOODENHEAD VINTNERS

Thoughtfully made small-production North Coast Pinot and Zinfandel are the focus at Nick Stez and Zina Bower's Woodenhead Vintners. Stetz's soulful wines reflect many of the light-handed Burgundian techniques he picked up while working as assistant winemaker to Burt Williams of Williams Selyem.

○ **Woodenhead French Colombard / 2010 / Russian River Valley / $$** This bracing white has lingering mineral tones.

● **Woodenhead Buena Tierra Vineyard Original Planting Pinot Noir / 2009 / Russian River Valley / $$$** Pomegranate notes and spicy floral nuances mark this fresh, light-bodied red.

● **Woodenhead Martinelli Road Vineyard Old Vine Zinfandel / 2007 / Russian River Valley / $$$** Well-balanced, despite its extreme ripeness, with plenty of spice and dried-berry layers.

OREGON

CLAIM TO FAME
That Oregon, with its wet weather and short summers, could ever be famous for wine was in doubt until as recently as 30 years ago, when it began to receive international acclaim. Today the damp Willamette Valley is the epicenter of a world-class wine region famous for some of the country's best Pinot Noir.

REGIONS TO KNOW

COLUMBIA GORGE & WALLA WALLA VALLEY Northeast of the Willamette Valley, these regions run along the Washington State border. The Walla Walla Valley AVA lies mostly in Washington, but, like the Columbia Gorge, it straddles the border into Oregon. Warm, dry summers mean that reds reign: Cabernet is the flagship grape; Syrah and Merlot are made in lesser volumes.

ROGUE & APPLEGATE VALLEYS Southern Oregon's Rogue Valley is actually three distinct valleys, one of which, Applegate Valley, is its own AVA. It specializes in Bordeaux and Rhône varieties.

UMPQUA Warmer than Willamette, cooler than Rogue, Umpqua produces small amounts of Pinots Noir and Gris, among others.

WILLAMETTE VALLEY Stretching from Portland in the north to Eugene in the south, this broad valley is home to most of the state's population as well as most of its wine. Protected against Pacific winds by the Coast Ranges, it's divided into six subregions: Chehalem Mountains, Dundee Hills, Eola-Amity Hills, McMinnville, Ribbon Ridge and the Yamhill-Carlton District.

☙ KEY GRAPES: WHITE

CHARDONNAY Not much Chardonnay is crushed in Oregon compared with Pinot Noir and Pinot Gris, but what does get made tends to be good, with subtle fruit flavors and lively acidity.

PINOT GRIS Oregon's principal white grape is Pinot Gris, and though it ranges in style, its typical expression in the state is generous and full-bodied with refreshing acidity.

RIESLING & PINOT BLANC Aromatic whites such as these are making headway, with a handful of small vintners achieving notable success in the Willamette Valley.

☙ KEY GRAPES: RED

PINOT NOIR Representing more than half of the state's wine production, Oregon Pinot Noir is silky smooth, with delicate berry flavors and firm acidity. Somewhere between the earthy, astringent style of Burgundy and the robust offerings characteristic of California, Oregon Pinot Noir can be outstanding.

Producers/
Oregon

ADELSHEIM VINEYARD

Adelsheim's small-lot Pinots helped pioneer Willamette Valley's fine-wine industry and remain among its best examples. David and Ginny Adelsheim founded their small estate in 1972; though David passed winemaking duties to Dave Paige 11 years ago, the focus on high-quality estate wines remains constant. The whites are silky, vibrant and more affordable than the reds.

○ **Adelsheim Auxerrois / 2010 / Ribbon Ridge / $$**
A pleasantly lean white made from Alsace's Auxerrois grape.

● **Adelsheim Elizabeth's Reserve Pinot Noir / 2009 / Willamette Valley / $$$** Blending a selection of the best barrels of the vintage created this graceful, ageworthy Pinot.

ARGYLE WINERY

Vintner Rollin Soles is as skilled at crafting seductive still wines as he is at making elegant sparkling cuvées (see p. 293). Their common denominator is superb Pinot Noir and Chardonnay grapes from 280 acres of estate-owned vines in the Dundee and Eola hills. Argyle is responsible for some of Oregon's finest wines; the Nuthouse Pinot Noir is among its most coveted bottlings.

● **Argyle Nuthouse Pinot Noir / 2009 / Eola-Amity Hills / $$$**
Soles made just 100 barrels of this excellent, savory red.

A TO Z WINEWORKS

A to Z Wineworks became Oregon's biggest wine producer just a few years after launching in 2002 (it's still one of the biggest). Its secret is simple: Along with winemaker Michael Davies, founders Bill and Deb Hatcher, Cheryl Francis and Sam Tannahill are master blenders. They source prime fruit from over 60 vineyards in order to achieve seamlessly balanced wines.

○ **A to Z Wineworks Pinot Gris / 2010 / Oregon / $**
This reliable bargain offers a fresh, aromatic take on Pinot Gris, with apricot and ginger notes.

● **A to Z Wineworks Pinot Noir / 2010 / Oregon / $$**
Zesty currant and spice tones reflect the cool 2010 season.

BEAUX FRÈRES

Wine critic Robert Parker and his brother-in-law Michael Etzel purchased a former pig farm in Willamette Valley in the late 1980s and converted it to a biodynamically farmed vineyard. Since then, Beaux Frères has been acknowledged as one of Oregon's finest Pinot Noir producers. Etzel makes just three pricey Pinots; they offer loads of smooth purity and polish.

● **Beaux Frères Pinot Noir** / 2010 / Willamette Valley / $$$
This lush, huckleberry-driven Pinot Noir is delicious now.

● **Beaux Frères The Beaux Frères Vineyard Pinot Noir** / 2010 / Ribbon Ridge / $$$$ This perfumed red is seductive and sleek, highlighted by upfront red fruit and spice.

BENTON-LANE WINERY

It may be Benton-Lane's eye-catching postage-stamp labels that first attract shoppers, but it's the juicy, well-made wines that keep them coming back. The winery's basic Willamette Pinot became popular in the 1990s as a go-to value red, and it still is. At the high end, its top Pinot is among Oregon's greatest wines.

○ **Benton-Lane Chardonnay** / 2009 / Willamette Valley / $$
An especially rich, creamy white from the warm 2009 vintage.

○ **Benton-Lane Pinot Gris** / 2010 / Willamette Valley / $$
Fermenting this racy white in tanks, not barrels, keeps its lime and green apple flavors fresh and pure.

● **Benton-Lane Pinot Noir** / 2010 / Willamette Valley / $$
Made with seven different Pinot clones, this estate-grown wine shows an energetic, herbal edge.

BERGSTRÖM WINES

This Willamette Valley winery has a short but impressive track record. Founded by Portland surgeon John Bergström and his wife, Karen, in 1999, Bergström is helmed by son Josh, who studied winemaking (and met his future wife) in Burgundy. Biodynamically farmed vineyards yield cool-climate wines— mainly Pinot Noir—of remarkable poise and depth.

○ **Bergström Sigrid Chardonnay** / 2010 / Willamette Valley / $$$$ Perfect for fans of buttery Chardonnay, this voluptuous white is named for the family's Swedish grandmother.

● **Bergström de Lancellotti Vineyard Pinot Noir** / 2010 / Chehalem Mountains / $$$$ From a sandy-soil vineyard with deep-rooted vines comes this especially elegant, earthy red.

BETHEL HEIGHTS VINEYARD

In 1977, twin brothers Ted and Terry Casteel and their partners, Patricia Dudley and Marilyn Webb, ditched their jobs to get back to the land. Specifically, to 75 acres in Eola-Amity Hills, a marine-influenced slice of Willamette Valley that's prime Pinot territory. It was the right move: Today family-owned Bethel Heights remains one of Oregon's most respected producers.

○ **Bethel Heights Vineyard Estate Grown Chardonnay / 2010 / Eola-Amity Hills / $$** This taut white has a zesty, green apple intensity reminiscent of some French Chardonnays.

● **Bethel Heights Vineyard Pinot Noir / 2010 / Willamette Valley / $$** Winemaker Ben Casteel (son of Terry) inherited his father's talent with Pinot Noir, as this succulent, raspberry-rich bottling attests.

DOMAINE SERENE

Domaine Serene lays claim to a collection of top Dundee Hills vineyards and produces some of America's most remarkable Pinot Noirs. Among these is the bold, rich Evenstad Reserve, named for owners Ken and Grace Evenstad. Its legacy is now in the hands of a new winemaker, Erik Kramer, who follows in the footsteps of his supertalented predecessor, Tony Rynders.

● **Domaine Serene Yamhill Cuvée Pinot Noir / 2009 / Willamette Valley / $$$** The winery's most affordable Pinot is still pricey but delivers impressive layers of plush, spicy fruit.

● **Domaine Serene Evenstad Reserve Pinot Noir / 2008 / Willamette Valley / $$$$** A top wine from a great year, this standout bottling is a blend of the vintage's finest barrels.

ELK COVE VINEYARDS

Over the past two decades, family-owned Elk Cove has steadily improved, becoming one of Oregon's finest producers. Winemaker Adam Campbell took the reins from his parents in 1995, and crafts precise, full-flavored Willamette Valley Pinot and a few whites. Elk Cove's single-vineyard and reserve Pinot Noirs are trophy wines worth the hunt—and the price.

○ **Elk Cove Vineyards Pinot Gris / 2010 / Willamette Valley / $$** Campbell's deft touch with Alsace varietals shines in this vivacious, appley white.

● **Elk Cove Vineyards Pinot Noir / 2009 / Willamette Valley / $$** Fantastically drinkable, with juicy, ripe raspberry fruit.

ERATH

Winemaker Gary Horner (formerly with Bethel Heights and Benton-Lane) continues the work that Dick Erath began at this venerable Oregon winery. Washington's Ste. Michelle Wine Estates purchased the property in 2006, but the wines haven't slipped a bit, still exhibiting an elegant style that's a welcome alternative to California's plumper Pinots.

● **Erath Pinot Noir / 2009 / Oregon / $$**
This widely available red delivers supple, straightforward berry and spice flavors at an approachable price.

KING ESTATE WINERY

The estate, founded by the King family in 1991, is known for two things: terrific Pinot Gris and a vast organic ranch, located southwest of Eugene, which includes gardens, orchards, a restaurant and wetlands. The brand's top wines are the estate-grown offerings made under the Domaine label. The Acrobat tier offers super value; the Signature wines are a step up.

> **WINE INTEL**
> Eco-friendly King Estate is reaping more than grapes from its hills: It's devoting over four acres to what is now the Pacific Northwest's largest solar array at a winery.

○ **Acrobat Pinot Gris by King Estate / 2010 / Oregon / $** This bright, tangerine-inflected white is a consistent steal.

● **King Estate Domaine Pinot Noir / 2008 / Oregon / $$$**
A serious, polished Pinot that clearly demonstrates wine-maker Jeff Kandarian's talent for crafting ageworthy reds.

PONZI VINEYARDS

In the early 1970s, Dick Ponzi helped jump-start Oregon's wine industry when he founded Ponzi Vineyards. His winemaker daughter Luisa follows in his footsteps, making Pinot Noir, Chardonnay and Pinot Gris from some of the state's oldest vines, as well as wines from obscure grapes like Dolcetto and Arneis.

○ **Ponzi Vineyards Pinot Gris / 2010 / Willamette Valley / $**
Ponzi was one of Oregon's first producers to focus on Pinot Gris; its expertise shows in this tangy, peachy example.

○ **Ponzi Vineyards Reserve Chardonnay / 2008 / Willamette Valley / $$** The fresh, minerally finish on this rich white imparts terrific balance and freshness.

● **Ponzi Vineyards Pinot Noir / 2009 / Willamette Valley / $$$**
This suave red delivers complexity along with bold fruit.

SCOTT PAUL WINES

Martha and Scott Paul Wright are so passionate about Pinot Noir that, after their first vintage of it in 1999 (supervised by Pinot guru Greg LaFollette), they moved from Sonoma to Oregon to create their own boutique brand (and even started importing some wines from Burgundy). They hired Eyrie Vineyards alum Kelley Fox to help craft their Burgundy-inspired wines.

● **Scott Paul La Paulée Pinot Noir / 2009 / Dundee Hills / $$$** Filigreed with notes of wild berries and sweet spice, this graceful red is named after a Burgundy harvest feast.

● **Scott Paul Audrey Pinot Noir / 2010 / Dundee Hills / $$$$** A seamless, extraordinary Pinot that recalls Burgundy's delicate Chambolle-Musigny wines.

ST. INNOCENT WINERY

A former physician's assistant in pediatrics, vintner Mark Vlossak takes a meticulous approach to winemaking, and it pays off. Vlossak's small-lot Pinots, which come from an all-star collection of vineyards across the Willamette Valley, are among the most sought-after in Oregon. Small amounts of Pinot Gris, Pinot Blanc and Chardonnay round out the compelling portfolio.

● **St. Innocent Villages Cuvée Pinot Noir / 2010 / Willamette Valley / $$** Vlossak makes this introductory, multivineyard blend from young and mature vines; it's tangy and elegant.

● **St. Innocent Temperance Hill Vineyard Pinot Noir / 2009 / Eola-Amity Hills / $$$** Temperance Hill's volcanic soil gives impressive structure to this lush, blackberry-driven cuvée.

WILLAMETTE VALLEY VINEYARDS

Founder and native Oregonian Jim Bernau bought a run-down plum orchard in 1983, cleared it himself and planted vines. Bernau eventually built Willamette Valley Vineyards into one of the state's largest producers, thanks also to late winemaker Forrest Klaffke, who made crafting terrific Pinot across the price spectrum look easy—as does current winemaker Don Crank III.

● **Willamette Valley Vineyards Elton Pinot Noir / 2009 / Eola-Amity Hills / $$$** Jim Bernau bottles fruit from the Elton vineyard on its own to showcase its unusual depth of flavor.

● **Willamette Valley Vineyards Signature Cuvée / 2009 / Willamette Valley / $$$** Blending prime barrels results in this velvety, cherry-rich cuvée of beautiful balance.

WASHINGTON STATE

CLAIM TO FAME

Washington is best known for its vast output of well-made and affordable red and white wines—it's the second-largest premium wine–producing state in the U.S. But it has also been building a reputation for complex reds that rival top California bottlings, often at half the price. The industry is growing, too: In the past decade, Washington has more than tripled its number of wineries and approved six new AVAs.

REGIONS TO KNOW

COLUMBIA GORGE Stunningly scenic Columbia Gorge isn't better known for its wine in part because its output is hard to define. Encompassing both sides of the Columbia River east of Vancouver, the region is warmer and drier inland and cool and rainy toward the west: No wonder so many grape varieties are planted here.

COLUMBIA VALLEY This huge southeastern region covers a third of the state and is responsible for 99 percent of its wine grapes; most other Washington AVAs (including Horse Heaven Hills and Walla Walla and Yakima valleys) are Columbia Valley subregions. Some 6,800 vineyard acres exist outside designated subzones.

HORSE HEAVEN HILLS Bordeaux-style reds and earthy, elegant Syrah are the calling cards of this southeast district, one of the state's premier regions.

LAKE CHELAN Approved in 2009, this newish AVA is defined by the influence of its eponymous 55-mile-long glacial lake in north-central Washington. Cool-climate varieties such as Riesling and Pinot Gris show terrific promise here.

WAHLUKE SLOPE Warm and dry, this up-and-coming district in south-central Washington is planted chiefly with heat-loving red grapes like Merlot, Cabernet and Syrah.

WALLA WALLA VALLEY Many of Washington's finest Cabernets come from this remote southeast region, which extends into Oregon. Merlot, Syrah and Chardonnay excel here as well.

YAKIMA VALLEY Established in 1983, Yakima Valley is the state's oldest AVA and home to most of its oldest grapevines and many prestigious vineyards. Important subregions include Red Mountain, Rattlesnake Hills and Snipes Mountain.

KEY GRAPES: WHITE

CHARDONNAY Washington Chardonnays are typically lighter and more refreshing than California versions, thanks to a generally cooler growing season.

PINOT GRIS This white variety is on the rise—nearly tripling in recent production. Most of it goes into large-production tank-aged wines made in a fresh, appley style.

RIESLING Washington growers produce slightly more Riesling—the No. 1 white grape in the state—than they do Cabernet. Cool nights allow the grapes to be crafted into a range of styles from dry to sweet.

SAUVIGNON BLANC, VIOGNIER & GEWÜRZTRAMINER These aromatic white varieties do well in Washington's northern climate and represent a little more than 10 percent of the state's white grape production. Gewürztraminer tends to yield ripe and floral wines, usually in an off-dry style.

KEY GRAPES: RED

CABERNET SAUVIGNON Washington's most planted red grape variety makes terrific wines up and down the price scale, with high-end cuvées competing with the world's best. Smooth-textured and bold, they're more restrained than California's dense, riper-style offerings.

MERLOT The state is arguably the best source in the country for delicious Merlot; its top bottles have a distinctive, spicy complexity and seductive depth.

SYRAH Columbia Valley's Walla Walla, Wahluke Slope, Rattlesnake Hills and Red Mountain subregions provide ideal conditions for Syrah. The grape yields wines with a mix of peppery, earthy flavors and a firm structure that follows a classic style of this Rhône variety.

Producers/ Washington State

ANDREW WILL

Winemaker Chris Camarda is renowned for his site-specific, Bordeaux-style red blends from some of Washington's greatest vineyards, like Ciel du Cheval (Red Mountain) and Champoux (Horse Heaven Hills). Their tiny quantities and high prices make them inaccessible to most. Fortunately, Camarda also makes a series of excellent, affordable wines that give a taste of his impressive talent.

● **Andrew Will Two Blondes Vineyard** / 2009 / Yakima Valley / $$$ A wonderfully complex, black cherry–inflected Bordeaux-style blend with terrific concentration and balance—it easily ranks as one of Washington's best.

● **Sorella** / 2009 / Horse Heaven Hills / $$$$ This outstanding Cabernet Sauvignon–based blend showcases the winery's signature style: fine-grained tannins, gorgeous fruit and restrained power.

BUTY WINERY

Superstar consultant Zelma Long is a mentor to Buty Winery's Caleb Foster and Nina Buty Foster, which helps explain how they achieved fame in so short a time. The couple founded their small Walla Walla winery in 2000, buying grapes from top vineyards while planting their own organically farmed site, Rockgarden. Look for their outstanding bottlings under both Buty and Beast labels.

○ **Buty Sémillon-Sauvignon-Muscadelle** / 2010 / Columbia Valley / $$ This attractive three-grape white blend features floral and citrus aromas followed by a plump body and brisk, lemon-infused acidity.

○ **Buty Conner Lee Vineyard Chardonnay** / 2010 / Columbia Valley / $$$ From a cool corner of a warm region, this lush, apricot-rich white is balanced by fresh acidity.

● **Buty Rediviva of the Stones** / 2009 / Walla Walla Valley / $$$ Expressive violet and black currant flavors have a kind of weightless density in this Syrah-Cabernet blend.

CADENCE

Gaye McNutt and Ben Smith make Cadence's stellar Bordeaux-style reds in a warehouse in a less-than-charming industrial Seattle business park. Their grapes, though, come from the Red Mountain region, including famous sites such as Ciel du Cheval, Tapteil and Klipsun, plus their own Cara Mia vineyard.

● **Cadence Coda / 2009 / Red Mountain / $$**
This juicy, tannic four-variety blend begs for hearty fare.

● **Cadence Camerata Cara Mia Vineyard / 2008 / Red Mountain / $$$** There's a savory, mineral and herb quality to this graceful blend that recalls Bordeaux's reds.

CHATEAU STE. MICHELLE

Few wineries combine scale and quality as successfully as Chateau Ste. Michelle. Head winemaker Bob Bertheau oversees the two-million-case annual production, which includes some of the most reliably high-quality value wines in the U.S. as well as top offerings such as the Eroica, Ethos and single-vineyard cuvées.

○ **Chateau Ste. Michelle Dry Riesling / 2010 / Columbia Valley / $** A fresh, light-bodied white at a bargain price, with tingly floral and apricot flavors.

● **Chateau Ste. Michelle Canoe Ridge Estate Cabernet Sauvignon / 2009 / Horse Heaven Hills / $$** This blackberry-driven red comes from a region well suited to Cabernet.

● **Chateau Ste. Michelle Meritage / 2008 / Columbia Valley / $$$** Blending five Bordeaux varieties creates a plush, layered red.

COLUMBIA CREST

Winemaker Ray Einberger worked at Napa's famous Opus One winery and at Bordeaux's Château Mouton Rothschild before joining this value-oriented producer in 1993. His luxury-wine experience set high standards for Columbia Crest, which he officially passed on to protégé Juan Muñoz Oca in 2011.

● **Columbia Crest Grand Estates Cabernet Sauvignon / 2009 / Columbia Valley / $** A wine as easy to swallow as its price, with lots of ripe, soft red cherry and plum notes.

● **Columbia Crest H3 Merlot / 2009 / Horse Heaven Hills / $** A supple, round red from a longtime Merlot expert.

DELILLE CELLARS

This smallish Woodinville-based winery raised the bar in Washington in the late 1990s with head-turning, ripe and ageworthy Bordeaux-style blends. Francophile winemaker Chris Upchurch has headed DeLille's cellar for 20 years, producing impeccably crafted Rhône- and Bordeaux-inspired wines under the Doyenne, Chaleur Estate, D2 and younger Grand Ciel labels.

○ **DeLille Cellars Chaleur Estate Blanc / 2010 / Columbia Valley / $$$** DeLille-labeled wines are Bordeaux-style blends, like this complex, spicy white.

● **Doyenne Aix / 2009 / Red Mountain / $$$**
A fantastically plush, spicy and energetic Syrah-Cab blend.

GRAMERCY CELLARS

A FOOD & WINE American Wine Award winner in 2010 for Best New Winery, Gramercy Cellars caused a sensation with its first 2007 Syrahs. Co-founder (along with his wife) and master sommelier Greg Harrington makes the kinds of wines he likes to drink: savory, refined reds that boast modest alcohol, bright acidity and subtle oak.

● **Gramercy Cellars Inigo Montoya Tempranillo / 2009 / Walla Walla Valley / $$$** Good U.S. Tempranillo is rare, which makes this fabulous, tobacco-infused wine worth seeking out.

● **Gramercy Cellars Syrah / 2009 / Walla Walla Valley / $$$**
This flamboyant Syrah is brimming with violet and bacon notes.

● **Gramercy Cellars The Third Man / 2009 / Columbia Valley / $$$** A hedonistic but deftly balanced Rhône-style blend loaded with seductive black cherry fruit and sweet spice.

HEDGES FAMILY ESTATE

The Hedges family has long promoted the Red Mountain district, where Tom and Anne-Marie Hedges broke ground in 1989. Cabernet and Merlot shine in the winery's two estate-grown reds. Prime grapes sourced from farther afield go into quirky CMS blends and minimalist Independent Producers offerings.

● **Independent Producers Bacchus Vineyard La Bourgeoisie / 2010 / Columbia Valley / $** Few Merlots at this price deliver as much character as this succulent, olive-infused bottling.

● **Descendants Liégeois Dupont Cuvée Marcel Dupont / 2010 / Red Mountain / $$** A stunning, minerally Syrah named for the French forebears of Anne-Marie Hedges (née Liégeois).

THE HOGUE CELLARS

Started in 1979 with fewer than six acres of Riesling vines planted on the Hogue family's Columbia Valley farm, Hogue was one of the state's largest producers by the time brothers Mike and Gary Hogue sold it to wine giant Constellation in 2001. The brand specializes in affordable, aromatic whites (with Riesling still the star), plus well-made Cabernet, Merlot and Syrah.

○ **Hogue Gewürztraminer / 2010 / Columbia Valley / $**
Exactly what an affordable Gewürztraminer should be: fresh, delicate and packed with flowers and fruit.

● **The Hogue Cellars Reserve Cabernet Sauvignon / 2007 / Wahluke Slope / $$** The warm climate in the Wahluke Slope gives this layered red extra richness.

K VINTNERS/CHARLES SMITH WINES

Rock-band manager turned vintner Charles Smith (FOOD & WINE's Winemaker of the Year in 2009) earned instant fame with his Syrah-based K reds. Those high-scoring wines are hard to find and expensive, so fans have been jubilant over Smith's introduction of affordable labels like Kung Fu Girl Riesling, Boom Boom! Syrah and the Charles & Charles red and rosé.

○ **Kung Fu Girl Riesling / 2011 / Columbia Valley / $**
A terrifically fresh white that drinks beautifully on its own and pairs well with a vast range of foods.

● **King Coal / 2008 / Columbia Valley / $$$$**
The first vintage of this costly red combines Cabernet and Syrah for a decadent, concentrated blend.

MILBRANDT VINEYARDS

Brothers Butch and Jerry Milbrandt sell 90 percent of the grapes they grow on their huge Columbia Valley farm; winemaker Josh Maloney uses the remaining 10 percent to make Milbrandt's wines. His incredible fruit selection, combined with Maloney's talent, mean that Milbrandt wines succeed at every level—from everyday bottlings to the ambitious Sentinel red.

● **Milbrandt Vineyards Brothers' Blend / 2009 / Columbia Valley / $$** An oddball blend of six varieties creates a surprisingly harmonious, berry-driven red.

● **Milbrandt Vineyards The Estates Cabernet Sauvignon / 2009 / Wahluke Slope / $$** Sourcing only from estate-grown grapes gives this Cabernet impressive depth.

RARITIES & COLLECTIBLES

CAYUSE VINEYARDS Syrah maestro Christophe Baron, who comes from a family of Champagne producers in France, produces powerful, site-specific reds in Walla Walla that tend to sell out before they're even ready for release.

LEONETTI CELLAR Three decades ago, this pioneering Washington cult winery helped convince an entire industry of the state's potential for greatness. It still concentrates on Cabernet Sauvignon and Merlot (along with a small amount of Sangiovese), using fruit from vineyards in the Walla Walla region.

QUILCEDA CREEK VINTNERS This Cabernet specialist's powerful reds are ageworthy classics. That should be no surprise, given that founder and winemaker Alex Golitzen's uncle was André Tchelistcheff, a legendary figure in American winemaking.

PACIFIC RIM

The internationally known Central Coast vintner Randall Grahm designed this Riesling-focused Columbia Valley brand to complement Asian cuisine. He also helped prove Washington State's tremendous potential for the grape. Winemaker Nicolas Quillé stayed on when the Mariani family bought Pacific Rim in 2011 and continues to turn out tasty, value-priced Rieslings that range from dry to sweet.

○ **Pacific Rim Dry Riesling / 2010 / Columbia Valley / $**
The lightly sweet flavors of this straightforward, pear-flavored white make it a perfect match for spicy foods.

POWERS WINERY

Greg Powers helped his dad plant Badger Mountain Vineyard, the state's first certified organic wine grape vineyard, before starting his own Powers label. Powers makes a handful of affordably priced wines with grapes sourced from all over the Columbia Valley, but it's his stellar single-vineyard reds that stand out.

● **Powers Reserve Sheridan Vineyard Cabernet Sauvignon / 2008 / Yakima Valley / $$** A big, brooding powerhouse red, this Cabernet offers tremendous structure and flavor concentration at a reasonable price.

● **Powers Reserve Champoux Vineyard / 2008 / Horse Heaven Hills / $$$** This wine's pedigreed origins show up in every sip, with fine, dusty tannins and vibrant, pure red fruit.

SPRING VALLEY VINEYARD

In a state that produces an outsize number of stunning Merlots, Spring Valley's Uriah Merlot blend is among the best. In 1993 Dean and Shari Derby planted their first vines amid wheat fields on the family's Walla Walla farm; these south-southwest-facing slopes turned out to be ideally suited to red Bordeaux grapes. All of Spring Valley's pricey, prestigious reds are estate-grown.

- ● Spring Valley Vineyard Nina Lee / 2009 / Walla Walla Valley / $$$ A full-bodied, succulent Syrah, this ripe, silky red is named for Shari Derby's mother, a former vaudevillian.
- ● Spring Valley Vineyard Uriah / 2008 / Walla Walla Valley / $$$ Full of velvety black currant, the 10th vintage of Uriah tastes balanced, even though its alcohol clocks in at 14.9 percent.

WATERS WINERY

Guitarist Jamie Brown moved to Seattle for the grunge scene but found himself loving good wine as much as great music. Today he's one of Washington's rising stars, thanks to his graceful Rhône- and Bordeaux-style Waters reds. Wines of Substance and 21 Grams—Brown's side projects with another up-and-coming talent, Greg Harrington—have been hits, too.

- ○ Waters Prelude / 2011 / Columbia Valley / $$ Brown ages this Roussanne-Viognier blend in neutral oak to keep its succulent peach flavors fresh and creamy.
- ● Waters Loess Syrah / 2009 / Walla Walla Valley / $$$ Grapes for this polished Syrah come from a vineyard owned by the esteemed Leonetti Cellar winery.
- ● 21 Grams / 2009 / Columbia Valley / $$$$ A fine Cabernet-led classic made from the year's best barrels.

OTHER U.S. STATES

REGIONS TO KNOW

MICHIGAN Savvy Midwestern sommeliers have known for years what the rest of the country is just finding out: Michigan's Rieslings are some of the country's best (the grape accounts for about a third of the state's wine grape plantings). Top vineyards hug the shores of Lake Michigan, on the Old Mission and Leelanau peninsulas, where the lake effect moderates the northern climate. Other whites like Gewürztraminer and Pinot Gris do well, too.

NEW YORK Long Island and the rural Finger Lakes region are located at opposite ends of New York State but they both produce high-quality wine. First planted with international grape varieties nearly 40 years ago, Long Island is best known for terrific examples of Sauvignon Blanc, Chardonnay, Merlot and Cabernet Franc, which are able to succeed in the uncertain maritime climate. Upstate, while hybrid grapes are still widely grown, quality-minded vintners in the Finger Lakes region are turning out sophisticated and complex dry Rieslings, Gewürztraminers and Pinot Noirs.

THE SOUTHWEST Thanks to cooler temperatures in its high deserts, **ARIZONA** has emerged as a fine-wine producer. Full-bodied reds such as Syrah, Cabernet Sauvignon and Sangiovese are succeeding in high-altitude vineyards, and the state's number of wineries has skyrocketed to nearly 50 in recent years. **TEXAS**, too, is in the midst of a significant wine boom. It ranks fifth among the states in terms of wine production and boasts an impressive number of wineries: some 232 in all. Its highest-quality wines—mostly those made from Cabernet Sauvignon, Merlot and Chardonnay—come from the Hill Country (a central district that's larger than the state of Maryland) and the High Plains, in the Panhandle. **COLORADO**'s rugged vineyards are some of the highest in the world. Bordeaux-inspired reds have become the state's signature pour, most of them produced in the Grand Valley AVA, while the West Elks region is gaining a solid reputation for cool-climate whites and reds. The most renowned of **NEW MEXICO**'s 40-odd wineries is Gruet, a family-owned producer of Champagne-style sparkling wine in North Albuquerque. Gruet's wonderfully tasty and low-priced wines have made it an increasingly widely available and delicious alternative to the big-name sparkling brands.

VIRGINIA Centuries after settlers planted vinifera grapes in Virginia in the early 1600s, the state has become a reliable source of well-made wines, especially aromatic Viognier, minty Cabernet Franc and lush Chardonnay, in addition to wines made with the native Norton grape variety. Investment has accelerated in recent years, with small winemaker-owners joined by ambitious newcomers such as Rutger de Vink and even renowned teetotaler Donald Trump.

Producers/ Other U.S. States

BECKER VINEYARDS

Quarter horses, a corral and a 19th-century bar from a San Antonio saloon set the Lone Star vibe at this successful Texas Hill Country property. Endocrinologist turned vintner Richard Becker and his wife, Bunny, founded their winery in 1992, planting small lots of many varieties to cover their bets. Cabernet and Viognier have emerged as their biggest stars, though Becker constantly continues to experiment.

○ **Becker Vineyards Viognier** / 2011 / Texas / $
There's just enough freshness in this Viognier to balance its full, satiny peach and ginger flavors.

BOXWOOD ESTATE

Former Washington Redskins owner John Kent Cooke recruited Bordeaux consultant Stéphane Derenoncourt to help make the wines at his ambitious Virginia estate, located in Middleburg. Daughter Rachel Martin manages the 16-acre vineyard, which produces a rosé and two Bordeaux-inspired reds.

● **Boxwood Estate Topiary** / 2010 / Virginia / $$
Virginia's calling card red variety, Cabernet Franc, combines with Merlot and Malbec in this juicy, red-fruited blend.

CHATEAU GRAND TRAVERSE

Chateau Grand Traverse and its affable owners, the O'Keefe family, deserve credit for helping to bring Michigan's Old Mission Peninsula—a skinny strip of land jutting into Grand Traverse Bay—to prominence. Son Sean studied winemaking in Germany, which helps explain his sure hand with whites: Grand Traverse's outstanding Rieslings are fruit-forward and crisp.

○ **Chateau Grand Traverse Dry Riesling** / 2010 / Old Mission Peninsula / $ Bright with a hint of sweetness, this fresh, apple-inflected white offers good value.

○ **CGT Whole Cluster Riesling** / 2010 / Old Mission Peninsula / $$ Picking grapes at different ripeness levels resulted in a wine with ripe apricot notes and zippy acidity.

DR. KONSTANTIN FRANK VINIFERA WINE CELLARS

If it weren't for Dr. Konstantin Frank, the stubborn, forward-thinking creator of this Finger Lakes estate, upstate New York might still be planted exclusively with uninteresting hybrid grape varieties. His early success with noble vinifera grapes, particularly Riesling, helped transform the region into fine-wine territory. Grandson Fred runs the acclaimed winery today.

○ Dr. Konstantin Frank Dry Riesling / 2011 / Finger Lakes / $
Racy, very dry and citrusy, this consistently outclasses its price.

○ Dr. Konstantin Frank Reserve Gewürztraminer / 2010 / Finger Lakes / $$ A stunning, subtly sweet white that rivals top Alsace versions of this grape.

THE INFINITE MONKEY THEOREM

Working out of a converted Quonset hut in a downtown Denver alley, Australian-trained, English-born vintner Ben Parsons has become an ambassador for Colorado wines. Parsons buys grapes and turns them into cheeky creations such as his Black Muscat, a fizzy rosé in a single-serving can. More serious wines—like the 100th Monkey blend—offer a lot of complexity for the price.

● The Infinite Monkey Theorem Syrah / 2010 / Grand Valley, Colorado / $$ This broad, luscious Syrah comes from Palisade, where most of the state's vineyards are located.

● The Infinite Monkey Theorem 100th Monkey / 2010 / Grand Valley, Colorado / $$$ A substantial portion of Petit Verdot adds tannic heft to this brambly, full-bodied red blend.

LENZ WINERY

One of the first wineries on Long Island's North Fork, Lenz claims some of the region's oldest vines, with the earliest dating to 1978. Winemaker Eric Fry arrived 11 years later and has been turning out its graceful estate wines ever since. Fry won't sell wines until he judges them ready to drink, meaning that Lenz's reds, especially, are often a few vintages behind those of his neighbors.

○ Lenz Gewürztraminer / 2007 / North Fork of Long Island / $$
Several years of bottle age have given this perfumed, creamy white additional spice notes.

● Lenz Estate Selection Merlot / 2007 / North Fork of Long Island / $$ A lively, beautifully balanced alternative to the winery's pricier, very limited Old Vines Merlot.

Australia

Wine Region

Australia's image, when it comes to wine, is defined by inexpensive, juicy Shiraz—millions and millions of bottles of it. But Australia's reality is far more complex and fascinating. Impressive reds and whites are produced from coast to coast, from the Yarra Valley's elegant Pinot Noirs to Margaret River's ageworthy Cabernet blends. And dry, intense Australian Rieslings can compete with the best the Old World has to offer.

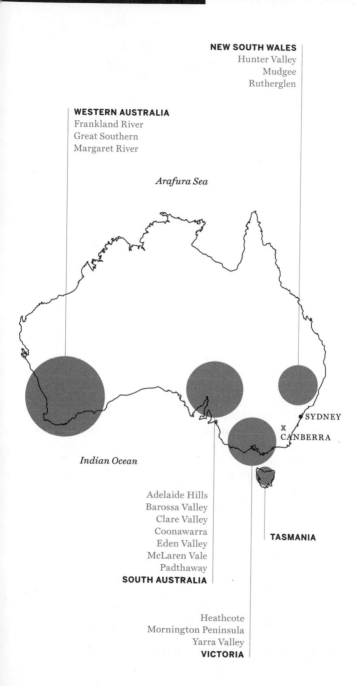

NEW SOUTH WALES
Hunter Valley
Mudgee
Rutherglen

WESTERN AUSTRALIA
Frankland River
Great Southern
Margaret River

Arafura Sea

Indian Ocean

● SYDNEY
X
CANBERRA

Adelaide Hills
Barossa Valley
Clare Valley
Coonawarra
Eden Valley
McLaren Vale
Padthaway
SOUTH AUSTRALIA

TASMANIA

Heathcote
Mornington Peninsula
Yarra Valley
VICTORIA

Australia

THERE'S MUCH MORE to Australian wine than bottles of easy-drinking Shiraz. Australia is the world's fourth-largest exporter of wine, and has more than 2,000 wineries across 65 designated growing regions in six states. South Australia is home to the country's most acclaimed wine regions, among them the Shiraz-centric Barossa Valley and McLaren Vale; the cooler Clare and Eden valleys, where Riesling thrives; and Coonawarra, synonymous with Cabernet Sauvignon. Pinot Noir excels in Victoria's Yarra Valley. Hunter Valley in New South Wales is known for its Shiraz, Sémillon, Cabernet and Chardonnay. Western Australia makes some of the country's finest, most balanced Chardonnays.

 KEY GRAPES: WHITE

CHARDONNAY The country's dominant white grape is most easily found in multiregion blends made in a full-bodied, often lightly sweet style. But aside from these industrial bottlings, Australian Chardonnays are generally fresher and less sweet these days. Look for examples from cooler regions, such as South Australia's Adelaide Hills, Victoria's Mornington Peninsula, Tasmania and especially Margaret River, which produces minerally, complex bottlings that can rival top Burgundies.

RIESLING The country's second most important high-quality white grape, Riesling here produces refreshing, dry wines with razor-sharp acidity. There are some ageworthy offerings from Clare and Eden valleys, Tasmania and Western Australia, while those from the Barossa Valley are riper and rounder.

SAUVIGNON BLANC Increasingly popular Sauvignon Blanc grows best in Australia's coastal zones, where it retains its citrusy acidity. Styles range from grassy and tart to ripe and tropical. In Margaret River, Sauvignon Blanc is commonly combined with Sémillon to create that region's Bordeaux-style blends.

SÉMILLON One reason wines made with this Bordeaux white grape are so underappreciated in the U.S. is that Australians keep most of the best bottles for themselves. Those from Hunter Valley are bright when they are young, and take on honeyed, nutty flavors as they age. Examples from Barossa are more opulent and oak-aged. Margaret River Sémillon hews to a style roughly between these extremes.

KEY GRAPES: RED

CABERNET SAUVIGNON In addition to the many straightforward, simple Cabernets made in Australia, there are a considerable number of complex, full-bodied bottlings; the finest are capable of extensive aging. Warmer areas tend to bring out berry and chocolate flavors, whereas cooler-climate places such as the Margaret River region produce more-refined versions. Tiny Coonawarra yields some of the country's greatest Cabernets.

GRENACHE & MOURVÈDRE These grapes—famous in France's Rhône Valley—thrive in many Australian regions. Grenache displays many of the same fruit-forward characteristics as Shiraz but with a lighter body, while Mourvèdre shows a smokier, spicier personality. Many vintners combine the two with Shiraz in blends labeled *GSM* (Grenache, Shiraz, Mourvèdre).

MERLOT Most Merlot in Australia is either used in blends, or to make soft, simple wines. Yet at the high end there are small amounts of firmer, herb-inflected Merlots from coastal areas like Yarra Valley and Margaret River, and denser, riper versions from warmer inland regions like Barossa.

PINOT NOIR Planted in several wine regions throughout Australia, Pinot Noir has succeeded mainly on the island of Tasmania and in Victoria's Yarra Valley and Mornington Peninsula, where cooler temperatures preserve its delicate fruit flavors, soft tannins and vibrant aromatics.

SHIRAZ Australia's leading red grape and signature wine is remarkably different from French Syrah (they are the same grape): Australian Shiraz has more explosive berry flavors as well as spice and eucalyptus notes. Grown throughout the country, Shiraz is at its best in the Barossa Valley and McLaren Vale, in South Australia; the Hunter Valley, in New South Wales; and several Victoria regions. It's typically aged in American oak (though many vintners are moving to French barrels), which complements its jammy, ripe fruit and adds to its affordability.

WINE TERMINOLOGY

Most Australian labels specify producer, region, vintage and grape. Blends tend to be named with the dominant grape listed first; sometimes only the initials are given, as in *GSM,* for Grenache, Syrah, Mourvèdre.

Producers/ Australia

BALGOWNIE ESTATE

Until local pharmacist-cum-winemaker Stuart Anderson started turning out unexpectedly stunning reds in the 1970s, Victoria's Bendigo subzone was best known as the center of a long-ago gold rush. Today grapes, not gold, count as the region's most famous product, and Anderson's label, Balgownie Estate, is still its leading winery. Now owned by brothers Des and Rod Forrester, Balgownie's portfolio is anchored by two estate reds.

● **Balgownie Estate Cabernet Sauvignon** / 2008 / Bendigo / $$
From Balgownie's original vineyard (planted in 1969), this savory, mint-edged Cabernet channels Bordeaux.

● **Balgownie Estate Shiraz** / 2008 / Bendigo / $$
This classy Shiraz shows Bendigo's potential for brilliant reds.

CHARLES MELTON WINES

Charlie Melton apprenticed under the legendary Barossa wine-maker Peter Lehmann, so it's no surprise that he shares Lehmann's fondness for dry-grown, old-vine Shiraz and Grenache. Soon after launching his own brand in 1984, Melton created Nine Popes, a Rhône-inspired blend that established Melton as a star in his own right. His bold reds have a fanatical following.

- **Charles Melton Nine Popes** / 2009 / Barossa Valley / $$$$
The name Nine Popes is a play on Châteauneuf-du-Pape, the region whose wines inspired this dense, spicy blend.

- **Charles Melton Richelieu** / 2009 / Barossa Valley / $$$$
Although it is aged in barrel for more than two years, this aromatic, full-bodied Grenache tastes lushly fruity, not oaky.

CORIOLE VINEYARDS

This McLaren Vale winery turns out brilliant old-vine Shiraz, plus a handful of worthwhile wines made from less-expected grapes. In fact, under its founder and current owner, the Lloyd family, Coriole was among Australia's first vintners to seriously tackle Sangiovese (Chianti's signature grape) and is one of the few to specialize in Chenin Blanc.

- **Coriole Sangiovese Shiraz** / 2009 / McLaren Vale / $
Sangiovese gives unusually juicy flavors to this easygoing, cherry- and herb-inflected red.

- **Coriole Estate Grown Shiraz** / 2008 / McLaren Vale / $$
Coriole has been making this wine for four decades; that experience shows in this polished, precise Shiraz.

CRAIGLEE

Encouraged by Craiglee's illustrious history (an 1872 red won an award in Vienna), Pat Carmody revived this boutique Victoria winery more than a century after its 1864 founding. Craiglee's vineyards are located near Melbourne, where they benefit from chilly winds blowing up from the Antarctic, and yield stunning cool-climate Shiraz and Chardonnay.

- ○ **Craiglee Chardonnay** / 2007 / Sunbury, Victoria / $$
Two years of bottle age plus aging on its lees have given this stylish, fresh white a nutty edge.

- **Craiglee Shiraz** / 2007 / Sunbury, Victoria / $$$
The perfect foil to many superfruity Barossa reds, this lithe Shiraz is gorgeously aromatic.

CULLEN WINES

Kevin and Diana Cullen were among the first modern vintners to take a chance on the remote Margaret River region; their 1971 vineyard helped put this western outpost on the map. Today their daughter Vanya farms the eco-friendly estate bio-dynamically. Her highly coveted reds and whites are made in extremely small quantities, which keeps the prices high.

O **Cullen Ephraim Clarke Sauvignon Blanc Semillon / 2010 / Margaret River / $$** Vanya Cullen partially ages this white in new French oak, which adds a toasty richness to its tangy citrus and apple tones.

O **Cullen Kevin John Chardonnay / 2008 / Margaret River / $$$$** Very small yields in the vineyard resulted in extra-dense flavors for this deliciously expressive Chardonnay.

D'ARENBERG

Chester Osborn's teetotaling great-grandfather founded the winery Chester now runs in McLaren Vale, where grapes are still basket-pressed and trod by foot. Don't be deceived by the wines' whimsical monikers, such as the Hermit Crab and the Laughing Magpie: The wines are seriously good, from the rock-solid d'Arenberg lineup to ambitious cuvées like Dead Arm Shiraz, one of Australia's best reds.

O **d'Arenberg The Hermit Crab Viognier Marsanne / 2010 / Adelaide Hills / $$** Rhône-style whites from Australia can be sweetly ripe, but this one is always refreshing and bright.

● **d'Arenberg The Galvo Garage / 2007 / Adelaide / $$** One way to end up with bold flavors is drought: This Cabernet-based red's concentration shows the effects of a dry year.

● **d'Arenberg The Dead Arm Shiraz / 2008 / McLaren Vale / $$$$** Made from d'Arenberg's best Shiraz barrels, this muscular red gets its name from old, "one-armed" grapevines.

GIANT STEPS/INNOCENT BYSTANDER

Jazz enthusiast and vintner Phil Sexton moved to Victoria's Yarra Valley after selling his successful Devil's Lair winery. He named his flagship venture Giant Steps, after a John Coltrane album; it also refers to his big leap into winemaking in Yarra Valley, where cooler temperatures mean riskier grape-growing. Sister label Innocent Bystander focuses on affordable wines sourced chiefly from purchased grapes.

RARITIES & COLLECTIBLES

BASS PHILLIP Australia's original cult Pinot Noir producer, Bass Phillip turns out minuscule amounts of benchmark wine from Victoria's cool south coast. Its Reserve Pinot Noir is generally considered not only to be Australia's greatest Pinot, but one of the country's greatest red wines.

BINDI WINEGROWERS The Dhillon family's Victoria estate specializes in Burgundy-inspired wines; its Chardonnays and Pinot Noirs are some of Australia's finest wines, particularly the graceful Block 5 Pinot Noir.

ROCKFORD WINES Using 19th-century equipment, Robert O'Callaghan makes legendary old-vine Barossa reds. The signature Basket Press Shiraz comes from vines that are up to 140 years old.

○ **Giant Steps Sexton Vineyard Chardonnay** / 2010 / Yarra Valley / $$$ Mild summer weather preserved the freshness in this toasty, single-vineyard Chardonnay.

● **Innocent Bystander Moscato** / 2011 / Victoria / $
A likeable, lightly frothy, slightly sweet rosé Moscato.

● **Innocent Bystander Pinot Noir** / 2010 / Victoria / $$
It's tough to make delicious Pinot at an affordable price, which is why this supple, tasty bottling is so impressive.

GLAETZER WINES

The Glaetzer family's roots in Barossa Valley viticulture date to the late 1800s, but it took Colin Glaetzer (creator of the famous E&E Black Pepper Shiraz at Barossa Valley Estate) to establish an eponymous label for the family, in 1995. Today his son Ben—an emerging winemaking star—creates its four sumptuous, small-production reds, all paragons of Barossa's brawny style.

● **Glaetzer Wallace** / 2009 / Barossa Valley / $$
Plump, fruity Grenache meets powerful Shiraz in Glaetzer's seductive entry-level red.

● **Glaetzer Amon-Ra** / 2010 / Barossa Valley / $$$$
Made from vineyards as old as 130 years, Amon-Ra fills out its formidable structure with deep, rich fruit.

● **Glaetzer Anaperenna** / 2010 / Barossa Valley / $$$$
This spicy Shiraz-Cabernet blend delivers terrific intensity and pronounced tannins that linger on the palate.

HARDYS

English immigrant Thomas Hardy planted a few acres of Grenache and Shiraz on a riverbank south of Adelaide in 1854, kick-starting the growth of the South Australia wine industry. Family-owned until 1992, Hardys is one of the world's biggest wine brands, and a source of value bottlings and some high-end cuvées. The HRB (Heritage Reserve Bin) wines reflect the company's ambitions for quality, not just quantity.

○ **Hardys The Gamble** / 2011 / South Australia / $
This blend of Chardonnay and Pinot Gris delivers an irresistible mix of pure, plump fruit and zesty acidity.

● **William Hardy Shiraz** / 2010 / South Australia / $$
Winemaker Paul Lapsley made the most of a terrific vintage with this gorgeously aromatic, seamlessly balanced red.

● **HRB D641** / 2007 / McLaren Vale & Clare Valley / $$$
Winery codes identify the HRB tier. This Shiraz starts sweet but finishes dry, with plush, intense fruit flavors and an appealing layer of cedary oak.

HENSCHKE

Although it's best known for its famous (and famously expensive) Hill of Grace Shiraz, this star Eden Valley winery offers an impressive selection of white wines and more affordable reds, too. Founded in 1868 by ancestors of current winemaker Stephen Henschke, its legacy is still in the hands of the family, including Stephen's wife, viticulturist Prue Henschke.

● **Henschke Henry's Seven** / 2009 / Barossa / $$$
Named for a Barossa pioneer, this seamless, Rhône-inspired red shows the freshness of the 2009 vintage.

● **Henschke Keyneton Euphonium** / 2008 / Barossa / $$$
This Shiraz-based blend of four red varieties stays suave and crisp despite its considerable power.

HEWITSON

Dean Hewitson is obsessed with old vines. He scours southeast Australia's long-established wine regions—Barossa Valley, Eden Valley, McLaren Vale and Adelaide Hills—for ancient, low-yielding vineyards, then uses their fruit to make a handful of superb, site-specific cuvées. These include some of Australia's best Mourvèdres as well as compelling (and reasonably priced) Shiraz, Sauvignon Blanc and Riesling.

- **Hewitson Miss Harry / 2010 / Barossa Valley / $$**
It's amazing that this silky, berry-rich blend, from historic vines, sells for such a reasonable price.
- **Hewitson Ned & Henry's Shiraz Mourvèdre / 2010 / Barossa Valley / $$** A luscious, spicy bottling that shows how perfectly Shiraz and Mourvèdre complement each other.
- **Hewitson Old Garden Mourvèdre / 2009 / Barossa Valley / $$$$** This wildly fragrant, dark chocolate- and cinnamon-inflected Barossa red comes from Mourvèdre vines planted in 1853, which makes them among the oldest in the world.

JACOB'S CREEK

Launched with a single red blend released in 1976, Jacob's Creek went on to become Australia's first international megabrand. Both its ubiquitous entry-level wines, made with grapes sourced across southeast Australia, and its reserve tiers offer lots of affordable drinking pleasure. Pricier, more complex wines, such as the Centenary Hill Shiraz, are worth seeking out.

- ○ **Jacob's Creek Moscato / 2010 / South Eastern Australia / $**
Jacob's Creek makes two Moscatos: a rosé and this lightly fizzy white, which has a kiss of sweetness.
- ○ **Jacob's Creek Reserve Chardonnay / 2009 / Adelaide Hills / $**
Using only grapes from the cooler Adelaide Hills boosts this white's freshness and appeal.
- **Jacob's Creek Reserve Shiraz / 2008 / Barossa / $**
The reserve tier's new focus on regional wines pays off incredibly well in this ripe, ambitious red.

JASPER HILL

This Heathcote winery's grapevines grow in soil that's half a billion years old, making it some of the oldest dirt on the planet. Founders Ron and Elva Laughton zeroed in on this incredible land in the 1970s for their boutique estate. Organic farming and brilliant winemaking result in wines that easily rank among Australia's very best.

- **Occam's Razor Shiraz / 2008 / Heathcote / $$$**
Emily Laughton assists her father with Jasper Hill wines and makes this intense, cherry-infused red on her own.
- **Jasper Hill Georgia's Paddock Shiraz / 2006 / Heathcote / $$$$** A few years of bottle age have opened up and softened this Shiraz's densely packed plum and spice flavors.

JIM BARRY WINES

With his wife, Nancy, Jim Barry helped pioneer modern Clare Valley winemaking in the 1960s and '70s, planting vineyards that have become some of the region's best-known sites. Among these is the Armagh Vineyard, the source of a monumentally full-bodied Shiraz that's arguably the Clare Valley's most acclaimed red wine. A handful of beautifully crafted Rieslings, the stunning Lodge Hill Shiraz and three Cabernets are highlights in the lineup.

- **Jim Barry The Cover Drive Cabernet Sauvignon / 2010 / Coonawarra / $$** Barry's least expensive Cabernet is marked by polished black currant and a smooth finish.
- **Jim Barry The Lodge Hill Shiraz / 2009 / Clare Valley / $$** This lively yet plush Shiraz hails from one of the highest vineyards in Clare Valley.

JOHN DUVAL WINES

John Duval's elegant wines defy the stereotype of supersize Aussie reds. As Penfolds's chief winemaker from 1986 to 2002, Duval was renowned for his blending expertise. At his own much smaller winery, he makes four wines each year from some of the highest-quality vineyards in the Barossa Valley: the Eligo and Entity Shirazes, plus two Rhône-inspired blends (a white and a red) under the Plexus label.

- **John Duval Wines Entity / 2009 / Barossa Valley / $$$** A brother to the prestigious Eligo bottling, this sophisticated, aromatic Shiraz is a superb introduction to Duval's restrained, seamless style.
- **John Duval Wines Eligo / 2008 / Barossa Valley / $$$$** Duval selects the best barrels of the vintage to create this rare, masterfully balanced Shiraz, one of Barossa's best reds.

KAESLER

A Swiss banker and an international trio of wine-loving colleagues teamed up with talented winemaker Reid Bosward in 1999 to start acquiring the Barossa Valley's historic Kaesler Vineyards, home to a collection of century-old vines. Combine prime vineyards and significant financial investment with Bosward's talents (before Kaesler, he worked all over the world as an in-demand consultant, including a stint in Moldova), and it's no surprise that these wines are thrilling every year.

- **Kaesler Stonehorse SGM** / 2008 / Barossa Valley / $$
  Aging in stainless steel and seasoned American and French oak keeps this Rhône blend pure, fresh and reasonably priced.
- **Kaesler Stonehorse Shiraz** / 2009 / Barossa Valley / $$
  Kaesler's two Stonehorse wines are affordable alternatives to the winery's rare old-vine reds. This dense Shiraz offers ripe tannins and deep blackberry flavors.
- **Kaesler The Bogan** / 2008 / Barossa Valley / $$$
  Barossa's extremely hot 2008 vintage brought out additional richness and spice character in the grapes from this ancient Shiraz vineyard, which was planted in 1899.

KANGARILLA ROAD

No, a kangarilla is not a mythical Australian hybrid of a kangaroo and a gorilla. Helen and Kevin O'Brien simply named their boutique winery after an actual road fronting their property in McLaren Vale. Terrifically high quality, fair prices and a balanced winemaking style make this one of the region's go-to labels; Kangarilla's Shiraz is an especially polished, well-crafted rendition of the grape.

- **Kangarilla Road Cabernet Sauvignon** / 2008 / McLaren Vale / $$ This black-fruit-dominated Cabernet is made in a rich, silky style that's typical of McLaren Vale reds.
- **Kangarilla Road Shiraz** / 2008 / McLaren Vale / $$
  Kevin O'Brien created a smooth, vibrant red by sourcing grapes from three microclimates.

KILIKANOON

This Clare Valley–based winery built its formidable reputation on its steely, mineral-rich Rieslings and polished reds. Most acclaimed are Kilikanoon's Mort's Block Riesling and a quartet of powerhouse Shirazes, from the Clare Valley (Oracle), Barossa Valley (Green's Vineyard and R Reserve) and McLaren Vale (M Reserve). Also worth looking for is Kilikanoon's affordable Killerman's Run label.

- ○ **Kilikanoon Mort's Block Watervale Riesling** / 2009 / Clare Valley / $$ Cold nights in the Watervale subregion produce zesty, pure whites, as this minerally example illustrates.
- **Kilikanoon The Lackey Shiraz** / 2008 / South Australia / $
  Blending grapes from the warm Barossa Valley and the cooler Clare Valley created this balanced, energetic Shiraz.

LANGMEIL

The Lindner family helped rescue the world's oldest surviving Shiraz vines when they purchased this neglected Barossa Valley estate in 1996, after making their name with the acclaimed St Hallett brand. The original Freedom Vineyard (planted in 1843) yields Langmeil's most famous Shiraz, though winemaker Paul Lindner excels with Grenache and Cabernet as well.

- ● **Langmeil Blacksmith Cabernet Sauvignon / 2008 / Barossa / $$** Blueberry and currant notes mark this sleek yet powerful Cab. Its name pays tribute to pioneer blacksmith Christian Auricht, who settled in the hamlet of Langmeil in the 1830s.
- ● **Langmeil Three Gardens SGM / 2010 / Barossa / $$** Vineyards (or "gardens") in three Barossa subzones provided grapes for this fruity, silky Rhône blend.

LEEUWIN ESTATE

Few names in Australian wine are as prestigious as Leeuwin Estate. This boutique winery, founded by the Horgan family in 1974, helped develop Western Australia's Margaret River wine region. Well known for its mineral-laden Chardonnays, Leeuwin has expanded its portfolio over the years, with the Siblings cuvées giving a taste of the racy, elegant house style at more wallet-friendly prices.

- ○ **Leeuwin Estate Siblings Sauvignon Blanc Semillon / 2011 / Margaret River / $$** Sémillon adds body to this zesty white's crisp citrus and herb character.
- ○ **Leeuwin Estate Art Series Chardonnay / 2008 / Margaret River / $$$$** This iconic Australian white is refined and pure, with gorgeous citrus and spicy apricot tones.
- ● **Leeuwin Estate Art Series Cabernet Sauvignon / 2006 / Margaret River / $$$** A coolly refined, intense Cabernet with the structure to age beautifully.

LINDEMAN'S

One of Australia's most enduring international successes, Lindeman's wines were exported as early as the 1850s, when former English navy surgeon Henry J. Lindeman sold Shiraz and Riesling to his homeland. Today this megawinery produces fruity, easy-drinking wines from across southeast Australia. Veteran winemaker Wayne Falkenberg provides continuity to a company that has grown in tandem with the Australian wine industry.

○ **Lindeman's Bin 90 Moscato** / 2011 / **South Eastern Australia** / **$** Fresh, floral-edged flavors make this spritzy white the perfect poolside sipper.

○ **Lindeman's Bin 65 Chardonnay** / 2010 / **South Eastern Australia** / **$** Many Chardonnays at this price are too sweet or oaky; this one is deftly balanced.

● **Lindeman's Bin 55 Shiraz-Cabernet** / 2010 / **South Eastern Australia** / **$** A straightforward, easy-drinking red blend that's priced to purchase by the case.

MITOLO

Frank Mitolo tapped up-and-coming winemaker Ben Glaetzer (see Glaetzer Wines, p. 233) in 2001 to help him turn his hobby label in McLaren Vale into a serious venture. Despite owning neither vineyards nor winery, they've had enormous success: Mitolo's red wines (four Shirazes and two Cabernets) have rocketed to the top of the region's offerings and spawned an overachieving entry-level line called Jester.

● **Mitolo Jester Cabernet Sauvignon** / 2010 / **McLaren Vale** / **$$** Winemaker Glaetzer concentrates the sweetness of this wine by drying some of the grapes before fermenting them.

● **Mitolo Jester Shiraz** / 2010 / **McLaren Vale** / **$$** This plush, blackberry-infused Shiraz is aged in barrels used previously for the pricier G.A.M. Shiraz, which gives it more subtle toasty oak flavors.

MOSS WOOD

This pioneering Margaret River estate was established in 1969 by Bill Pannell and soon earned a reputation for some of Australia's most elegant Cabernet Sauvignons. Keith Mugford, who first took over winemaking and later ownership of Moss Wood, does wonders with other grape varieties, too: Don't overlook the less famous (though just as beautifully made) Chardonnay, Sémillon and Pinot Noir bottlings.

○ **Moss Wood Ribbon Vale Vineyard Semillon Sauvignon Blanc** / 2011 / **Margaret River** / **$$** The Sémillon in this crisp 50/50 blend was picked relatively early and imparts a savory edge to its waxy, citrus profile.

● **Moss Wood Amy's** / 2010 / **Margaret River** / **$$$** Look for 2010 reds from Margaret River, like this Bordeaux-style blend—the warm summer ripened grapes perfectly.

PENFOLDS

In the early 1950s, Penfolds created a red blend that eventually became Australia's most famous wine: the Shiraz-based Penfolds Grange. Today this historic Barossa Valley producer (established in 1844) makes an array of wines across multiple price levels, employing a team of skilled winemakers led by the eminent Peter Gago.

- **Penfolds Bin 28 Kalimna Shiraz** / 2008 / **South Australia** / **$$** Although no longer exclusively sourced from the famed Kalimna Vineyard, this suave Shiraz is still delicious.

- **Penfolds RWT Shiraz** / 2008 / **Barossa Valley** / **$$$$** Penfolds makes a handful of world-class reds; this profound, French oak–aged Barossa Shiraz is one of them.

PETALUMA

Since its founding by Brian Croser in the late 1970s, Petaluma has been a great example of the wisdom of matching grape to place. The winery sources Chardonnay grapes from the cool Piccadilly Valley in the Adelaide Hills (the winery's home). Riesling comes from the Clare Valley, and Cabernet and Merlot from warmer Coonawarra. Croser is no longer involved, but winemaker Andrew Hardy stays true to the mission.

- ○ **Petaluma Hanlin Hill Riesling** / 2011 / **Clare Valley** / **$$** The Hanlin Hill vineyard yields fresh, minerally Rieslings.

- ○ **Petaluma Piccadilly Valley Chardonnay** / 2009 / **Adelaide Hills** / **$$$** A ripely styled Chardonnay for this cool region, this white is loaded with citrus and nectarine.

PETER LEHMANN WINES

Fifth-generation Barossan Peter Lehmann started his winery as a way to save Barossa growers facing bankruptcy during a massive grape glut in the 1970s. Owned since 2003 by Swiss entrepreneur Donald Hess, Peter Lehmann Wines is now one of the valley's largest producers. A focus on quality and access to some of the region's oldest vines mean that it's hard to go wrong with this brand, especially when it comes to Shiraz.

- **Peter Lehmann Clancy's Red** / 2009 / **Barossa** / **$$** Winemaker Andrew Wigan's expert blending is on display in this affordable, herb-edged Cab-Shiraz-Merlot.

- **Peter Lehmann Portrait Shiraz** / 2009 / **Barossa** / **$$** Lehmann's mint-inflected Shiraz is always a reliable bet.

PEWSEY VALE VINEYARD

Pewsey Vale wines come from one of South Australia's oldest vineyard sites, a plot 1,600 feet above the Barossa Valley floor that was first planted in 1847. Riesling thrives in this cool region, and that's what Pewsey Vale co-founder Geoffrey Parsons wisely planted in 1961. The winery's outstanding Rieslings benefit from their small and focused production.

○ Pewsey Vale The Contours Riesling / 2006 / Eden Valley / $$
Although the winery ages this famous white in bottle for five years before release, it tastes amazingly fresh.

○ Pewsey Vale Riesling / 2011 / Eden Valley / $$
Pewsey Vale's high-altitude vineyard yields mineral-rich Rieslings with vibrant, lemony acidity.

REYNELLA

John Reynell planted South Australia's first commercial wine grapes in the 1830s and crushed his first vintage in 1842, an event that marked the birth of South Australia's wine industry. While other brands soon outstripped Reynella in size, it remains a McLaren Vale stalwart. Despite modern ownership changes, Reynella's top wines maintain a steady grip on quality.

● Reynella Cabernet Sauvignon / 2007 / McLaren Vale / $$$
A few years of bottle age have mellowed the deep fruit and cedar tones in this rich Cabernet.

● Reynella Shiraz / 2009 / McLaren Vale / $$$
Reynella still uses small, old-fashioned basket presses to crush its grapes, resulting in this bold Shiraz with remarkably fine-grained tannins.

ROLF BINDER VERITAS WINERY

Siblings Rolf and Christa Binder grew up in the wine business: Their immigrant parents created Barossa's Veritas Winery, which Rolf took over and soon took to new heights with bottlings like the excellent Hanisch Shiraz. Today he makes the reds at the renamed family winery, while Christa crafts the whites.

○ Rolf Binder Highness Riesling / 2011 / Eden Valley / $$
Best known for her Sémillons, Christa Binder also makes this lovely, lime-inflected Riesling.

● Rolf Binder Halliwell Shiraz Grenache / 2007 / Barossa Valley / $$ Ripe, mellow tannins and rich cherry flavors define this Shiraz-Grenache blend.

ST HALLETT

This long-established, midsize winery is synonymous with classic Barossa Shiraz, with the rare Old Block Shiraz its most celebrated cuvée. Easier to find are the Faith and Gamekeeper's bottlings, made by veteran winemaker Stuart Blackwell. But St Hallett's white wines are the stealth choice in the portfolio: Fragrant and bright, they make a refreshing, affordable counterpoint to the powerful reds.

○ **St Hallett Riesling / 2009 / Eden Valley / $$**
Consistently terrific, this assertive Riesling offers racy lime, floral and mineral tones.

● **St Hallett Gamekeeper's Reserve Shiraz Grenache Touriga / 2009 / Barossa / $** A touch of the Portuguese Touriga Nacional grape gives this easygoing red a spicy note.

● **St Hallett Blackwell Shiraz / 2008 / Barossa / $$$**
This velvety red is the baby brother to the famous Old Block Shiraz; its hint of coconut comes from American oak.

TAHBILK

Few people get the chance to taste Tahbilk's famous 1927 Vines Marsanne and 1860 Vines Shiraz, which are made with grapes from this landmark Central Victoria winery's oldest vines. Fortunately, Tahbilk also turns out a range of compelling wines in relatively greater abundance, all from estate vineyards in the lush Nagambie Lakes subregion. Its basic Marsanne is both affordable and ageworthy, while its reds display rare elegance.

○ **Tahbilk Marsanne / 2010 / Central Victoria / $**
A portion of the grapes for this waxy, melon- and citrus-driven white comes from Tahbilk's historic 1927 vineyard, which explains its complexity.

● **Tahbilk Eric Stevens Purbrick Shiraz / 2005 / Central Victoria / $$$** Named for the grandfather of owner Alister Purbrick, this rich, silky Shiraz displays impressive balance.

VASSE FELIX

Vasse Felix was the first winery to start up production in the cool, coastal Margaret River region, and it remains one of the best. Perth cardiologist Tom Cullity planted the original vines back in 1967. Now known for its top-notch Chardonnay and Cabernet, Vasse Felix has thrived under the stewardship of its current owners, the Holmes à Court family.

○ **Vasse Felix Chardonnay / 2010 / Margaret River / $$**
This showcases the vibrant, citrusy flavors typical of the
region and melds them gracefully with toasty oak.

● **Vasse Felix Cabernet Sauvignon / 2009 / Margaret River /
$$$** Produced in a sleek, refreshing style, this minty Cabernet
is very food-friendly.

WOLF BLASS

Although Wolf Blass is more famous for red wines (its Black
Label Cabernet-Shiraz has won Australia's prestigious Jimmy
Watson Trophy four times), this megawinery also produces good-
quality Rieslings and Chardonnays. The Yellow and Gold labels
are value-oriented; Gray, Black and Platinum tiers are pricier.

○ **Wolf Blass Yellow Label Dry Riesling / 2009 / South
Australia / $** Packed with sweet-savory quince, lime and floral
tones, this reliable Riesling is a steal.

YALUMBA

At age 164, Yalumba is Australia's oldest family-
owned winery, but this Barossa-based producer is no stodgy operation. Led by dynamic
scion Robert Hill Smith, Yalumba is constantly
innovating. Its portfolio of more than 50 wines
includes many lesser-known varietals such
as Tempranillo, Viognier and Vermentino,
although Barossa stalwarts Shiraz and Cabernet Sauvignon remain the focus.

> **WINE INTEL**
> Yalumba wine-
> maker Louisa
> Rose helped create
> TempraNeo, a
> society that
> promotes Rioja's
> signature grape,
> Tempranillo, in
> Australia (Tempra
> Neo.com.au).

○ **Yalumba Y Series Viognier / 2011 / South Australia / $**
Here's a refreshing, delicately floral Viognier with pronounced
stone-fruit aromatics.

● **Yalumba Y Series Shiraz Viognier / 2010 / South Australia / $**
This deep red is enhanced by a bit of fragrant Viognier, a
marriage that works to beautiful effect.

● **Yalumba Patchwork Shiraz / 2008 / Barossa / $$**
A richly styled and fruit-forward Barossa Shiraz loaded with
inviting blackberry flavors.

New Zealand

Wine Region

New Zealand Sauvignon Blanc is one of the world's great wine success stories. The popularity of the country's signature zesty style continues to rise, and vineyard plantings have tripled in the past decade. Yet red wine production here is increasing, too, driven by world-class Pinot Noirs from Central Otago and Martinborough and outstanding Syrahs from up-and-coming districts like the North Island's Gimblett Gravels.

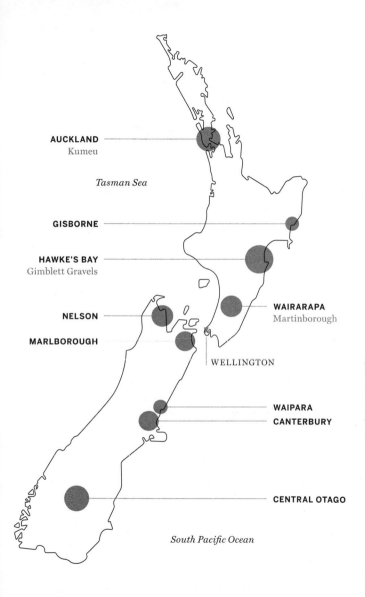

AUCKLAND
Kumeu

Tasman Sea

GISBORNE

HAWKE'S BAY
Gimblett Gravels

WAIRARAPA
Martinborough

NELSON

MARLBOROUGH

WELLINGTON

WAIPARA
CANTERBURY

CENTRAL OTAGO

South Pacific Ocean

New Zealand

U NLIKE NEIGHBORING AUSTRALIA, whose wine industry dates to the 1800s, the first modern commercial vineyards weren't planted in New Zealand until the 1970s. Today the country's winegrowing areas extend from the tip of subtropical Northland to Central Otago, one of the world's southernmost wine regions. Climate ranges from humid, rainy and temperate on the North Island to nearly continental in the South Island's Central Otago, where hot, dry summers follow cold winters.

KEY GRAPES: WHITE

CHARDONNAY A trend toward less oak aging has improved New Zealand's Chardonnays, which showcase apple and citrus. Riper, oaked versions are still produced, full of vanilla and melon notes.

PINOT GRIS, RIESLING & GEWÜRZTRAMINER Increasingly fashionable alternatives to the ubiquitous Sauvignon Blanc and Chardonnay, these Alsace grapes thrive in Waipara and Gisborne.

SAUVIGNON BLANC Few countries are as identified with a single grape as New Zealand is with Sauvignon Blanc. While the traditional style here is zingy and unoaked, with green pepper, lime and grapefruit notes, warmer vintages and a move toward fruitier wines have resulted in a wider array of styles. North Island Sauvignon Blancs tend to be riper and fruitier than those from Marlborough, the most prolific region for the grape.

🌿 KEY GRAPES: RED

CABERNET SAUVIGNON & MERLOT One of the few spots in New Zealand warm enough for these heat-loving reds is Hawke's Bay, on the North Island. Look for examples from its Gimblett Gravels subregion, where vintners make superb Bordeaux-style blends.

PINOT NOIR Vibrant acidity is a hallmark of New Zealand's most popular red. Cool regions like Marlborough offer tangy, berry-flavored versions, whereas Central Otago yields richer examples. Martinborough produces the North Island's best Pinots.

SYRAH Most of New Zealand is too cold for Syrah, but examples from Hawke's Bay's Gimblett Gravels subzone can be excellent, with seductive floral, spice and black-fruit notes.

WINE TERMINOLOGY
New Zealand labels generally list region, grape, vintage and, in some cases, vineyard name. The term *reserve* may be used to designate higher-quality wines but has no legal meaning.

Producers/ New Zealand

BRANCOTT ESTATE
With its vast vineyard holdings on the South Island and beyond, Brancott has a geographical reach that helps make it one of New Zealand's most successful producers. Brancott Vineyard is credited with being the birthplace of commercial Marlborough Sauvignon Blanc (the first plantings date back to 1975). Although Sauvignon Blanc remains the estate's signature wine, its lineup also includes a cross section of popular varietals.

○ **Brancott Estate Sauvignon Blanc / 2011 / Marlborough / $**
Winemaker Patrick Materman leaves the grape skins to steep with the juice, which boosts this grapefruity white's intensity.

CARRICK

Steve and Barbara Green gave up careers in local government and nursing, respectively, to become novice vintners in Central Otago in 1993. They bet wisely: Two decades later the fame of their estate-grown wines (now organically farmed) has grown in tandem with that of Otago itself. Though the Greens are known for their layered, polished Pinot Noirs, lately their white wines have been outshining the reds.

○ Carrick Chardonnay / 2009 / Central Otago / $$
All the grapes for this supple, judiciously oaked Chardonnay come from Carrick's prime estate vineyards in the elite Bannockburn subregion.

○ Carrick Riesling / 2010 / Central Otago / $$
A hint of sweetness balances the tangy peach and apple character of this easy-drinking Riesling.

CLOUDY BAY

This famous Marlborough winery put New Zealand on the world's wine map with its iconic citrus- and green bell pepper–inflected Sauvignon Blanc. Arguably the country's best-known wine brand, Cloudy Bay has toned down its herbaceous style in recent years. At the helm today, Nick Blampied-Lane and Tim Heath turn out vibrant Sauvignon Blancs, plus crisp Chardonnay and Pinot Noir.

○ Cloudy Bay Sauvignon Blanc / 2011 / Marlborough / $$
Very cool fermentation entirely in stainless steel highlights the vibrancy and tropical aromatics of the winery's flagship Sauvignon Blanc.

● Cloudy Bay Pinot Noir / 2009 / Marlborough / $$$
Destemming grapes before they're crushed yields a bright, fruit-forward and intense Pinot Noir underscored by earthy notes of mushroom.

CRAGGY RANGE

New Zealand's climate favors whites, but Craggy Range founder Terry Peabody is a big believer in the country's ability to produce world-class reds. Acclaimed winemaker Steve Smith cherry-picks fruit from vineyards all over New Zealand, then crafts single-vineyard bottlings from each. The resulting wines are outstanding, though Peabody confesses that Craggy Range's Martinborough Sauvignon Blanc is actually his favorite.

○ **Craggy Range Kidnappers Vineyard Chardonnay** / 2011 / Hawke's Bay / $$ A cool vineyard on Cape Kidnappers produced grapes for this lithe, citrusy, lightly oaked white.

○ **Craggy Range Te Muna Road Vineyard Sauvignon Blanc** / 2011 / Martinborough / $$ Sourced from blocks planted in stone- and limestone-rich soils, this white evokes Loire Sauvignons with its intense minerality.

● **Craggy Range Le Sol Gimblett Gravels Vineyard Syrah** / 2009 / Hawke's Bay / $$$$ This powerful, gorgeously aromatic Syrah competes in quality with top Rhône reds.

DOG POINT VINEYARD

Dog Point Vineyard's wines debuted in 2002 to much anticipation, thanks to the fame of founders James Healy and Ivan Sutherland, the talents behind New Zealand's emblematic Cloudy Bay brand. Ten years later, Dog Point wines, from the Marlborough region, have lived up to the hype, with Healy's minimalistic winemaking approach teasing out new levels of complexity from familiar grapes.

○ **Dog Point Sauvignon Blanc** / 2011 / Marlborough / $$ Most of the grapes for this vibrant, lime-inflected Sauvignon Blanc were handpicked—a relatively rare practice in the Marlborough region.

FELTON ROAD

The most famous winery in Central Otago, Felton Road helped establish New Zealand's reputation for extraordinary Pinot Noir in the 1990s with its coveted Block 3 cuvée. Skilled vintner Blair Walter uses fruit from organic and/or biodynamic estate vineyards for Felton Road's graceful wines, which also include small-lot Chardonnays and Rieslings.

● **Felton Road Bannockburn Pinot Noir** / 2010 / Central Otago / $$$ Redolent of cherries and Asian spice, this prized red comes from select lots from three vineyards.

● **Felton Road Calvert Vineyard Pinot Noir** / 2010 / Central Otago / $$$ Grapevines in the Calvert Vineyard are just a little more than a decade old but yield fruit of outstanding, mineral-rich depth.

● **Felton Road Cornish Point Pinot Noir** / 2010 / Central Otago / $$$ Cornish Point's sandy soil is known for growing aromatic Pinots, with lots of spice and dense tannins.

FROMM WINERY

On a vacation in New Zealand in the late 1980s, Swiss wine-maker Georg Fromm found the country's wines so compelling that he started his own Marlborough winery. Fromm teamed up with a fellow Swiss winemaker already working in New Zealand, Hätsch Kalberer (who is still in charge of the cellar). Together they honed the Fromm style, which combines pure, succulent fruit flavors with minerally depth.

○ **Fromm La Strada Sauvignon Blanc** / 2011 / Marlborough / $$
This crisp white's softer texture and terrific intensity come from fermenting part of the grapes in old barrels.

● **Fromm Clayvin Vineyard Pinot Noir** / 2010 / Marlborough / $$$ Named for the clay soil from which it comes, this small-lot Pinot offers a dense texture and seductive red fruit.

MARTINBOROUGH VINEYARD

Martinborough Vineyard occupies a privileged slice of Waira-rapa geography: It lies in a rain shadow created by the Tararua Range, which creates long, dry summers; and vines dig their roots into the cobblestones of an ancient river terrace, which helps give small, extra-flavorful berries. The resulting wines show unusual concentration.

○ **Martinborough Vineyard Sauvignon Blanc** / 2011 / Martinborough / $$ A single site just behind the winery provided grapes for this grassy, citrusy white.

● **Martinborough Vineyard Pinot Noir** / 2008 / Martinborough / $$$ This spicy, dark and fruity red comes from some of New Zealand's oldest Pinot Noir vines.

MATUA VALLEY

Visionaries Ross and Bill Spence were the first to plant Sauvignon Blanc in New Zealand. Today the Matua Valley winery, now run by Treasury Wine Estates, is one of the country's larger producers, with a range of mostly mid-priced wines. But its focus on quality comes across most clearly in its Estate Series offerings. The basic Sauvignon Blanc is a terrific value.

○ **Matua Valley Sauvignon Blanc** / 2011 / Marlborough / $
A vivacious, citrus- and herb-inflected white at a nice price.

○ **Matua Valley Paretai Sauvignon Blanc** / 2011 / Marlborough / $$ Selected from the best estate blocks, the Paretai features fragrant minerality and tangy citrus tones.

MT. DIFFICULTY WINES

Though planted only in 1992, Mt. Difficulty's vineyards are among Central Otago's oldest. Made by the affable Matt Dicey, who comes from a family of South African vintners, the terrific lineup includes the famous Pinot Noir–focused Mt. Difficulty label, plus the more affordable Roaring Meg bottlings.

○ **Mt. Difficulty Estate Pinot Gris / 2011 / Central Otago / $$**
Five vineyards near the town of Bannockburn contribute fruit to this creamy, peach-driven white.

● **Mt. Difficulty Roaring Meg Pinot Noir / 2010 / Central Otago / $$** A warm autumn and late harvest created an especially opulent cherry-scented red.

> **WINE INTEL**
> Wines are not the only draw at Mt. Difficulty: A new tasting room has joined a well-regarded restaurant on the estate. Both offer dramatic mountain views.

NAUTILUS ESTATE

Owned by Australia's Hill Smith family, which also owns that country's venerable Yalumba winery, Nautilus makes a fabulous Wairau Valley Pinot Noir. For its noteworthy Sauvignon Blancs, winemaker Clive Jones blends riper fruit from sites throughout Marlborough to capture a complex range of flavors, from green nuances to lusher fruit character.

○ **Nautilus Estate Sauvignon Blanc / 2011 / Marlborough / $$**
Three months of aging on its lees (spent yeast) gives depth to this refreshing Sauvignon.

● **Nautilus Estate Pinot Noir / 2010 / Marlborough / $$**
Nautilus makes its Pinot Noir in a separate winery from its white wines; the dedication shows in this succulent bottling.

PEGASUS BAY

Neurologist Ivan Donaldson moonlighted as a *garagiste* wine-maker (a French term for vintners who craft small wine lots in nontraditional wineries) for decades until 1985, when he and his wife, Christine, founded Pegasus Bay, in the Waipara Valley. Their boutique winery quickly became one of the region's finest estates. Today their son, Matthew, and his wife, Lynnette Hudson, make Pegasus Bay's seductive Pinot Noirs and elegant Rieslings.

● **Pegasus Bay Pinot Noir / 2009 / Waipara Valley / $$$**
Made from 25-year-old vines and 10 different Pinot clones, this is bright yet weighty, with vibrant black cherry flavors.

PEREGRINE WINES

Lindsay McLachlan left a business career to found this Central Otago winery with Greg Hay in 1998. Thanks to top vineyards and to former winemaker Pete Bartle, Peregrine rocketed to the top ranks of South Island producers. In 2010, replacement Nadine Cross arrived with serious Pinot Noir cred, including stints at California's DuMOL and Buena Vista.

○ **Peregrine Pinot Gris / 2011 / Central Otago / $$**
Though it tastes dry, this white possesses a touch of residual sugar that helps soften its zippy acidity.

○ **Peregrine Riesling / 2009 / Central Otago / $$**
Reminiscent of an Alsace Riesling, with lush apricot and dried apple tones.

● **Peregrine Pinot Noir / 2009 / Central Otago / $$$**
Warm, dry harvest weather in 2009 gave this Pinot its dark berry flavors and fragrant spice.

RIPPON VINEYARD & WINERY

Situated on the pristine shores of Otago's Lake Wanaka, Rippon produces graceful, richly textured wines—chiefly Pinot Noir and Riesling. Founded by Lois and the late Rolfe "Tink" Mills, the winery is now in the hands of son Nick, who polished his winemaking chops in Burgundy for four years before bringing that region's traditionalist techniques back home.

○ **Rippon Riesling / 2010 / Central Otago / $$$**
Pronounced apple, floral and petrol tones feature just a kiss of sweetness, balanced by tangy, lingering acidity.

● **Rippon Vineyard Mature Vine Pinot Noir / 2009 / Central Otago / $$$** Mature Otago vines are rare; here, they give depth to this spicy, supple red.

● **Rippon Emma's Block Mature Vine Pinot Noir / 2009 / Central Otago / $$$$** Rippon makes only one barrel of this gorgeous and sophisticated Pinot each year.

SERESIN ESTATE

Michael Seresin left New Zealand for Italy in the 1960s to pursue his dream of becoming a cinematographer. While there, he developed a love of wine that ultimately led him back home to the booming Marlborough region in the early 1990s. Though he still keeps his hand in cinema (with a Harry Potter film to his credit), it's his elegant wines that have brought him fame.

○ **Seresin Sauvignon Blanc** / 2010 / Marlborough / $$
A touch of Sémillon lends fullness to this fresh, tropical white.

● **Seresin Leah Pinot Noir** / 2009 / Marlborough / $$$
Seresin blends eight different Pinot parcels to create this
seductive red, full of heady aromatics and silky tannins.

SPY VALLEY WINES

Named for a mysterious U.S. spy station located near this Marlborough estate, Spy Valley relies primarily on its single (albeit
enormous) 360-acre vineyard. Owners Bryan and Jan Johnson,
along with winemaker Paul Bourgeois, have earned Spy Valley
a reputation for bright, richly styled whites (such as its Chardonnay, Gewürztraminer and Riesling) and aromatic reds, all
at reasonable prices.

○ **Spy Valley Riesling** / 2011 / Marlborough / $$
Picking grapes at different ripeness levels gives this succulent
Riesling a mix of citrus, apple and floral tones.

● **Spy Valley Pinot Noir** / 2010 / Marlborough / $$
Supple and satisfying, this mouth-filling cherry-scented Pinot
gets finesse from extra-gentle fermentations, with grapes
punched down by hand.

VILLA MARIA ESTATE

A son of Croatian immigrants, George Fistonich sold his car to
help fund Villa Maria's first vintage in 1962. Thanks to a knight-
hood, he's "Sir George" these days, and he runs one of New
Zealand's largest wine companies. The estate crafts four tiers,
with offerings that range from reliable, everyday wines to often
outstanding Estate Line cuvées.

○ **Villa Maria Estate Cellar Selection Dry Riesling** / 2010 /
Marlborough / $$ The cool 2010 growing season kept this
citrusy Riesling's flavors vibrant.

○ **Villa Maria Estate Cellar Selection Sauvignon Blanc** / 2011 /
Marlborough / $$ An invigorating, lime-inflected white that's
a step up from the winery's basic Private Bin Sauvignon.

● **Villa Maria Estate Cellar Selection Pinot Noir** / 2010 /
Marlborough / $$ Typical of Marlborough Pinot Noir, this
showcases fresh, sweet berry and herb tones.

Argentina

Wine Region

Argentine Malbec, characterized by dark fruit, spiciness and almost always a low price, has seduced American wine drinkers—it's been one of the fastest-growing red wines in the U.S. over the past decade. But there's more to Argentina than Malbec. Lively, aromatic Torrontés is a white wine that's well worth investigating, and the cool-climate Patagonian desert has become one of the world's newest sources of outstanding Pinot Noir.

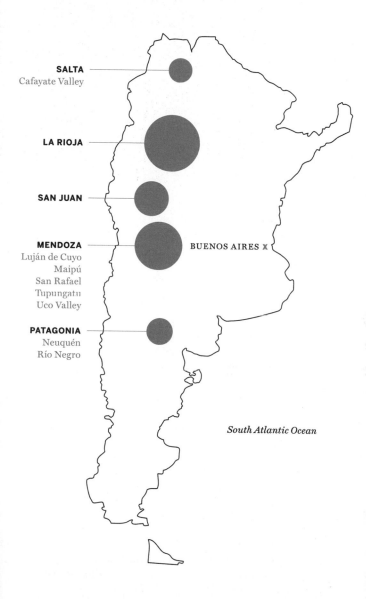

SALTA
Cafayate Valley

LA RIOJA

SAN JUAN

MENDOZA
Luján de Cuyo
Maipú
San Rafael
Tupungatu
Uco Valley

BUENOS AIRES X

PATAGONIA
Neuquén
Río Negro

South Atlantic Ocean

Argentina

FOR A PICTURE of Argentina's vineyards, envision three elements: high altitudes, bright skies and dry air. Argentina's arid climate and brilliant sunshine mean that its best wine regions cling to the foothills of the Andes, where temperatures are cooler and there is ample irrigation. More than 80 percent of the country's wine comes from the vast west-central region of Mendoza. Of its major growing areas, Maipú and Luján de Cuyo are the oldest and best known, while the newer, higher-altitude Uco Valley yields structured reds and whites. North of Mendoza, in the remote Salta Province, are some of the highest-altitude vineyards in the world; that region's Cafayate Valley is a source of refreshing white wines. La Rioja and San Juan are traditional wine regions that have been moving gradually from bulk production to high-quality winemaking. The current buzz, though, is about remote Patagonia, where the world's most southerly vineyards have begun producing truly impressive wines from Malbec and Pinot Noir.

❦ KEY GRAPES: WHITE

CHARDONNAY Widely produced Argentine Chardonnay ranges in style from crisp, lightly oaked and light-bodied to rich, full-bodied and creamy.

PINOT GRIS (PINOT GRIGIO), SÉMILLON & VIOGNIER Small amounts of these aromatic whites are finding a foothold in Argentina's cooler regions.

SAUVIGNON BLANC This crisp variety ripens easily in Argentina's sunny climate, yielding medium-bodied, melony whites.

TORRONTÉS The country's most distinctive white grape variety, Torrontés makes refreshing wines that showcase crisp and inviting citrus flavors and exuberant floral aromas.

❧ KEY GRAPES: RED

BONARDA A staple in many Argentine vineyards and historically used in blends, Bonarda is a deeply colored red grape that's now being taken more seriously by winemakers, with polished, single-variety bottlings joining rustic, cherry-inflected blends.

CABERNET SAUVIGNON Look for Cabernets from Mendoza, where sunny, arid days and cool nights result in wines packed with powerful cassis and a hint of bell pepper.

MALBEC While it yields tough, tannic wines in its native France, this grape becomes alluringly supple in Argentina, producing reds with peppery black-fruit notes.

PINOT NOIR Most of Argentina's wine regions are too warm to grow this thin-skinned grape. Patagonia has turned out to be ideal Pinot Noir territory, however, and examples from this remote region are velvety and aromatic.

SYRAH Argentinean vintners often blend Syrah with other red grapes, most often Malbec. But on its own Syrah can yield great wines full of dark, brooding fruit and spice.

WINE TERMINOLOGY

Most Argentine wine labels identify grape variety, the region where the grapes were grown, the producer's name and the vintage. Wineries are known as *bodegas;* the word *finca* refers to a particular vineyard or estate. Many wineries apply the designation *reserva* to their higher-quality bottlings, although this term has no legal meaning.

Producers/ Argentina

ACHAVAL-FERRER

Italian winemaker Roberto Cipresso and his four partners in Achaval-Ferrer are obsessed with two things: old vines and Malbec. Their winery makes three highly sought-after, single-vineyard Malbecs from ancient vines. Cipresso also crafts two more accessibly priced bottlings: Quimera, a polished red made from three sites, and a basic Mendoza Malbec.

● **Achaval-Ferrer Quimera** / 2009 / Mendoza / $$$
This smoky, dense blend gets its spice from Malbec, its lush fruit flavors from Merlot and its structure from Cabernet.

BODEGA CATENA ZAPATA

Nicolás Catena transformed the bulk-focused wine property he inherited in 1989 into one of Argentina's most successful fine-wine pioneers. Today his children help manage what has become an iconic estate. Its Mendoza wines include the Catena, Alta and Zapata tiers, plus the well-made, entry-level Alamos line.

○ **Bodega Catena Zapata Catena Chardonnay** / 2010 / Mendoza / $$ Low yields in 2010 gave this clean, richly textured Chardonnay terrific intensity.

● **Bodega Catena Zapata Catena Malbec** / 2009 / Mendoza / $$ Powerful, meaty, black-fruit flavors make this mid-priced Malbec a good value.

● **Bodega Catena Zapata Catena Alta Malbec** / 2008 / Mendoza / $$$ Alta wines are made from Catena's best vineyard blocks; this is a muscular, ageworthy example.

BODEGA CHACRA

Few wineries have as interesting a backstory as this Patagonia estate: Piero Incisa della Rochetta, Italian winemaking nobility of Sassicaia fame, was bewitched after tasting an oddity, an old-vine Pinot Noir from the Patagonia region. He visited the remote, barren spot and quickly bought and resuscitated three neglected Pinot vineyards dating from 1932, 1955 and 1967. Today, each site produces a unique, small-lot wine.

- **Barda Pinot Noir** / 2010 / Patagonia / $$
  Chacra's most affordable Pinot Noir is also its lightest, with fresh red-fruit flavors and a long finish.
- **Bodega Chacra Cinquenta y Cinco Pinot Noir** / 2009 / Patagonia / $$$$ Named for the amazing Cinquenta y Cinco vineyard planted back in 1955, this Pinot Noir offers deep layers of red berry flavors and a hint of spice.

BODEGA COLOMÉ

Swiss-born wine entrepreneur Donald Hess and winemaker Thibaut Delmotte are pushing the boundaries of high-altitude winemaking in the Salta region. Hess's Colomé winery and biodynamically farmed vineyards lie at elevations of up to about 10,000 feet; the resulting wines display terrific freshness and purity.

> **WINE INTEL**
> A remote Andean mountaintop is an unlikely location for cutting-edge art, but Bodega Colomé's airy James Turrell Museum is an ideal showcase for the work of this renowned Light and Space artist.

- **Colomé Amalaya** / 2010 / Calchaqui Valley, Salta / $$ An unusual blend of Malbec, Cabernet, Syrah and Tannat that's fresh and minerally, with dark-fruit tones.
- **Colomé Estate Malbec** / 2009 / Salta / $$
  Totally different from Malbecs grown in Mendoza, this features succulent red-fruit flavors and soft tannins.

DOMINIO DEL PLATA/BENMARCO

Argentina's premier wine power-couple, Susana Balbo and Pedro Marchevsky, produce a handful of high-profile labels from their Mendoza facility. These include winemaker Balbo's affordable Crios line (whose Torrontés helped catapult this grape to international stardom) and her namesake reds, which have set standards for balance and precision. Marchevsky, a top viticulturist, crafts red wines under his well-regarded BenMarco label.

- **BenMarco Cabernet Sauvignon** / 2010 / Mendoza / $$
  This cassis-inflected Cabernet delivers more structure and concentration than similar reds of its price.
- **Susana Balbo Signature Malbec** / 2010 / Mendoza / $$
  The combination of juicy black cherry and smoky spice notes make this an ideal barbecue wine.
- **BenMarco Expresivo** / 2009 / Mendoza / $$$
  This big, toasty red blend of Malbec, Cabernet, Syrah, Tannat and Petit Verdot showcases ripe black-fruit flavors.

LUCA

For most of the year, Luca's energetic owner, Laura Catena, is an emergency-room doctor and mother of three in San Francisco. She spends the remainder of her time back home in Argentina running Luca and consulting for her family's famous winery, Bodegas Catena Zapata. Catena's brilliance is on display in Luca's lineup: exquisite, small-lot wines made from old vines.

● **Luca Laborde Vineyard Double Select Syrah / 2010 / Mendoza / $$** Catena made this dense, full-throttle Syrah from 48-year-old vines, which helps explain its intensity.

MENDEL

Roberto de la Mota made his name crafting superbly balanced and complex wines at prestigious labels Terrazas de los Andes (owned by luxury giant LVMH) and Cheval des Andes. Mendel is de la Mota's personal project, focusing on just four wines: three reds and a Sémillon sourced mostly from old vines planted in the gravelly soils of Luján de Cuyo.

● **Mendel Malbec / 2010 / Mendoza / $$** This decadent Malbec showcases de la Mota's opulent winemaking style, with plush, balanced plum and spice notes.

● **Mendel Unus / 2009 / Mendoza / $$$** Cabernet Sauvignon bolsters Malbec in this penetrating red that's loaded with rich black-fruit flavors.

● **Mendel Finca Remota Malbec / 2007 / Mendoza / $$$$** The winery's top cuvée is one of Argentina's most outstanding, complex Malbecs, and priced accordingly.

RUTINI WINES

Like many of Argentina's oldest wineries, Rutini was founded by emigrants from Italy—in this case Don Felipe Rutini, who planted Cabernet vines in Mendoza's Maipú area in 1885. Now part-owned by vintner Nicolás Catena, the largish producer operates vineyards in five Mendoza subregions. Its wines include the entry-level Trumpeter line and the Felipe Rutini label.

● **Trumpeter Malbec / 2010 / Mendoza / $** The consistent best bet in the Trumpeter lineup is this affordable, spice-inflected Malbec.

● **Rutini Malbec / 2009 / Mendoza / $$** More concentrated than the Trumpeter Malbec, with sweet red-fruit flavors and a light floral accent.

RARITIES & COLLECTIBLES

BODEGA NOEMÍA DE PATAGONIA This exciting winery, owned by an Italian noblewoman and run by a Dutch winemaker, proves that the remote Patagonian desert is capable of producing world-class Pinot Noir.

CHEVAL DES ANDES A joint venture between St-Émilion's Cheval Blanc—one of Bordeaux's greatest châteaus—and Mendoza's Terrazas de los Andes, this winery produces a single, stellar red from a blend primarily of Malbec and Cabernet Sauvignon.

NOSOTROS Superstar winemaker Susana Balbo's best bottling, Nosotros, is a voluptuous, extraordinarily rich old-vine Malbec that she produces with grapes from the very best blocks of the Dominio del Plata estate.

TERRAZAS DE LOS ANDES

Hervé Birnie-Scott made sparkling wines for Champagne Moët et Chandon's Argentine venture, Bodegas Chandon, before heading up this sister winery. Its vines grow in terraces (*terrazas*) and grapes are matched to specific altitudes to encourage ideal ripeness. Offerings range from the basic Terrazas to the more refined *reserva* and single-vineyard (Afincado) cuvées.

- **Terrazas de los Andes Reserva Malbec / 2009 / Mendoza / $$** High-altitude vines (3,500 feet) yield this cherry-driven red.
- **Terrazas de los Andes Single Vineyard Las Compuertas Malbec / 2008 / Mendoza / $$$** From a vineyard that dates to 1929, this old-vine red is luscious and deeply flavored.

VIÑA COBOS

Celebrated California winemaker Paul Hobbs fell in love with Argentina on a visit in 1989, and has been returning ever since as a consultant. In 1999 he founded this Mendoza winery with two Argentinean enologists. His Viña Cobos label showcases Hobbs's classic style—rich, indulgent, crowd-pleasing wines that have impressive poise and balance.

- **Viña Cobos Felino Cabernet Sauvignon / 2010 / Mendoza / $$** Cobos's entry-level Felino line delivers lots of power for the price, as this tobacco-edged red shows.
- **Viña Cobos Bramare Malbec / 2009 / Luján de Cuyo / $$$** The Bramare Luján de Cuyo Malbec displays plush black fruit.

Chile
Wine Region

The image of Chile as a source for value wine is becoming outdated. There's no question that excellent, affordable Chilean wines can still be found, but that's only part of what the country offers. Top Cabernet-based reds can challenge premier California wines. Sauvignon Blancs from cool-climate regions are among the world's best. And recent ventures into other grape varieties—Syrah, Pinot Noir—are a testament to the ambitions of Chile's top winemakers.

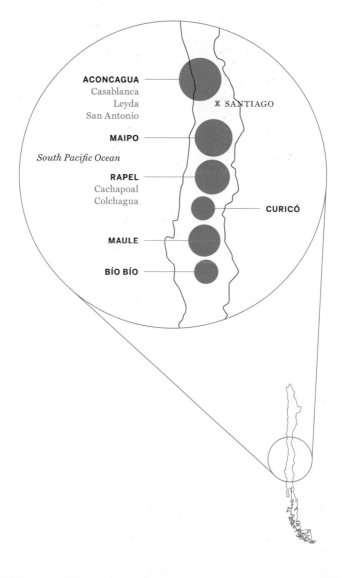

ACONCAGUA
Casablanca
Leyda
San Antonio

✗ SANTIAGO

MAIPO

South Pacific Ocean

RAPEL
Cachapoal
Colchagua

CURICÓ

MAULE

BÍO BÍO

Chile

MONG OTHER QUALITIES, Chile is undoubtedly the world's skinniest wine country. Wedged between the Andes and the Pacific, Chile is nearly 3,000 miles long, but it's fewer than 300 miles across at its widest point. Yet the country is packed with great vineyards. Since the beginning of Chile's wine renaissance in the early 1990s, the sunny Central Valley has been a source for solid, value-oriented wines—chiefly reds—while quality Cabernet Sauvignon from the Alto Maipo district has earned prestige. More recently, Chilean winemakers have pioneered cool-climate winemaking in young areas such as Bío-Bío, Casablanca, San Antonio (and its Leyda district) and, in far nothern Chile, Limarí Valley and Elqui. Chile also has a growing number of independent vintners.

 ## KEY GRAPES: WHITE

SAUVIGNON BLANC & CHARDONNAY Though known for its red wines, Chile is rapidly gaining attention for its whites, led by these international varieties. The cooler air of ocean-influenced zones near the coast, such as Casablanca and the Limarí and San Antonio valleys, produces bright, fragrant Sauvignon Blancs and the country's best Chardonnays. The southern Bío-Bío Valley has become an important source as well.

🍇 KEY GRAPES: RED

CABERNET SAUVIGNON A disproportionate number of the planet's greatest bargains in Cabernet Sauvignon come from Chile. The grape is by far the country's most widely planted variety. Examples from two important subzones in the Central Valley—Alto Maipo and the Rapel Valley's Colchagua—have garnered the most international fame.

CARMENÈRE Like Merlot, the grape for which it was long mistaken, Carmenère came to Chile from France's Bordeaux region. The confusion is understandable: Both varieties possess plummy fruit and fine-grained tannins, but Carmenère expresses an alluring spicy accent that's distinctively Chilean. Some of the best examples come from the Rapel Valley, especially its Cachapoal and Colchagua subzones.

MERLOT Often combined with Cabernet Sauvignon or Carmenère grapes in blends, Chilean Merlot is typically juicy, supple and loaded with ripe plum and black cherry flavors. The Colchagua subregion, a part of the Central Valley's Rapel district, has clay soil and warm temperatures that make it a particularly good source for the variety.

PINOT NOIR This famously finicky grape variety grows best in marginal climates with cooler temperatures, which in Chile means regions like Bío-Bío, a remote, emerging region in the country's far southern reaches, as well as coastal zones like Casablanca and Leyda.

SYRAH The Chilean wine industry's Francophile bent shows in its Syrahs, which at their best combine powerful dark-fruit flavors with cooler notes of pepper and violets, similar in many ways to renditions from France's Rhône Valley. Young plantings in regions like the Elqui and Limarí valleys are turning out impressive new wines from cool-climate vineyards.

WINE TERMINOLOGY

Chilean labels list the name of the winery (*viña*) or brand, grape variety and often a proprietary name for blends. Producers are increasingly using single-vineyard designations and adding the term *reserva* to top-quality wines.

Producers/ Chile

ALMAVIVA

Chilean powerhouse Concha y Toro and Bordeaux's esteemed Château Mouton Rothschild teamed up to create this ambitious label, which turns out a single Bordeaux-inspired blend each year. Sourced in part from a legendary Maipo Valley vineyard called Puente Alto and based on Cabernet Sauvignon, Almaviva has stood as one of the country's most important benchmark reds since its first vintage, in 1996.

● **Almaviva** / 2009 / Puente Alto, Maipo Valley / $$$$
A significant portion of Carmenère helps soften the firm tannins in this ageworthy, Cabernet-based blend, which offers ripe black fruit and velvety depth.

ARBOLEDA

This Aconcagua estate is the pet project of Eduardo Chadwick, head of his family's Errazuriz brand and one of the most influential figures in Chilean wine. Thanks to vast vineyards, the region's coolish climate and talented winemaker Carolina Herrera, Arboleda offers a broad and finely crafted tour of Chile's major varieties at reasonable prices.

○ **Arboleda Chardonnay** / 2010 / Aconcagua Costa / $$
From a vineyard whose name means "the place of seagulls" in the local native language, this citrusy, vivid Chardonnay has the freshness typical of coastal whites.

● **Arboleda Carmenère** / 2009 / Aconcagua Valley / $$
Lower yields in 2009 created an especially intense Carmenère bursting with juicy plum and berries.

CARMEN

Carmen's two biggest claims to fame are being Chile's first winery (1850), and almost 150 years later "rediscovering" in its vineyards what would soon become Chile's signature grape variety, Carmenère. Today winemaker Sebastian Labbé sources fruit from top regions throughout the country for Viña Carmen's cleanly styled and affordable wines.

○ **Carmen Gran Reserva Chardonnay** / 2010 / **Casablanca Valley** / **$** Fermenting just a quarter of this Chardonnay in oak kept its pear and citrus flavors vibrant.

● **Carmen Gran Reserva Apalta Carmenère** / 2009 / **Colchagua Valley** / **$** Grapes grown in the cool Apalta subzone retain more acidity, as evidenced by this juicy, food-friendly red.

CONCHA Y TORO

The largest producer in Chile, Concha y Toro makes wine from every major grape variety in every major region of the country. Of its dizzying lineup—there are 12 separate sub-brands—the affordable Casillero del Diablo and mid-priced Marques de Casa Concha lines offer particularly great value. Two flagship reds, the Don Melchor Cabernet Sauvignon and Carmín de Peumo Carmenère, top the portfolio.

○ **Concha y Toro Casillero del Diablo Reserva Sauvignon Blanc** / 2011 / **Chile** / **$** Blending grapes from two coastal regions—Leyda and Casablanca—gives this lime-inflected white its mouthwatering crispness.

● **Concha y Toro Marques de Casa Concha Carmenère** / 2009 / **Cachapoal Valley** / **$$** Cachapoal Valley is a top spot for Carmenère; this plump, currant-infused bottling shows why.

● **Concha y Toro Don Melchor Cabernet Sauvignon** / 2008 / **Puente Alto** / **$$$$** An iconic Chilean wine, this muscular, tightly wound red comes from the historic Tocornal Vineyard in the Maipo Valley.

COUSIÑO-MACUL

Cousiño-Macul helped create Chile's reputation as a source of great low-priced wines. Founded in 1856, it's now run by a sixth-generation owner, Arturo Cousiño. Though Cousiño-Macul still produces tasty value wines, its top cuvées, such as the Finis Terrae Cabernet blend, compete with the country's best.

○ **Cousiño-Macul Sauvignon Gris** / 2010 / **Maipo Valley** / **$** Sauvignon Gris is a pink-skinned relative of Sauvignon Blanc—one can taste the relationship in this refreshing, grapefruit-flavored example.

● **Cousiño-Macul Finis Terrae** / 2009 / **Maipo Valley** / **$$** The sweet tannins and lush finish in this red-fruit-dominated blend of Cabernet, Merlot and Syrah mean that it's drinking beautifully right now.

KINGSTON FAMILY VINEYARDS

The Kingston family turned its Michigan-born patriarch's unsuccessful 1920s gold mine on the chilly Casablanca coast into farmland and vineyards. Planting reds like Syrah and Pinot on the windblown hills makes for challenging grape-growing but can yield thrilling cool-climate wines—particularly when they're made by consulting California winemaker Byron Kosuge and local talent Evelyn Vidal.

- **Kingston Family Vineyards Lucero Syrah / 2010 / Casablanca Valley / $$** This red's seamless, spicy, dark-fruit flavors make it one of Chile's greatest Syrah values.
- **Kingston Family Vineyards Tobiano Pinot Noir / 2010 / Casablanca Valley / $$** Kingston's introductory Pinot is another terrific value, full of vibrant cherry and toast notes.
- **Kingston Family Vineyards Alazan Pinot Noir / 2010 / Casablanca Valley / $$$** Kosuge creates this fragrant, flagship Pinot Noir by blending the 10 best barrels of the vintage.

LAPOSTOLLE

Alexandra Marnier Lapostolle (as in Grand Marnier, the French liqueur) cofounded this Colchagua estate and imported a French winemaking team that includes superstar consultant Michel Rolland and winemaker Jacques Begarie. Lapostolle's bold, rich wines include the terrific, bargain-priced Casa wines, the mid-priced Cuvée Alexandre tier and the much-celebrated Bordeaux-style blend Clos Apalta. As of 2011, all Lapostolle vineyards are certified organic.

- **Lapostolle Casa Carmenère / 2010 / Rapel Valley / $** It may not be complex, but this affordable red is packed with appealingly juicy berry and herb flavors.
- **Clos Apalta / 2009 / Colchagua Valley / $$$$** This famous blend gets its dense fruit from old-vine Carmenère and its powerful structure from Cabernet Sauvignon.

MONTES

Consistently dependable wines made in a clean, fruity style are the Montes hallmark. Visionary winemaker Aurelio Montes grows heat-loving Bordeaux varieties in the Colchagua Valley, and Pinot Noir and white grapes in coastal regions like Casablanca and Leyda. His top cuvée, Purple Angel, is one of Chile's priciest Carmenères, but smart values round out the portfolio.

○ **Montes Alpha Chardonnay / 2010 / Casablanca Valley / $$**
Montes uses different yeast strains on its various lots of
Chardonnay, a technique that gives complexity to this creamy,
apple- and pear-inflected white.

● **Montes Alpha Apalta Vineyard Syrah / 2009 / Colchagua
Valley / $$** The smallest-production wine in the Alpha line,
this Syrah-dominated red is also the best, with silky tannins
and plush blackberry fruit.

SANTA EMA

Founded by an Italian emigrant from Piedmont, Santa Ema
began as a grape-growing business, then morphed into a winery
in the 1950s. Today this family-owned producer is one of Chile's
great value brands, with a range of reliably delicious wines. Best
bets include the reserve tier wines, which, despite their modest
prices, get aged in oak barrels; and the Selected Terroir bottlings, which highlight key subregions' star varietals.

○ **Santa Ema Selected Terroir Sauvignon Blanc / 2011 / Maipo
Valley / $** A ripe, zesty white that's fabulous with shellfish.

● **Santa Ema Reserve Merlot / 2009 / Maipo Valley / $**
The Maipo Valley is a good source of affordable, tasty Merlot,
as this plummy, spicy bottling attests.

● **Santa Ema Selected Terroir Carmenère / 2010 / Cachapoal
Valley / $** Carmenère's exuberant, accessible side is showcased
here, with supple, vanilla-tinged berry flavors.

SANTA RITA

Australian winemaking guru Brian Croser consults for this
Maipo Valley mainstay, one of Chile's most recognizable names,
thanks to its large production and more than 130-year history.
Forays into newer growing regions such as Limarí and Leyda
are paying off with crisp white wines and structured, elegant
reds, though the savory, iconic Casa Real Cabernet Sauvignon
remains the portfolio's star.

○ **Santa Rita Medalla Real Gran Reserva Sauvignon Blanc /
2010 / Leyda Valley / $$** A big step up from basic Sauvignon
Blancs, this *reserva* has a lovely concentration to its brisk
grass and grapefruit tones.

● **Santa Rita 120 Carmenère / 2011 / Central Valley / $**
Santa Rita's 120 line offers some terrific values, including this
smooth yet substantial Carmenère.

UNDURRAGA

Founded just outside Santiago in 1885, Undurraga began exporting its wines to the U.S. as early as 1903, making it the first Chilean winery to do so. Sold by the Undurraga family to an investment group in 2005, Undurraga still produces the wines that helped build the country's international reputation as a go-to source for well-made, inexpensive whites and reds.

○ **Undurraga T.H. Sauvignon Blanc / 2010 / Leyda / $$** This succulent, exuberantly fruity white is among Undurraga's T.H. ("Terroir Hunter") wines, which are made with grapes sourced from small, exceptional sites.

● **Undurraga T.H. Pinot Noir / 2010 / Leyda / $$** Delicious, reasonably priced Pinot Noir isn't easy to find, but here is a great example, loaded with vibrant cherry flavors and delicate spice.

VERAMONTE

Veramonte was a Casablanca Valley trailblazer in the early 1990s; its refreshing Sauvignon Blancs helped put both the winery and this cool region on the map. Founded by the Huneeus family (Chilean natives who also own Napa's Quintessa winery), Veramonte specializes in cool-climate Chardonnay, Sauvignon Blanc and Pinot Noir, plus reds from the warmer Colchagua Valley.

○ **Veramonte La Gloria Sauvignon Blanc / 2011 / Chile / $** Fermenting this delicious Sauvignon Blanc entirely in stainless steel, not oak, keeps its mouthwatering grapefruit flavors zingy and bright.

VIÑA FALERNIA

Italian vintner and Falernia founder Giorgio Flessati pioneered winemaking in the remote, northerly Elqui Valley. With a number of international observatories, Elqui attracts astronomers for the same reasons it attracts vintners: clear skies, boundless sunshine and crystalline-pure air. Throw in well-draining soil, snow-melt irrigation and huge temperature swings and you get the crisp, flavorful—and amazingly well-priced—wines of Falernia.

○ **Falernia Reserva Pedro Ximénez / 2011 / Elqui Valley / $**
The grape used to make pisco also yields this dry white whose medium-bodied flavors have a lemony tang.

○ **Falernia Reserva Sauvignon Blanc / 2010 / Elqui Valley / $**
Exactly what an affordable Sauvignon Blanc should be, this is packed with delicious lime, herb and passion fruit tones.

● **Falernia Reserva Syrah / 2008 / Elqui Valley / $**
More than half of this Syrah was aged in new oak—rare for a wine this inexpensive; the result is a luscious, seamless red.

VIÑA LOS VASCOS

France's Rothschild family—owners of Pauillac's fabled Château Lafite and five other Bordeaux wineries—purchased this Colchagua property in 1988. Its portfolio reflects traditional winemaking on a grand scale, with a single vineyard of more than 1,400 acres supplying fruit for five Bordeaux-inspired reds. Le Dix, a suavely structured luxury cuvée, tops the portfolio; the winery's Casablanca Sauvignon Blanc is a consistent value.

○ **Los Vascos Sauvignon Blanc / 2011 / Casablanca Valley / $**
Purchased grapes from the cooler Casablanca and Curicó districts go into this fresh, tropical fruit–accented white.

● **Le Díx de Los Vascos / 2009 / Colchagua Valley / $$$**
A seductive, ageworthy red blend that's made from the best barrels of the vintage.

VIÑA MORANDÉ

While Pablo Morandé was head winemaker at Concha y Toro in the 1980s, he convinced the company to invest heavily in the Casablanca Valley. It was a bold move: Casablanca's cool, maritime climate seemed like a risky bet. Today Morandé's successful label, which he debuted in 1996, offers vibrant, energetic whites that showcase the fabulous qualities of Chile's coastal zones; his reds come chiefly from the warmer Maipo district.

○ **Morandé Reserva Sauvignon Blanc / 2011 / Casablanca Valley / $** Serve this bright, citrusy white well chilled.

● **Morandé Edición Limitada Carignan / 2008 / Loncomilla Valley / $$** Sixty-year-old vines have yielded a silky, sweet-tart red that will improve for a few years but is also terrific now.

● **Morandé Gran Reserva Cabernet Sauvignon / 2009 / Maipo Valley / $$** This cherry-driven Cabernet delivers loads more depth than the basic Reserva, for just a small jump in price.

South Africa / Wine Region

Though South Africa's winemaking history stretches back more than 350 years, only in the past two decades have the country's wines truly come of age. South Africa now boasts delicious Chenin Blancs, ageworthy Cabernets and powerful Syrahs, and is home to a new generation of talented young winemakers pushing boundaries in less-heralded regions such as Elgin and Swartland.

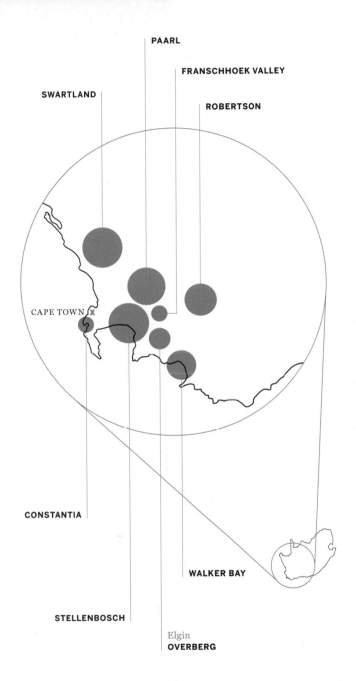

- PAARL
- FRANSCHHOEK VALLEY
- ROBERTSON
- SWARTLAND
- CAPE TOWN
- CONSTANTIA
- WALKER BAY
- STELLENBOSCH
- Elgin
- OVERBERG

South Africa

SOUTH AFRICA IS another wine country defined by the ocean. Cooled by Atlantic winds and Antarctic currents, South Africa's best districts are located around its southwestern tip. Stellenbosch and Paarl turn out most of the top red wines. Sauvignon Blanc, Chardonnay and Pinot Noir production is focused in cooler Constantia, a Cape Town suburb, and in Walker Bay, Overberg and especially the latter's subzone, Elgin.

❧ KEY GRAPES: WHITE

CHENIN BLANC South Africa's most important white grape (also known here as Steen) yields wines ranging in style from zippy to lush, with more tropical flavors than French Chenin Blancs.

SAUVIGNON BLANC & CHARDONNAY South African Chardonnays often hew to a line midway between the ripe fruitiness of California and the leaner, mineral-driven flavors of France; Sauvignon Blancs range from herbal and tart to exotically fruity.

❧ KEY GRAPES: RED

CABERNET SAUVIGNON & SHIRAZ (SYRAH) Wines produced from these powerful grapes make South Africa's most convincing case for greatness. Cabernet is the country's dominant red variety, and plantings of Shiraz (also called Syrah here) have more than doubled in the past decade. These reds tend to split into two camps: Some vintners aim for ripe, plush styles akin to California's and Australia's, while others make earthier, herb-inflected versions that evoke comparisons with French bottlings.

PINOTAGE Once South Africa's preeminent red grape, Pinotage— a crossing of Pinot Noir and Cinsaut—now ranks behind Cabernet and Merlot in terms of plantings. Pinotage's distinctively pungent, funky flavors have limited its appeal abroad, though a few vintners craft fruitier versions of the grape.

PINOT NOIR With an increase in plantings in cool-climate regions, Pinot Noir production is on the rise, although not much of it is exported yet to the U.S.

WINE TERMINOLOGY
South African winemakers use straightforward labels that list winery name, variety, region and vintage. Blends may be given proprietary names, and the varieties that went into them usually appear on the back label.

Producers/ South Africa

BOEKENHOUTSKLOOF
Winemaker Marc Kent has a deft hand with Syrah, fashioning it into some of South Africa's finest renditions of the grape. Best known is his dark and savory, Syrah-based Chocolate Block blend. Just as worth seeking out are Boekenhoutskloof's (*BOOK-n-HOWD-skloof*) entry-level wines, such as its admirable and affordable Wolftrap bottlings.

○ **The Wolftrap Viognier Chenin Blanc Grenache Blanc** / 2010 / Franschhoek / $ An unusual combination of grape varieties yields a plump, pleasing white with fresh fig and peach flavors.

● **The Chocolate Block** / 2010 / Franschhoek / $$$
Kent styles this Syrah-based blend to emphasize the grapes' savory side, making it complex and supremely food-friendly.

BUITENVERWACHTING

One of the grand, if consonant-heavy, old names in Constantia, Buitenverwachting (*BAY-ten-fur-VACHK-ting*) boasts a history dating back to 1796 and a stunning setting cooled by the winds of False Bay, eight miles away. Cellar master Hermann Kirschbaum and winemaker Brad Paton excel with minerally, characterful Sauvignon Blancs.

○ **Buitenverwachting Beyond Sauvignon Blanc / 2011 / Coastal Region / $** Fermenting grapes with several types of yeast adds complexity to this crisp, lemony white.

○ **Buitenverwachting Chardonnay / 2010 / Constantia / $$** Low yields in 2010 resulted in greater flavor depth for this graceful, orange-driven Chardonnay.

○ **Buitenverwachting Husseys Vlei Sauvignon Blanc / 2010 / Constantia / $$** A single-vineyard wine that displays the herbal side of Sauvignon Blanc, with bell pepper and lime notes.

DEMORGENZON

DeMorgenzon's owners, investment guru Wendy Appelbaum and her husband, Hylton, are so passionate about music that they pipe classical tunes through their vineyards and cellar, 24 hours a day. How much the sound energy influences the wines is debatable, but what's certain is that DeMorgenzon makes one of South Africa's greatest Chenin Blancs. Also look for their stellar bargains under the winery's DMZ label.

○ **DeMorgenzon DMZ Chardonnay / 2011 / Western Cape / $** It's hard to find Chardonnay under $15 that's as stylish as this vibrant, apricot-inflected example.

○ **DeMorgenzon Reserve Chenin Blanc / 2010 / Stellenbosch / $$** Older vines yield a stunning combination of silkiness, power and freshness in this full-bodied, citrus-infused wine.

FAIRVIEW/GOATS DO ROAM

Charles Back's Fairview estate was the first in South Africa to plant Viognier and is still the only one making Petite Sirah. Back and vintner Anthony de Jager experiment with other grapes uncommon to the region (Tannat and Tempranillo), but their passion is Rhône grapes, used for Back's Goats do Roam value label, a cheeky homage to France's Côtes-du-Rhône district.

○ **Fairview Chenin Blanc / 2010 / Darling / $**
De Jager fashions this wine in a reliably juicy, citrus-driven style that highlights Chenin's zesty character.

○ **Goats do Roam White / 2010 / Western Cape / $**
Using more estate-grown fruit has bumped up the concentration in this invigorating, tangerine-accented blend of Viognier, Roussanne and Grenache Blanc.

● **Goats do Roam Red / 2011 / Western Cape / $**
Blending six different grape varieties yields a succulent, easy-drinking—and bargain-priced—red.

HAMILTON RUSSELL VINEYARDS

Hamilton Russell's wines compete with world-class whale-watching as a compelling reason to visit the fishing village of Hermanus, which lies on Walker Bay and is home to one of the continent's southernmost vineyards. Tim Hamilton Russell purchased this property in 1975; today son Anthony oversees its two wines, estate-grown Pinot Noir and Chardonnay.

○ **Hamilton Russell Vineyards Chardonnay / 2010 / Hemel-en-Aarde Valley / $$$** Bright acidity and minerals are on display in this elegant and exhilaratingly crisp (yet luscious) white.

● **Hamilton Russell Vineyards Pinot Noir / 2009 / Hemel-en-Aarde Valley / $$$** Pricey but worth it, this fragrant, cherry-driven Pinot has the structure to age beautifully.

KEN FORRESTER VINEYARDS

Ken Forrester's labels display the date 1689, the year the land was granted for what became his flagship vineyard. But Forrester himself jumped into winemaking only in 1993, after a career as a restaurateur. The success of his old-vine Chenins turned Forrester into a poster boy for the variety, though today the brand's diverse portfolio includes as many Rhône-style reds as whites.

○ **Ken Forrester Reserve Chenin Blanc / 2010 / Stellenbosch / $**
This delivers the winery's creamy, spice-infused Chenin style at an easy-to-swallow price.

○ **Ken Forrester The FMC / 2009 / Stellenbosch / $$$$**
A touch of botrytis ("noble rot"; see p. 305) gives this juicy, apple- and pear-driven Chenin Blanc a lightly honeyed edge.

● **Ken Forrester Petit Pinotage / 2010 / Western Cape / $**
Priced to buy by the case, this plummy, plush red makes a great introduction to Pinotage.

MEERLUST ESTATE

This prominent Stellenbosch estate has been owned by the Myburgh family since 1756, and the property (including dove-cote and family cemetery) is a national monument. Meerlust's top wine, the Bordeaux-style Rubicon red, was one of the country's first blends of its type and might be considered another kind of national gem. Quality across the portfolio has risen impressively under Chris Williams, the winemaker since 2004.

● **Meerlust Merlot** / 2007 / Stellenbosch / $$
By cutting away some grapes before they're ripe, Meerlust concentrates flavors into the remaining bunches—a practice evident in this velvety Merlot's deeply plummy fruit.

● **Meerlust Rubicon** / 2007 / Stellenbosch / $$$
Chris Williams blends Cabernet with a bit of Merlot and Cabernet Franc for this seamless, classically structured red.

MULDERBOSCH VINEYARDS

Launched 24 years ago, Mulderbosch quickly gained a reputation for turning out some of South Africa's best white wines. Founding winemaker Mike Dobrovic established the winery's vibrant, citrusy style, which has continued under new owner Terroir Capital, an investment group founded by former Screaming Eagle co-owner Charles Banks.

○ **Mulderbosch Chenin Blanc** / 2011 / Western Cape / $
About 20 percent of this vivid Chenin Blanc was fermented in barrel, which adds a nice richness; a touch of late-harvest (i.e., superripe) grapes contributes density as well.

○ **Mulderbosch Sauvignon Blanc** / 2011 / Stellenbosch-Elgin / $$ Picking grapes at different levels of ripeness gives this zesty white a range of grassy, lemony flavors.

● **Mulderbosch Cabernet Sauvignon Rosé** / 2011 / Coastal Region / $ This neon pink, pomegranate-inflected rosé has a tiny hint of sweetness and a lot of character.

RUSTENBERG WINES

Encompassing nearly 3,000 acres in Stellenbosch, this vast estate was founded in 1682 and overhauled in the late 1980s. Its size offers owner Simon Barlow an enviable range of grape-friendly sites, with heat-loving red varieties planted on the sunny, red clay slopes of Simonsberg and Helderberg mountains, and white grapes in cooler territory close to False Bay.

RARITIES & COLLECTIBLES

A.A. BADENHORST FAMILY WINES In 2008, acclaimed Rustenberg winemaker Adi Badenhorst restored a ruined 19th-century winery in the up-and-coming Swartland region (displacing a sizable bat population in the process). From it, he now produces some of the country's most sought-after red and white blends.

DE TRAFFORD This remote estate at the top of a valley above Stellenbosch is arguably South Africa's greatest Shiraz producer; winemaker/owner David Trafford also makes stunning whites.

SADIE FAMILY Eben Sadie, the *enfant terrible* of South African wine, is known for his phenomenal old-vine Rhône blends and Chenin Blancs from Swartland. (He also makes top-quality reds from Spain's Priorat region under the Terroir al Limit label.)

○ **Rustenberg Chardonnay / 2010 / Stellenbosch / $$**
Rustenberg offers several Chardonnays; this one's made in a richer style, with broad apple tones, fresh acidity and an appealing creamy texture.

● **Rustenberg Peter Barlow / 2006 / Simonsberg-Stellenbosch / $$$** The winery's flagship red is a bold, single-vineyard Cabernet packed with toasty black cherry fruit.

THELEMA MOUNTAIN VINEYARDS

"Hell's Heights" (Helshoogte) may not be an auspicious-sounding spot for a new business. But it proved to be a brilliant location for Gyles and Barbara Webb's ambitious winery built in 1983 on Simonsberg Mountain, near Stellenbosch. The Webbs and rising star winemaker Rudi Schultz craft exceptional cool-climate wines from the home estate and a newer site in Elgin.

○ **Thelema Sauvignon Blanc / 2010 / Stellenbosch / $$**
Crisp summer nights result in extra-bright acidity for this silky, lime- and lychee-flavored white.

● **Thelema Cabernet Sauvignon / 2008 / Stellenbosch / $$$**
Thelema's wines combine richness with savory notes and food-friendly acidity, like this expertly balanced, black currant–inflected Cabernet.

● **Thelema Shiraz / 2008 / Stellenbosch / $$$**
One of the country's most consistent Shirazes, this estate-grown red is polished and bold, with cherry and mineral tones.

Champagne & Other Sparkling Wines

Most Americans serve sparkling wines only for special occasions, cocktail parties or dessert, which is a missed opportunity. Few wines are as food-friendly or refreshing as Champagne and its international counterparts, such as Prosecco and cava. With excellent examples at every price, sparkling wine is an ideal choice for everyday drinking.

THERE ARE SEVERAL ways to make sparkling wine. The finest is the traditional method—*méthode traditionnelle*—whereby vintners create carbon dioxide bubbles in a still wine by activating a second fermentation in the bottle. The pinnacle of all sparkling wine regions is Champagne, located in northern France, but France's Loire Valley, northern Italy, northeastern Spain and Northern California also make exceptional examples, as do many other places with cool climates and mineral-rich soils. The best of these other sparkling wines are made using the *méthode traditionnelle;* less expensive versions typically employ other methods.

CHAMPAGNE

CLAIM TO FAME

The French went to court (and won) to keep wineries outside the Champagne region from labeling their sparkling wines as Champagne. But the word's enduring ubiquity as a casual synonym for any effervescent wine reflects the phenomenal success of Champagne: Few (if any) sparkling wines can match Champagne's best bottles in complexity and finesse. Chalk and limestone soils and a cool Atlantic climate—along with centuries of winemaking trial and error—mean that these wines are in a category of their own, no matter how liberally the Champagne moniker is applied elsewhere.

REGIONS TO KNOW

AUBE A crucial source of fruit for large producers in the more prestigious districts of Reims and the Côtes des Blancs, the Aube is located almost 70 miles southeast of central Champagne and has a slightly warmer climate and soil that is richer in clay. The grape of choice here is Pinot Noir, which represents most of the region's acreage. Increasingly, its top growers—chiefly located in the Côte des Bar, the Aube's primary subregion—are vinifying their own wines rather then selling their grapes.

CÔTES DES BLANCS Chardonnay dominates this region, which lies south of the city of Epernay and produces wines renowned for freshness and delicacy. Its southernmost tip, called Côte de Sézanne, also focuses on Chardonnay.

MONTAGNE DE REIMS This stretch of wooded hills and vineyards follows a mountain ridge south from Reims to Epernay and focuses primarily on Pinot Noir. Most of Champagne's *grand cru* vineyards for red grapes are found here.

VALLÉE DE LA MARNE Pinot Meunier is the main grape in Champagne's largest growing region. Encompassing the city of Epernay as well as land west of it, Vallée de la Marne is home to many acclaimed grower-producers, with its best vineyards located on sloping hillsides above the Marne River.

KEY GRAPES: WHITE
CHARDONNAY Thanks to the Champagne region's cool climate and stony soil, its Chardonnay yields fresh, zesty whites. The variety accounts for less than a third of the region's vineyards. Most Champagnes are blends of Chardonnay, Pinot Noir and Pinot Meunier; blends based on Chardonnay offer citrusy mineral flavors, but are scarcer than those dominated by red grapes.

KEY GRAPES: RED
PINOT MEUNIER This grape is prized for its ability to ripen early (a lifesaver for vintners in cooler vintages) and for its fruity, floral flavors, which round out a traditional Champagne blend.

PINOT NOIR Used to make both rosé and white wines, this black-skinned grape lends body, richness and bright berry flavors to Champagne. Pinot Noir is the main grape of the Montagne de Reims and Aube subregions.

WINE TERMINOLOGY
BLANC DE BLANCS Most Champagnes are made from a blend of red and white varieties, but Blanc de Blanc ("white from white") cuvées are made entirely from white grapes—Chardonnay—and represent less than 5 percent of all Champagne.

BLANC DE NOIRS These are white Champagnes produced using only red grapes (Pinot Noir and Pinot Meunier). To create the wine, the clear juice of red grapes gets drained from the skins before it gains any color. (Rosés are created by blending a bit of red wine into white sparkling wine or by leaving the red grape skins in the pressed juice for a short time to bleed in some color.)

DISGORGEMENT Fermenting sugar inside a bottle gives Champagne its fizz but also creates lees, a yeasty sediment. The disgorgement process removes the lees without losing the fizz. The disgorgement date is a key indicator of a wine's age.

DOSAGE The sugary syrup added to most Champagne after it's disgorged (see above). It maintains the bottle's fill level (some wine is lost during disgorgement) and adds some sweetness.

SWEETNESS LEVELS Bone-dry cuvées that had no dosage added after disgorgement (see above) are labeled brut *nature* (or brut *zéro, pas dosé* or *sans dosage), brut* meaning "dry." The second-driest of all Champagne styles, extra brut wines are bright and zesty. The next category, brut, is the most widely produced style. Extra sec bottlings are one step up from brut wines and have a hint of sweetness. Though translating as "semi-dry," demi-sec wines are actually fairly sweet.

PREMIER CRU Champagne ranks wines by the village from which they come. Forty-three villages, chiefly in the Montagne de Reims and the Côtes des Blancs, have *premier cru* status.

GRAND CRU Seventeen Champagne villages rate high enough to call their wines *grand cru,* the most prestigious designation.

TÊTE DE CUVÉE A Champagne house's top-tier bottling, usually sold under a proprietary name, such as Moët's Dom Pérignon.

GROWER CHAMPAGNE Champagnes made by vintners who bottle their own wines, rather than selling grapes to large producers. Instead of supplying fruit for enormous blends made to reflect a house style, grower-producers highlight the qualities imparted to wine by the particular plot where it was grown (its *terroir*).

NONVINTAGE/NV Most Champagnes are nonvintage, which means they are blends of wines from different vintages, a practice designed to maintain a consistent taste from year to year.

VINTAGE Producers make vintage Champagnes only in exceptional years; these wines are typically aged longer and priced higher than their nonvintage counterparts (see above).

Producers/ Champagne

BILLECART-SALMON

One of Champagne's most respected midsize producers, Billecart-Salmon crafts wines that emphasize fruit and finesse over power. The nonvintage brut rosé is the most famous example of the house style, but the estate's most impressive and complex offering is the prestige Nicolas François Billecart cuvée. Brothers François and Antoine Roland-Billecart pick grapes on the early side, resulting in especially fresh wines.

○ **Billecart-Salmon Brut Réserve / NV / Champagne / $$$**
Although made mostly from red grapes that usually yield bolder wines, this basic brut is elegant and subtle.

○ **Billecart-Salmon Blanc de Blancs Grand Cru / NV / Champagne / $$$$** Using only *grand cru* fruit gives this racy Chardonnay-based white its chalky minerality.

○ **Billecart-Salmon Cuvée Nicolas François Billecart Brut / 2000 / Champagne / $$$$** First produced in 1955, this fabulous brut displays precise apple and mineral tones.

BOLLINGER

Founded in 1829 and still family-owned, Bollinger is known for its full-bodied style, a result of fermenting some wines in barrel. Most of Bollinger's grapes come from estate vineyards—a key factor in its wines' reliable quality. Its famous reserve and vintage bottlings are some of the most long-lived in Champagne.

○ **Bollinger Special Cuvée / NV / Champagne / $$$**
Bollinger's Pinot Noir–based introductory wine delivers impressively dense flavors that make it a relative bargain.

DEUTZ

Deutz's wines manage to combine delicacy and refinement with underlying richness—a tightrope act that translates to whites and rosés with deep fruit, bright acidity and pronounced minerality. Started as a *négociant* business in 1838, Deutz has been owned since 1983 by deep-pocketed Champagne Louis Roederer, which continues the winery's tradition of excellence.

○ **Deutz Brut Classic / NV / Champagne / $$$**
Wonderfully crisp and aromatic, this is a fabulous go-to choice for modestly priced Champagne.

○ **Deutz Blanc de Blancs / 2004 / Champagne / $$$$**
The 2004 vintage produced wines of terrific vitality and freshness, qualities evident in this silky, citrusy Champagne.

KRUG

Krug produces some of the world's most breathtakingly expensive wines, such as its Clos d'Ambonnay, introduced at $3,500 per bottle. Scarcity and prestige drive up the prices, but the wines can be truly thrilling, with extraordinary complexity and endless layers of flavors. This results partially from Krug's practice of adding very high amounts of reserve (i.e., older) wines; fermenting them in oak barrels adds a signature richness, too.

○ **Krug Brut / 2000 / Champagne / $$$$**
Aged in cellars for more than a decade before its release, this sleek, powerful vintage Champagne will improve in bottle for many years to come.

● **Krug Rosé Brut / NV / Champagne / $$$$**
The addition of reserve wines from multiple vintages gives this creamy, fragrant rosé its intensity, though it's equally finessed.

LOUIS ROEDERER

Louis Roederer sources 70 percent of its grapes from estate-owned vineyards, more by far than most major Champagne houses. That kind of quality control contributes to Roederer's remarkable consistency; another factor is winemaker Jean-Baptiste Lécaillon, who has been with the winery since 1989. Roederer's esteemed prestige cuvée, Cristal, was first created for Russian czar Alexander II, in 1876.

○ **Louis Roederer Brut Premier / NV / Champagne / $$$**
Rich yet wonderfully fresh, this has a touch of creaminess to counter its bright fruit profile.

○ **Louis Roederer Cristal Brut / 2004 / Champagne / $$$$**
Champagne's first prestige cuvée is still one of its greatest, showcasing an incredible balance of full-bodied richness and taut, chalky minerality.

○ **Louis Roederer Vintage Brut / 2005 / Champagne / $$$$**
Warm weather in 2005 created Champagnes with dense fruit, as this bold example shows.

MOËT & CHANDON/DOM PÉRIGNON

Moët & Chandon's debonair *chef de cave*, Benoît Gouez, oversees Champagne's largest cellar, turning out five major cuvées sourced from a vast collection of 2,500 acres of estate vines, plus purchased fruit. The three nonvintage Impérial wines include a brut, a rosé and Nectar, made in a sweeter style. Moët's legendary tête de cuvée, Dom Pérignon, became so successful that it is now its own brand, crafted by winemaking genius Richard Geoffroy.

○ **Moët & Chandon Impérial Brut / NV / Champagne / $$$**
Moët recently reduced the dosage in its best-selling flagship brut to give it a drier, crisper taste.

NICOLAS FEUILLATTE

Value in Champagne is relative—the least expensive wines are still pricey. But this young brand, founded in 1976 by coffee baron and diplomat Nicolas Feuillatte, always delivers exactly that. Feuillatte gave the brand glamour by popularizing it among his jet-set friends, but the wines' continued quality is due to Champagne's oldest cooperative, which acquired the brand in 1986.

○ **Nicolas Feuillatte Blanc de Blancs Millésime / 2004 / Champagne / $$$** Crisp green apple and citrus fruit define this all-Chardonnay vintage bottling.

○ **Nicolas Feuillatte Brut / NV / Champagne / $$$**
Made chiefly from red grapes, this floral-edged white is still light enough to drink as an aperitif.

● **Nicolas Feuillatte Brut Rosé / NV / Champagne / $$$**
This pretty, pale pink rosé is full of strawberries and spice.

PIPER-HEIDSIECK

In less than a century, starting in 1785, the Heidsieck family founded three Champagne houses: Piper-Heidsieck, Charles Heidsieck and what is now Heidsieck & Co. Monopole. Piper-Heidsieck wines are lighter-bodied than the others, with refined fruit and zesty freshness. Winemaker Rémi Camus has stayed with the winery since its sale to a luxury goods firm in 2011.

○ **Piper-Heidsieck Brut / NV / Champagne / $$$**
Older reserve wines make up about 15 percent of this fresh, lightly floral bottling.

● **Piper-Heidsieck Rosé Sauvage / NV / Champagne / $$$**
This vivid, ruby-colored rosé is a value as far as rosé Champagnes go, with bold, firm red berry and cherry tones.

RARITIES & COLLECTIBLES

JACQUES SELOSSE Vintner Anselme Selosse has influenced a generation of younger talents with his uncompromising Champagnes, which are made with indigenous yeasts and minimal use of sulfur and are fermented in wooden barrels.

PHILIPPONNAT The remarkably long-lived, vintage-dated Clos des Goisses cuvée is made with grapes sourced from one of Champagne's most renowned vineyards, an incredibly steep, warm hillside parcel of vines in Mareuil-sur-Aÿ.

VOUETTE & SORBÉE From the first vintage, 2001, sommeliers fell in love with the wines of Bertrand Gautherot, a naturalist grower in the Aube region. Production is tiny, which makes bottles hard to find except in restaurants with extraordinary cellars—but the quality is stratospheric.

POL ROGER

Pol Roger—now in its fifth generation of family ownership—is responsible for some of the finest wines in Champagne. These bottlings include its impressive prestige bottling, Cuvée Sir Winston Churchill (the English statesman was a devoted fan of Pol Roger and a friend of the owners), plus the gorgeously balanced nonvintage Brut Réserve.

○ **Pol Roger Brut Réserve / NV / Champagne / $$$**
Nicknamed the White Foil bottling, this refreshing offering is remarkably crisp yet luscious—exactly what great brut Champagne should be.

○ **Pol Roger Brut Blanc de Blancs / 2000 / Champagne / $$$$**
A powerful white that combines the fruity richness of the 2000 vintage with a stony minerality.

SALON

Nearly all Champagne houses produce wines in several different styles, but Salon creates just one, and that only in great vintages. It is made with grapes from a single year, variety (Chardonnay) and village (Le Mesnil), and its rarity and extraordinary longevity have made Salon one of the most coveted and expensive white wines in the world.

○ **Salon Le Mesnil Blanc de Blancs Brut / 1999 / Champagne / $$$$** Famous for its penetrating mineral depth, Salon takes years of aging to develop its true complexity.

TAITTINGER

One of the few large Champagne houses that's still family-owned, Taittinger, whose roots date back to 1734, is headquartered above a spectacular network of Gallo-Roman chalk mines in Reims. The chalk-pit cellars provide a perfect environment for aging the house's wines, which weave delicate flavors with enough creamy lushness to keep them from tasting austere.

○ **Champagne Taittinger Prélude Grands Crus / NV / Champagne / $$$$** First released to celebrate the last millennium, this *grand cru* is equal parts Chardonnay and Pinot Noir.

● **Champagne Taittinger Prestige Rosé / NV / Champagne / $$$** Taittinger's superb rosé costs just a few more dollars than its basic brut, and is well worth the price.

VILMART & CIE

A darling of sommeliers, this boutique grower and producer made its reputation with powerful, biodynamically grown sparkling wines that mature in barrels, not in tanks, which gives the wines an opulent, round texture. Laurent Champs, the fifth generation of his family to direct the estate, favors a style that is equal parts freshness and richness.

○ **Vilmart & Cie Coeur de Cuvée Premier Cru / 2003 / Champagne / $$$$** Vilmart's top cuvée is sourced from premier vineyards that yield great wine even in lesser years like 2003.

○ **Vilmart & Cie Grand Cellier d'Or Brut Premier Cru / 2006 / Champagne / $$$$** Chiefly Chardonnay, this exquisite wine needs time to unwind its bold, tightly packed flavors.

● **Vilmart & Cie Grand Cellier Rubis Brut Premier Cru / 2006 / Champagne / $$$$** A stunning rosé made only in exceptional vintages, this bursts with creamy red fruit.

OTHER SPARKLING WINES

REGIONS TO KNOW

FRANCE Beyond Champagne, France abounds with sparkling wines, most made with grapes typical to each region. Seven of the country's sparkling wine appellations—the largest is the Loire—are able to use the term *crémant* to indicate they are produced by the *méthode traditionnelle*. Other wines labeled *brut* or *Mousseux* may or may not have been made this way.

ITALY Italy's northern regions are the main source of the country's *spumante* (sparkling) wines. One of the best, very similar in taste to Champagne, comes from Lombardy's Franciacorta zone. Also noteworthy are Piedmont's flowery Moscato d'Asti and light red, berry-scented Brachetto d'Acqui. The Veneto's affordable and popular Proseccos are made using a process called the Charmat method, in which the wine undergoes its second fermentation in tanks rather than bottles. The effervescent liquid is then drained from its spent yeast and bottled.

SPAIN Long marketed as less costly substitutes for Champagne, Spanish cavas by law must be made using traditional techniques (see p. 281). Most cavas come from the Catalonia region near Barcelona and are based largely on the white Macabeo grape.

UNITED STATES The quality of American sparkling wines has been steadily improving. While the best bottlings still come from the cooler regions of Northern California—such as Carneros, Sonoma and the Anderson and Green valleys—Washington State, Oregon, New York and New Mexico are making a growing number of complex, vibrant sparklers.

Producers/Other Sparkling Wines

FRANCE
LANGLOIS-CHATEAU

Bollinger brought Champagne expertise to the Loire when it acquired this *crémant* producer in 1973. The superb wines evoke Champagne in their minerally depth but are firmly Loire-based in *terroir* and grape selection, with Chenin Blanc largely replacing Chardonnay and Cabernet Franc standing in for Pinot Noir. Even better, they can cost half of what most Champagne does.

○ **Langlois Brut / NV / Crémant de Loire / $$**
Aging this gently sparkling, pear-scented *crémant* on its lees for two years, rather than the legally mandated minimum of nine months, gives it unusual richness.

SIMONNET-FEBVRE

Simonnet-Febvre has specialized in the production of sparkling wines since it was founded in 1840, and it's still the only winery in the Chablis region that produces Crémant de Bourgogne—sparkling Burgundy wines made using the traditional method. Based on Chardonnay and Pinot Noir, the winery's *crémants* gain lovely freshness and depth from the district's unique clay and limestone soils.

○ **Simonnet-Febvre Brut / NV / Crémant de Bourgogne / $$**
White wines from the Chablis region boast a hallmark minerality that is clearly on display in this invigoratingly brisk, dry, pear-scented sparkler.

● **Simonnet-Febvre Brut Rosé / NV / Crémant de Bourgogne / $$** A light wine perfect for hot days (or as a predinner sipper), this strawberry-scented rosé reflects the cool climate of Chablis in its lean, tangy fruit.

VIGNEAU-CHEVREAU

This small, fifth-generation estate is located in the Loire Valley's Vouvray region, where brothers Christophe and Stéphane Vigneau fashion sparkling and still wines from the Chenin Blanc grape. Unusually graceful and precise, their three bottlings come from old, biodynamically farmed vines. The wines are aged on their lees for two years, which softens their acidity and gives them an almost creamy texture.

○ **Domaine Vigneau-Chevreau Brut / NV / Vouvray Pétillant / $$**
Redolent of fresh crushed apples, this dry, *pétillant* (lightly effervescent) white has the complexity and finesse of a wine costing twice as much.

ITALY
BISOL

The highest-quality Prosecco comes from Valdobbiadene, a small town north of Venice where the Glera variety (the new name for the Prosecco grape) grows best. The Bisol family has been growing grapes in Valdobbiadene since the 16th century (though they didn't start selling their own wine until 1875), meaning that they farm their vines with several centuries of accumulated wisdom. The combination of premier vineyards and phenomenal expertise means that Bisol's Proseccos set benchmarks at every price level.

○ **Bisol Crede Brut / NV / Valdobbiadene Prosecco Superiore /
$$** Creamy-textured yet crisp, this floral-inflected Prosecco
is made with grapes grown in *crede*, the region's moisture-
retaining clay soil.

○ **Bisol Cartizze Dry / NV / Valdobbiadene Prosecco Superiore
di Cartizze / $$$** Bisol's top bottle comes from a famous
hilltop, Cartizze, that yields unusually rich wines, like this
aromatic, pineapple-edged example.

CA' DEL BOSCO

Italian Maurizio Zanella has channeled his considerable energy,
talent and ambition into coaxing outstanding, refined sparkling
wines from his vineyards. In the process, he helped galvanize
the entire Franciacorta region, a zone near Milan that became
the country's most prestigious sparkling wine region. Made
using *champenoise* techniques (*metodo classico*), Ca' del Bosco's
best wines rival those of Champagne.

○ **Ca' del Bosco Cuvée Prestige Brut / NV / Franciacorta / $$$**
Older, reserve wines make up 20 percent of this entry-level
white, giving its bright apple flavors a lightly honeyed edge.

○ **Ca' del Bosco Brut / 2007 / Franciacorta / $$$$**
Made since the 1970s, this single-vintage wine ages in bottle
for more than four years before release.

○ **Ca' del Bosco Cuvée Annamaria Clementi / 2004 /
Franciacorta / $$$$** The crème de la crème of Franciacorta,
this prestige bottling achieves rare complexity and power.

LINI 910

It takes an exceptional producer to resuscitate a tired style of
wine, and that's exactly what Italian Fabio Lini did for fresh,
fizzy Lambrusco (see Emilia-Romagna, p. 96) in all its incarna-
tions: red, white and rosé. Unlike the cloyingly sweet and simple
Lambruscos of past years, Lini's wines display the kind of bal-
ance and flavors that make them refreshingly good. Today
daughter Alicia Lini has taken up the reins in the winery.

● **Lini 910 In Correggio / NV / Lambrusco Scuro / $$**
Bursting with supple, lively blueberry flavors, this ranks
among the world's most food-friendly red wines.

● **Lini 910 Labrusca / NV / Lambrusco Rosso Emilia / $$**
This opaque, aromatic red is juicy and sleek, with a spicy
huckleberry character.

JUVÉ Y CAMPS

Joan Juvé's family had grown grapes for generations, but it wasn't until he and his wife, Teresa Camps, produced their first batch of sparkling wine in the cellar of the family house in 1921 that the Juvé y Camps label was born. Today it's a midsize family firm that turns out some of Spain's best cavas, thanks in part to a massive number of ideally located, estate-owned vines.

○ **Juvé y Camps Cinta Purpura Reserva Brut / NV / Cava / $** Some inexpensive cavas are simple and boring, but this one offers loads of refreshing apple and floral flavors.

○ **Juvé y Camps Gran Reserva de la Familia Brut Nature / 2007 / Cava / $$** This makes an ideal house sparkler at a great price, with bright, silky almond and tangerine tones.

RAVENTÓS I BLANC

The Raventós family aren't just cava experts—they invented it. An ancestor traveling through Champagne brought the idea back to Spain, and in 1872 the successful Cordoníu brand (and an entire industry) was born. Raventós i Blanc is the family's smaller project, where they craft fine cavas from estate grapes.

○ **Raventós i Blanc L'Hereu Reserva Brut / 2009 / Cava / $$** A blend of Macabeo, Xarello and Parellada grapes, this Raventós reserve is peachy, citrusy and floral.

● **Raventós i Blanc de Nit Brut / 2009 / Cava / $$** This beautifully refined rosé cava looks more like a white wine, but strawberry and red apple notes give away the Monastrell (Mourvèdre) in the blend.

SEGURA VIUDAS

Now owned by the Freixenet Group, cava specialist Segura Viudas maintains a distinct identity and a reputation for high quality. Its longtime winemaker Gabriel Suberviola ages the top *reserva* wines in bottle for up to four years before releasing them, which imparts a toasty richness. The entry-level bottlings are fantastically crisp, refreshing values.

○ **Segura Viudas Aria Estate Brut / NV / Cava / $** This zesty, citrus-driven cava offers more richness and weight than the winery's basic *reserva*, for just a few dollars more.

○ **Segura Viudas Reserva Heredad / NV / Cava / $$** Bone-dry and bright, this has a nutty, creamy complexity.

UNITED STATES
ARGYLE WINERY

This pioneering winery released its first sparkling wines in 1987, when the idea of fine, Champagne-style wines from Oregon raised more eyebrows than enthusiasm among potential buyers. Vintner Rollin Soles persevered, and today his elegant sparklers rank among the country's best. Made in six styles using traditional Champagne techniques and varieties (Pinot Noir, Chardonnay and Pinot Meunier), they are all vintage-dated.

○ **Argyle Brut / 2008 / Willamette Valley / $$**
Always delicious, this shows even more concentration than usual, thanks to Oregon's stellar 2008 vintage.

● **Argyle Brut Rosé / 2008 / Dundee Hills / $$$**
Soles bases this coral-colored rosé on the less common Pinot Meunier grape. It's rich, with apricot and raspberry notes.

DOMAINE CHANDON

A California branch of LVMH Group's Moët & Chandon, Domaine Chandon farms a massive 1,000 acres of vineyards in Yountville, Carneros and Mount Veeder. An extensive line of sparkling wines offers good value across the board, from the basic nonvintage Brut Classic to the prestige cuvée line Étoile. More unusual offerings include three single-appellation bruts and a sparkling red produced with Pinot Noir and Zinfandel.

○ **Chandon Brut Classic / NV / California / $$**
Winemaker Tom Tiburzi sources grapes for this reliably good wine from cool sites up and down the California coast.

○ **Étoile Brut / NV / Sonoma and Napa counties / $$$**
Made from roughly equal parts Chardonnay and Pinot Noir, this gets its toasty notes from five years of aging on its lees.

DOMAINE STE. MICHELLE

Sparkling wine represents nearly half the production of the well-known Washington winery Chateau Ste. Michelle (see p. 218). Labeled as Domaine Ste. Michelle and made at the winery's facility in Paterson, the sparkling wines come in five styles. The formula for their success is simple: Grow great grapes, handle them gently and sell the wines at an affordable price.

○ **Domaine Ste. Michelle Blanc de Blancs / NV / Columbia Valley / $** This pear-scented bottling is the driest, crispest sparkler in the winery's lineup and features an attractively low price.

GLORIA FERRER CAVES & VINEYARDS

Spanish wine maven José Ferrer (of the Freixenet sparkling wine empire) founded this estate in Sonoma's Carneros region in 1986, naming it after his wife, Gloria. In short order the estate was turning out some of California's best sparkling wines, chiefly from Pinot Noir. That grape takes the lead role in most Gloria Ferrer wines, from the fruity Sonoma Brut to the long-lived Carneros Cuvée.

○ **Gloria Ferrer Sonoma Brut / NV / Sonoma County / $$**
There's a delicate tinge of pink to this lovely, appley white, which is made chiefly from Pinot Noir.

○ **Gloria Ferrer Carneros Cuvée / 2000 / Carneros / $$$**
Although it's 13 years old, the winery's top offering tastes fresh and vibrant, with rich baked pear and lemon notes.

IRON HORSE VINEYARDS

Located at the end of a winding dirt road in Green Valley, the coolest subzone in California's Russian River Valley, this boutique winery produces sophisticated wines in a homey setting. Iron Horse was founded by Audrey and Barry Sterling and is run today by their children, Joy and Laurence. The bright, vibrant style of their wines reflects the unique microclimate of Green Valley, where summer days begin and end in fog.

○ **Iron Horse Brut X / 2007 / Green Valley of Russian River Valley / $$$** Racy and sleek, this extremely dry offering delivers lean, tart citrus and green apple flavors.

○ **Iron Horse Russian Cuvée / 2007 / Green Valley of Russian River Valley / $$$** More opulent than the Classic Brut, this luscious, zesty sparkler was first produced for the Reagan-Gorbachev Cold War summit meetings.

J VINEYARDS & WINERY

Created in 1986 by Judy Jordan, daughter of the founder of Sonoma's Jordan Vineyard, J has been dedicated almost from the start to producing Russian River sparkling wine by the *méthode traditionnelle*. J Vineyards' ultra-rich and elegant Late-Disgorged series benefits from extra aging on lees.

○ **J Cuvée 20 25th Anniversary Brut / NV / Russian River Valley / $$$** (1.5 liters) J has released its signature "Cuvée 20" bottling under a commemorative anniversary label, yet the wine remains consistent in style: fruity, bright and suave.

ROEDERER ESTATE

Louis Roederer's outpost in California's Anderson Valley sticks closely to Champagne tradition. All vineyards are estate-owned, and the cuvées benefit from the addition of reserve wines, aged in French oak casks. The two nonvintage Brut and vintage white and rosé L'Ermitage wines could rival true Champagne.

○ **L'Ermitage by Roederer Estate / 2003 / Anderson Valley / $$$**
This 2003 white, marked by expressive dried pear and hazelnut tones, is drinking beautifully right now.

● **Roederer Estate Brut Rosé / NV / Anderson Valley / $$**
Roederer adds a portion of oak-aged reserve wines to give this alluring, strawberry-scented rosé its vanilla notes.

SCHRAMSBERG VINEYARDS

Skeptics thought that Jack and Jamie Davies were crazy to purchase this dilapidated Napa Valley property in 1965 and turn it into a high-end sparkling wine estate. Just seven years later, Richard Nixon served a Schramsberg Brut during his trip to China; today the wines are benchmarks of their type. Son Hugh Davies continues to focus on quality, aging the wines in hillside caves that were dug in the 1870s.

○ **Schramsberg Mirabelle Brut / NV / North Coast / $$**
Schramsberg's most affordable wine is slightly rounder and sweeter than its other bruts, though it's still dry.

○ **Schramsberg Blanc de Blancs / 2008 / North Coast / $$$**
Consistently one of the country's best all-Chardonnay sparklers, this is made in a pure, refined style with firm acidity and white-fruit flavors.

SOTER VINEYARDS

Tony Soter first gained fame as a California winemaker, helping to propel such revered labels as Spottswoode, Araujo and his own brand, Etude, to cult status. But this Oregon native returned to his roots when he founded Soter Vineyards in the Willamette Valley, where he makes ethereal, sparkling Pinot Noirs in addition to still wines.

● **Soter Vineyards Brut Rosé / 2006 / Yamhill-Carlton / $$$**
Intense yet delicate, this strawberry- and orange-inflected bottling is one of America's best sparkling rosés.

Fortified & Dessert Wines

Though few people drink them in the U.S., fortified wines are finally beginning to generate some buzz. Mixologists are promoting port in cocktails, and sherry seems to be the latest enthusiasm for young, adventurous sommeliers. Unfortunately, traditional dessert wines haven't yet lucked out in that way—a shame, given their alluring flavors and impressive complexity.

FORTIFIED WINES

The practice of fortifying wines involves adding a neutral spirit before bottling. Traditional fortified wines include sherry, port, Madeira and Marsala, although variations abound. These wines have a higher alcohol content—usually 16 to 20 percent—than most unfortified wines. A fortified wine's style depends largely on when the spirit is added. Adding it during fermentation, as is the case with most port and Madeira, yields wines with a lot of natural grape sugar. When brandy is added after fermentation, the result can be drier, such as a fino sherry.

FORTIFIED WINES

SHERRY

CLAIM TO FAME

Made only in southern Spain's Jerez region, sherry gets stereotyped as an aperitif but is actually a vastly underrated food wine. Dry fino styles complement salty, savory dishes, while sweeter olorosos are delicious with desserts. Sherry gains its distinctive flavors from the Jerez area's chalky soils and, in most cases, from *flor*, a unique yeast that appears on the surface of the wine while it is fermenting. *Flor* helps give sherry its nutty, appley tones, while neutral spirit—added after fermentation finishes—increases its alcohol and body.

❦ KEY GRAPES

Sherry's chief grape variety is Palomino, though sweeter styles sometimes contain Pedro Ximénez or Moscatel. Except for a handful of rare, vintage-dated wines (called *Añadas*), all sherries are blends of wines from different years, combined in a fractional blending system called solera. In the solera system, small amounts of younger wines get blended into older wines, which in turn get blended into a set of even older wines, and so on. A typical bodega ages three to nine levels of wine at the same time. Because only a small portion of wine is removed from each barrel each year, the oldest level contains a blend of wines from decades—and sometimes more than a century—of different vintages. The blending and long aging results in consistent, complex sherries that come in two basic types, fino and oloroso, and a range of sweetness levels.

WINE TERMINOLOGY

FINO Dry, pale and delicate, with flavors of green apples and straw, fino sherry ages under a protective blanket of *flor*. The yeast covers the surface of the wine as it ages, preventing it from oxidizing and keeping it fresh. Like white table wine, fino tastes best chilled and loses its appeal within a few days of opening.

AMONTILLADO This nutty sherry starts out as fino, then loses its *flor* and ages in barrel for many years (at least for high-quality versions). The resulting oxidation is what gives amontillados their darker color. The finest examples are dry; "medium" amontillado is sweeter, though not as sweet as most olorosos.

MANZANILLA A fino sherry made around the port city of Sanlúcar de Barrameda, this is racy and bone-dry. Its lighter alcohol and salty tang make it terrific with seafood or tapas.

OLOROSO Darker than finos and shading from dark gold to amber, olorosos are more highly fortified, which prevents the formation of *flor*. Exposure to oxygen darkens their color and creates nutty, earthy flavors. Most olorosos are sweet, though dry examples are usually high quality and worth seeking out.

PALO CORTADO With the freshness of an amontillado and an oloroso's body and depth, this relatively rare sherry is exposed to oxygen as it ages. Some vintners create inexpensive shortcuts to the style by blending amontillado and oloroso.

PEDRO XIMÉNEZ/PX Made from partially raisined grapes, this rich, viscous and ultra-dark sherry can stand in for dessert.

CREAM SHERRY These sweet, often simple sherries are typically made from a blend of young sherries—usually oloroso—that are sweetened with partially fermented, fortified Pedro Ximénez wines. "Pale" versions are lighter in color and taste.

ALMACENISTA An *almacenista* is a small-scale sherry producer who doesn't grow grapes or bottle sherry, but instead buys young wines, refines them in a solera system and sells finished wines to large producers. Some of the best sherries are released as small-lot bottlings bearing an *almacenista* family name.

VOS This term designates any sherry with a minimum average age of 20 years. Made in a smooth and complex style, these wines offer dark, intensely nutty flavors. Although VOS officially stands for *Vinum Optimum Signatum,* a Latin phrase meaning "certified best wine," it's much easier to remember the category as "very old sherry."

VORS Although this designation is reserved for sherries with a minimum average age of 30 years, some VORS (*Vinum Optimum Rare Signatum,* or "certified best rare wine") bottlings are considerably older. They are most often used by producers to boost the complexity of younger wines, but small amounts of these mellow, savory and sometimes acidic wines are increasingly bottled and sold on their own.

Producers/ Sherry

ALVEAR

Family-run for nearly 300 years, Alvear produces exquisite wines from some of Spain's oldest solera systems (see Key Grapes, p. 297), including traditional fino and oloroso-style offerings. But because it's located in Montilla-Moriles, not Jerez, Alvear's wines can't technically be called sherry. Another point of difference: For most of its wines Alvear dries grapes before fermenting them, to create powerful, complex flavors and naturally higher alcohol contents, with no alcohol added.

○ **Alvear Fino en Rama / 2006 / Montilla-Moriles / $**
(500 ml) Trendy unfiltered *en rama* sherries (*en rama* wines are minimally processed) taste dry and incredibly fresh, like this tongue-tingling, lemon-edged example.

○ **Alvear 1927 Pedro Ximénez Solera / NV / Montilla-Moriles /**
$$ (375 ml) One of the region's star wines, this molasses-colored, toffee-scented sherry is dessert in liquid form.

○ **Alvear Solera Cream / NV / Montilla-Moriles / $$**
(500 ml) The combination of nutty oloroso and a small dash of dark, rich Pedro Ximénez results in a terrifically well-balanced and complex cream sherry.

BODEGAS HIDALGO LA GITANA

Hidalgo's flagship La Gitana brand is quintessential manzanilla-style sherry—a completely dry, slightly briny white that's best consumed young and fresh (ideally with a platter of salty snacks or seafood). But don't overlook this centuries-old producer's other wines, which include outstanding aged sherries crafted in a range of styles.

○ **Bodegas Hidalgo Napoleón Amontillado** / NV / Sherry / $$
The Hidalgo family once sold sherry to Napoleon's troops; this completely dry amontillado is silky and caramel-infused.

○ **La Gitana Manzanilla** / NV / Sherry / $$
(500 ml) Like all manzanilla sherries, this tangy, delicate bottling tastes best within a week or two of opening.

LUSTAU

Emilio Lustau was founded in 1896 as an *almacenista,* a sherry wholesaler selling to larger companies. Today, however, it's Lustau that does the buying. Its stunning portfolio includes more than 40 wines, encompassing every style from cream sherry to the limited 30-year-old VORS bottlings.

○ **Lustau East India Solera** / NV / Sherry / $$
A revival of an old style, this cream (sweet) sherry gets aged in hot, humid cellars, creating a luxuriously rich, smooth wine.

○ **Lustau Papirusa Manzanilla Solera Reserva** / NV / Sanlúcar de Barrameda / $$ The briny freshness of this invigorating, bone-dry sherry makes it fantastic with seafood.

○ **Lustau Pata de Gallina Oloroso** / NV / Sherry / $$$
Lustau led the way in showcasing sherries from small *almacenistas;* this rare bottling is intensely nutty and dry.

FORTIFIED WINES

PORT

CLAIM TO FAME

Portugal's second-largest city, Oporto, gave its name to the country's emblematic wine. Ranging from light, juicy ruby ports to decadent, powerful vintage bottlings, port's lush fruit and sweetness make it the quintessential after-dinner drink. Experimental bartenders are discovering its versatility in cocktails, too, and in the process freshening up port's dusty image.

♣ KEY GRAPES

Port is a blended wine, made chiefly from five major red grapes (although more than 80 kinds are allowed). The most important of these is Touriga Nacional, with Touriga Franca, Tinto Cão, Tinta Barroca and Tinta Roriz (Tempranillo) valued for bringing qualities like fragrance, fruit, spice and tannins to the blend. Port comes in two main styles, ruby and tawny, as well as the occasional white, made from a handful of mostly obscure local grapes.

WINE TERMINOLOGY

RUBY The most common style of port, ruby is a juicy, fruity blend of young wines. Ruby reserve ports are more complex, often bearing proprietary names such as Graham's Six Grapes. Late Bottled Vintage (LBV) ports are thick-textured, single-vintage rubies that have been aged four to six years in barrel and are drinkable upon release. The most famous rubies are vintage ports, which are made from grapes harvested in a single year; they spend only two years in cask and age primarily in bottle. Producers declare a vintage only in the best years, usually just two or three times a decade. Decadent vintage ports are big, black, densely flavored wines that need time or rich food to tame their powerful tannins—they age effortlessly for decades. Single-quinta (vineyard) vintage ports are made with grapes from one vineyard, usually in nondeclared vintages.

TAWNY Ready to drink on release and often served lightly chilled, tawny ports are aged in wood and offer delicate, nutty aromas and dried-fruit flavors. In theory, a tawny has been aged in wood longer than a ruby and has thus taken on a lighter, tawny hue. In reality, many inexpensive tawny ports are the same age as most rubies; they are just made with lighter wines. Aged tawny ports, however, are very different: Seductive and complex, they're made from blends of the highest-quality ports. They are released in 10-, 20-, 30- and 40-year-old versions, with the number referring to the average age of the blend's component wines. (For example, a 20-year tawny might be a blend of wines ranging in age from five to 50 years old.)

WHITE With its bright, citrusy flavors, white port is a terrific aperitif or warm-weather drink, especially when it's served chilled with tonic or over ice.

Producers/ Port

COCKBURN'S

After changing hands several times in recent years, this venerable port house was acquired by the Symington family (W. & J. Graham's, Dow's, Warre's) in 2010. Cockburn's ports are marked by warm spice notes, a house style that works beautifully for both its aged tawnies and bargain Special Reserve Port.

● **Cockburn's Special Reserve Port / NV / Douro Valley / $$**
Made from a blend of ruby and vintage ports, this velvety, fruit-packed bottling outperforms its price.

● **Cockburn's Quinta dos Canais Vintage Port / 2003 / Douro Valley / $$$** Grapes from the spectacular Canais vineyard go into this outstanding, mocha-flavored bottling.

CROFT

Most great port brands rely on a keystone estate vineyard, or quinta, to deliver a consistent character to their vintage wines and to seed the rest of their line with a signature personality. For Croft, owned by the port giant Taylor Fladgate & Yeatman, that vineyard is Quinta da Roêda, which imbues Croft wines with decadent fruit and great structure.

● **Croft Pink / NV / Douro / $$**
Croft invented a radically new style of port when it created this strawberry-scented rosé in 2008. It's best served over ice.

● **Croft Distinction Porto / NV / Douro / $$**
A spicy, cherry-infused blend of four- and five-year-old wines.

● **Croft 10 Year Old Tawny Porto / NV / Douro / $$**
Still young after about a decade of aging, this polished red bursts with luscious red fruit and nuts.

NIEPOORT

Dirk Niepoort leads this family winery (see p. 135), lightening up port's stodgy image with a sense of humor (as in a 10-year-old tawny called Drink Me). But don't doubt the firm's seriousness: Its aged tawnies are among the best; the second-label Secundum is excellent, and ready to drink sooner than true vintage port.

- **Niepoort Late Bottled Vintage Port / 2007 / Douro / $$**
  The stellar 2007 vintage yielded some serious bargains, like this intensely fragrant, spicy blend.
- **Niepoort 10 Years Old Tawny Port / NV / Douro / $$$**
  Cellarmaster José Nogueira combines old and young wines averaging 10 years of age to create this reliably delicious tawny port full of toffee, nut and dried-fruit notes.
- **Niepoort Vintage Port / 2007 / Douro / $$$$**
  Stash this in a dark, cool place and forget about it for a decade or two to let its powerful, velvety flavors unwind.

QUINTA DO CRASTO

Leonore and Jorge Roquette's famed Crasto estate is one of the Douro's finest vineyards, climbing the right bank of the river between Régua and Pinhão. Crasto produces not only fine vintage port (its grapes still foot-trodden in *lagares* in the traditional fashion), but also first-rate table wines (see p. 136). The dynamic, well-known "Douro Boys," brothers Miguel and Tomás Roquette, now manage production and marketing.

- **Quinta do Crasto Late Bottled Vintage Port / 2006 / Douro / $$** Handpicked grapes were crushed by foot to make this firm, fresh LBV port.
- **Quinta do Crasto Vintage Port / 2007 / Douro / $$$**
  Crasto's vintage port offers a taste of the quality of the 2007 vintage at a more accessible price than many.

SMITH WOODHOUSE

Smith Woodhouse is less famous than many of its counterparts in the Douro Valley, but its expertly made wines are generally wonderful—consequently, they often deliver great value for the money. Founded in 1784 by Christopher Smith, a member of the British Parliament and lord mayor of London, Smith Woodhouse is now owned and operated by the Symington family.

- **Smith Woodhouse Late Bottled Vintage Port / 2000 / Douro / $$** The winery typically ages this LBV port for an additional three years after it is bottled, which makes it especially mellow and refined.
- **Smith Woodhouse Colheita / 1994 / Douro / $$$**
  Colheitas are relatively rare tawny ports produced from a single vintage; this graceful, amber-hued bottling was aged 15 years before release.

WARRE'S

Named for William Warre, an early partner in the firm who came to Portugal in the first part of the 18th century, this leading estate dates back even further than that, to 1670. It's now part of the Symington family's portfolio, which also includes several of the Douro's strongest brands.

○ **Warre's Fine White Porto / NV / Douro Valley / $**
Mixed with tonic and served over ice, white port—like this lightly sweet one—makes a refreshing summer cocktail.

● **Warre's Otima 10 Year Old Tawny Port / NV / Douro / $$**
Warre's introduced this silky, toffee-edged tawny with the unorthodox suggestion that it be served chilled.

W. & J. GRAHAM'S

The Symingtons are the second family of Scottish origin to helm this house, following the original Grahams. The Quinta dos Malvedos property, the estate's star vineyard, merits its own bottling in years when its wines are not needed to make a vintage port. It also contributes to the much-loved Six Grapes, an accessibly priced reserve ruby.

● **W. & J. Graham's Natura Organic Reserve Port / NV / Douro / $$** Softer and fresher than Six Grapes, this reserve ruby comes from organically farmed sites.

● **W. & J. Graham's Six Grapes Reserve Port / NV / Douro / $$**
This ruby epitomizes Graham's richly fruity style, with sweet licorice and cherry extract flavors.

● **W. & J. Graham's Quinta dos Malvedos Vintage Port / 2009 / Douro / $$$** This offers the intensity expected of quality vintage port, with dark, spicy fruit and supple structure.

DESSERT WINES

The longest-lived wines in the world are sweet. Legendary bottlings of Bordeaux's Sauternes wines and Hungary's Tokaji routinely outlive the people who made them, and offer luscious, honey-tinged flavors of incredible complexity (as well as price tags to match their prestige). But great sweet wines are made all over the world, often at affordable prices. Whether from California, Italy, Australia or elsewhere, they're characterized by ample sweet fruit and enough bright acidity to keep them from tasting heavy or overly rich.

WINE TERMINOLOGY

BOTRYTIS Botrytized wines owe their unique flavors to *Botrytis cinerea,* a mold ("noble rot") that concentrates the wine's sugars and adds smoke and truffle notes. The finest are Bordeaux's Sauternes, made of Sémillon, Sauvignon Blanc and Muscadelle. Superb examples come from Bordeaux's Barsac subregion, while nearby Loupiac and Cadillac yield less-costly versions. Loire Valley vintners make terrific botrytized sweet wines with Chenin Blanc; in Alsace, they're identified by the designation Sélection de Grains Nobles. German and Austrian vintners use mainly Riesling to craft sublime botrytized wines, labeled *Beerenauslese* (BA) or *Trockenbeerenauslese* (TBA), depending on sugar levels (see p. 142). California, Australia and South Africa also make botrytized wines, many of them terrific.

LATE HARVEST These wines rely on grapes harvested very late in the season, when they have developed extremely high sugar levels. The best known come from Germany (marked *Auslese* or *Beerenauslese,* indicating progressively greater sweetness) and Alsace (where they're called Vendanges Tardives). California, Australia, South Africa, Chile and the Greek island of Samos make good versions, too.

ICE WINE/EISWEIN This wine is made by pressing grapes that froze on the vine, a process that yields very small amounts of sweet, concentrated juice. The finest ice wines are made from Riesling in Germany and Austria; many great examples also come from Canada.

PASSITO An Italian specialty, *passito* wines are made from grapes that have been dried before pressing. Tuscan vintners use Trebbiano and/or Malvasia to make the local version, *vin santo,* while Sicilian vintners use the Zibibbo grape (a.k.a. Muscat of Alexandria) for their delicious *passito* wines.

DOUX This term refers to the sweetest wines made in the Loire region. Doux wines often have an almost syrupy consistency.

MOELLEUX The less sweet of the Loire's two dessert wine categories, *moelleux* wines often gain complexity and sweetness from botrytis, a "noble rot" affecting grapes.

VIN DOUX NATUREL Fortified with brandy during the fermentation process, these wines are produced mainly in southern France. The two most noteworthy white examples are Muscat de Beaumes-de-Venise from the Rhône Valley and Muscat de Rivesaltes from the Roussillon region; Banyuls is the most famous red Vin Doux Naturel.

TOKAJI This distinctive wine is infused with a mash of botrytis-affected (*aszú*) grapes (see p. 305). Produced mainly in Hungary, Tokaji is graded by the amount of crushed grapes added to the base, on a scale measured by *puttonyos*—the more *puttonyos,* the more intense the wine. Every Tokaji tends to exhibit delicious ripe apricot, orange and almond flavors, and high acidity.

Producers/ Dessert Wines

CANTINA DE BARTOLI

Former race-car driver Marco De Bartoli took over his family's Marsala estate in the 1970s. He worked hard to improve the wines and to make Marsala sexy again, even delivering orders in vintage sports cars. In addition to the famous Marsalas, the winery—now run by De Bartoli's children—makes aromatic, *passito*-style whites on the island of Pantelleria.

○ Marco De Bartoli Bukkuram / NV / Passito di Pantelleria / $$$$ The native Zibibbo variety gives an intense sweetness to this *passito* white's decadent raisin and walnut flavors.

○ Marco De Bartoli Vecchio Samperi Ventennale / NV / Marsala / $$$$ This nut-brown, caramel-inflected Marsala is made using a traditional solera system (see Key Grapes, p. 297).

CHÂTEAU GUIRAUD

This first-growth Sauternes estate encompasses more than 200 acres of grapes, most of which go into a single, eponymous *grand vin*. Well regarded for decades, Guiraud gained new attention after its sale in 2006 to a prominent team of four owners—including Guiraud's general manager, Xavier Planty, and Stephan von Neipperg, of Bordeaux's Château Canon la Gaffelière.

○ **Petit Guiraud / 2009 / Sauternes / $$** With its buoyant fruit
and accessible price, this sibling bottling to Guiraud's *grand
cru* is a fantastic introduction to Sauternes.

○ **Château Guiraud Premier Grand Cru / 2009 / Sauternes /
$$$$** Guiraud uses an unusually high proportion of Sauvi-
gnon Blanc in its wines, which gives its unctuous, lightly
honeyed flagship bottling lovely freshness.

OREMUS

This historic Hungarian estate may have crafted the world's first
botrytized late-harvest wine in the mid-17th century. Spain's
Vega-Sicilia purchased Oremus in 1993 and provided the capital
for vineyard and winery upgrades that dramatically improved
the sweet Tokaji Aszú dessert bottlings as well as the fine dry
white Mandolás cuvée. Today its luscious, long-lived sweet
wines rank among the world's most admired.

○ **Oremus Late Harvest / 2008 / Tokaji / $$**
(375 ml) Aged in a network of tunnels dating from the 13th to
17th centuries, this luscious white gets its concentration from
botrytized Furmint grapes.

○ **Oremus 5 Puttonyos / 2003 / Tokaji Aszú / $$$$**
(500 ml) Sugar levels in Tokaji go up to six *puttonyos*, meaning
that this viscous, lightly honeyed bottling is superripe.

SARACCO

Sales of Moscato, a light and often sweet white wine, have
exploded recently, and a lot of mediocre bottlings are flooding
the market. For benchmark dessert-worthy Moscatos from a
longtime expert, look to Paolo Saracco, whose deft touch with
the grape earned him the nickname "the maestro of Moscato."
His graceful, gently effervescent wines come from Italy's
Moscato heartland, in Piedmont's Asti district, and have a touch
of sweetness that's fantastic with light desserts.

○ **Saracco Moscato d'Asti / 2011 / Moscato d'Asti / $$**
Try this juicy Italian sparkling wine with not-too-sweet
desserts such as fruit tarts or sorbets.

Pairing
Wine & Food

These days the adage "White wine with fish and red with meat" seems to have been replaced with "Drink whatever you like with whatever you want." Both approaches have advantages, but neither is an absolute. The truth is that there is no one principle for creating perfect wine matches beyond the fact that you want to bring together dishes and wines that highlight each other's best qualities rather than obscure them. To help make delicious matches at home, the following pages provide five basic strategies for matching and tips for pairing based on the main course and cooking technique. The specific bottle recommendations are all from this guide.

WINE-PAIRING GUIDELINES

THINK ABOUT WEIGHT One simple approach to pairing wine and food is to match lighter dishes with lighter wines and richer dishes with richer wines. We all know that a fillet of sole seems "lighter" than braised beef short ribs. With wine, the best analogy is milk: We know that skim milk feels lighter than whole milk, and wine is similar. So, for instance, Cabernet Sauvignon or Amarone feels richer or heavier than a Beaujolais or a crisp rosé from Provence.

TART GOES WITH TART Acidic foods—like a green salad with a tangy vinaigrette—work best with similarly tart wines: a Sauvignon Blanc, say, or a Muscadet from France. It might seem as though a richer, weightier wine would be the answer, but the acidity in the food will make the wine taste bland.

CONSIDER SALT & FAT Two things to keep in mind about how your palate works: First, salt in food will make wine seem less sour, softening the edge in tart wines; and fat in a dish—whether it's a well-marbled steak or pasta with a cream sauce—will make red wines seem lighter and less tannic.

SPLIT THE DIFFERENCE In restaurants, a group of people will rarely order the same entrees; instead, someone will order fish, another person a steak, a third the pasta with duck ragù, and so on. In instances like this, go for a wine that follows a middle course—not too rich, not too light, not too tannic. For reds, Pinot Noir is a great option; for whites, choose an unoaked wine with good acidity, like a dry Riesling or a Pinot Gris from Oregon.

MOST OF ALL, DON'T WORRY Pairings are meant to be suggestions. Play around with possibilities and don't get caught up in absolutes. After all, Cabernet may go well with a cheeseburger, but if you don't like cheeseburgers, that doesn't matter at all.

Pairing /Cheat Sheet

	DISH	BEST WINE MATCH
CHICKEN	**STEAMED OR POACHED**	Medium white or light red
	ROASTED OR SAUTÉED	Rich white or medium red
	CREAMY OR BUTTERY SAUCES	Rich white
	TANGY SAUCES MADE WITH CITRUS, VINEGAR, TOMATOES	Medium white
	EARTHY FLAVORS LIKE MUSHROOMS	Light or medium red
	HERBS	Light white
PORK	**GRILLED OR SEARED, LEAN**	Medium red
	GRILLED OR SEARED, FATTY	Rich red
	BRAISED OR STEWED	Rich red
	SWEET SAUCES OR DRIED FRUIT	Medium white
	SPICY INGREDIENTS	Medium white or light red
	CURED OR BRINED	Medium white or rosé

GREAT VARIETIES	BOTTLE TO TRY
Chardonnay (unoaked), Gamay	2010 Foxglove Chardonnay / p. 183
Chardonnay, Marsanne, Tempranillo	2006 Montecillo Reserva Rioja / p. 116
Chardonnay, Viognier	2010 Cambria Katherine's Vineyard Chardonnay / p. 178
Verdicchio, Sauvignon Blanc	2011 Domaine Vacheron Blanc Sancerre / p. 52
Pinot Noir, Cabernet Franc	2010 Maison Joseph Drouhin Côte de Beaune / p. 42
Pinot Grigio, Albariño, Vermentino	2011 Martín Códax Albariño / p. 119
Sangiovese, Cabernet Franc	2010 Lang & Reed Cabernet Franc / p. 190
Grenache blends, Merlot	2008 Swanson Vineyards Merlot / p. 205
Cabernet Sauvignon, Malbec	2010 Susana Balbo Signature Malbec / p. 259
Riesling, Pinot Gris (Alsace)	2011 Domaine Zind-Humbrecht Pinot Gris / p. 23
Riesling (off-dry), Pinot Noir	2011 Dr. Bürklin-Wolf Estate Riesling / p. 143
Verdicchio, Sauvignon Blanc, rosé	2010 Bucci Verdicchio Classico dei Castelli di Jesi / p. 101

DISH	BEST WINE MATCH
BEEF	
GRILLED OR SEARED STEAKS, CHOPS, BURGERS	Rich red
BRAISED OR STEWED	Rich red
SWEET SAUCES LIKE BARBECUE	Rich red
SPICY INGREDIENTS	Medium red
LAMB	
GRILLED OR ROASTED	Rich red
BRAISED OR STEWED	Rich red
SPICY INGREDIENTS	Light red
FISH	
GRILLED	Medium white, rosé or light red
ROASTED, BAKED OR SAUTÉED	Medium white or light red
FRIED	Light white or rosé
STEAMED	Light white
SPICY INGREDIENTS	Medium white
HERB SAUCES	Light or medium white
CITRUS SAUCES	Light or medium white
SHELLFISH, COOKED	Medium or rich white
SHELLFISH, RAW	Light white

GREAT VARIETIES	BOTTLE TO TRY
Cabernet Sauvignon, Malbec	2008 Ladera Napa Valley Cabernet Sauvignon / p. 189
Cabernet Sauvignon, Nebbiolo	2008 Vietti Castiglione Barolo / p. 79
Zinfandel, Grenache	2010 Buehler Vineyards Zinfandel / p. 177
Tempranillo, Sangiovese	2010 Emilio Moro Finca Resalso Ribera del Duero / p. 128
Zinfandel, Grenache, Syrah	2009 Jim Barry The Lodge Hill Shiraz / p. 236
Syrah, Malbec, Cabernet Sauvignon	2009 Vidal-Fleury St. Joseph / p. 62
Pinot Noir, Gamay, Dolcetto	2010 Saintsbury Carneros Pinot Noir / p. 200
Chardonnay (unoaked), rosé, Pinot Noir	2010 Domaine Christian Moreau Chablis / p. 37
Pinot Gris (Oregon), Gamay	2010 Georges Duboeuf "Flower Label" Fleurie Beaujolais / p. 46
Vermentino, rosé	2011 Jean-Luc Colombo Cape Bleue Rosé / p. 61
Sauvignon Blanc	2011 Cloudy Bay Sauvignon Blanc / p. 248
Riesling (off-dry)	2010 Weingut Leitz Leitz Out Riesling / p. 146
Arneis, Grüner Veltliner	2011 Domäne Wachau Terrassen Grüner Veltliner / p. 152
Pinot Grigio, Chenin Blanc	2010 Ken Forrester Reserve Chenin Blanc / p. 277
Chardonnay (unoaked), Grenache Blanc	2010 Bonny Doon Vineyard Le Cigare Blanc / p. 176
Muscadet, Albariño, Vinho Verde	2010 Château de La Ragotière Muscadet / p. 49

DISH	BEST WINE MATCH
GAME	
VENISON	Rich red
DUCK OR GAME BIRDS, ROASTED OR PAN-ROASTED	Medium red
DUCK OR GAME BIRDS, RAGÙ OR STEW	Medium or rich red
PASTA	
BUTTER OR OIL	Medium white or rosé
CREAMY, CHEESE SAUCES	Medium white or red
TOMATO-BASED SAUCES	Medium red
SPICY SAUCES	Medium white or light red
MEAT SAUCES	Rich red
FISH AND SEAFOOD SAUCES	Medium white
EGGS	
PLAIN OR WITH HERBS	Sparkling
WITH CHEESE (QUICHE)	Sparkling, medium white or rosé
SALADS	
TART DRESSINGS LIKE VINAIGRETTE	Light white
CREAMY DRESSINGS	Medium white
PASTA & OTHER STARCHY SALADS	Rosé or light red

GREAT VARIETIES	BOTTLE TO TRY
Monastrell, Syrah	2008 Casa Castillo Las Gravas / p. 122
Pinot Noir	2010 Hirsch Vineyards The Bohan-Dillon / p. 187
Sangiovese, Touriga Nacional	2009 Quinta do Crasto Douro Red / p. 136
Pinot Blanc, Fiano di Avellino	2010 Tiefenbrunner Pinot Bianco / p. 85
Chardonnay (unoaked), Barbera	2009 Pio Cesare Barbera d'Alba / p. 78
Sangiovese	2008 Castello di Monsanto Chianti Classico Riserva / p. 91
Riesling (off-dry), Dolcetto	2008 Ca' Viola Barturot Dolcetto d'Alba / p. 74
Aglianico, Corvina	2008 Masi Campofiorin Rosso del Veronese / p. 84
Vermentino	2010 Sella & Mosca La Cala Vermentino di Sardegna / p. 107
Champagne or other dry sparkling	NV Louis Roederer Brut Premier / p. 285
Champagne or other dry sparkling, Riesling (dry), rosé	2008 Argyle Brut Rosé / p. 293
Sauvignon Blanc, Vinho Verde	2010 Brander Santa Ynez Valley Sauvignon Blanc / p. 176
Chenin Blanc, Pinot Gris	2010 Elk Cove Vineyards Pinot Gris / p. 212
Rosé, Beaujolais	2011 LIOCO Indica Rosé / p. 190

Index
of Producers